EDI DEVELOPMENT STUDIES

G000147484

Trade, Technology, and International Competitiveness

Irfan ul Haque

in collaboration with

Martin Bell
Carl Dahlman
Sanjaya Lall
Keith Pavitt

The World Bank
Washington, D. C.

The Economic Development Institute (EDI) was established by the World Bank in 1955 to train officials concerned with development planning, policymaking, investment analysis, and project implementation in member developing countries. At present the substance of the EDI's work emphasizes macroeconomic and sectoral economic policy analysis. Through a variety of courses, seminars, and workshops, most of which are given overseas in cooperation with local institutions, the EDI seeks to sharpen analytical skills used in policy analysis and to broaden understanding of the experience of individual countries with economic develop- ment. Although the EDI's publications are designed to support its training activities, many are of interest to a much broader audience. EDI materials, including any findings, interpre- tations, and conclusions, are entirely those of the authors and should not be attributed in any manner to the World Bank, to its affiliated organizations, or to members of its Board of Executive Directors or the countries they represent.

Because of the informality of this series and to make the publication available with the least possible delay, the manuscript has not been edited as fully as would be the case with a more formal document, and the World Bank accepts no responsibility for errors. Some sources cited in this book may be informal documents that are not readily available.

The material in this publication is copyrighted. Requests for permission to reproduce portions of it should be sent to the Office of the Publisher at the address shown in the copyright notice above. The World Bank encourages dissemination of its work and will normally give permission promptly and, when the reproduction is for noncommercial purposes, without asking a fee. Permission to copy portions for classroom use is granted through the Copyright Clearance Center Inc., Suite 910, 222 Rosewood Drive, Danvers, Massachusetts 01923, U.S.A.

The backlist of publications by the World Bank is shown in the annual *Index of Publications*, which is available from Distribution Unit, Office of the Publisher, The World Bank, 1818 H Street, N.W., Washington, D.C. 20433, U.S.A., or from Publications, Banque Mondiale, 66, avenue d'Iéna, 75116 Paris, France.

Irfan ul Haque is principal economist in the Macroeconomic Policy and Management Division of the World Bank's Economic Development Institute.

Library of Congress Cataloging-in-Publication Data

Irfan-ul-Haque.
    Trade, technology, and international competitiveness / Irfan ul
Haque in collaboration with Martin Bell ... [et al.].
        p.   cm. — (EDI development studies, ISSN 1020-105X)
    Includes bibliographical references and index.
    ISBN 0-8213-3418-2
    1. Competition, International.   2. Comparative advantage
(International trade)   3. Technological innovations—Economic
aspects. I. Bell, Martin (R. Martin N.)   II. Series.
HF1414.I73   1995
382'.1042—dc20   95-33307
                                                  CIP

Contents

Foreword

A remarkable feature of the discussion of economic policy during the last decade has been the recognition given to the importance of international trade and competition in the world market. There is hardly a country today that does not seek to be more closely integrated into the global economy, where the mobility of goods, services, and capital has increased to a point unforeseen only two decades ago. However, it is also becoming clear that the ability to compete in the world market differs widely across countries, industrial as well as developing. Although international competitiveness depends on a variety of factors (notably, the macroeconomic environment), there is an increasing appreciation that in the long term the ability to master technology and to manage and generate technological change is decisive in determining an economy's competitive strength and capacity to grow.

The Economic Development Institute of the World Bank organized a series of seminars during 1991–95 that focused on the issues of trade, technology, and international competitiveness. This book presents the views of some of the resource persons who participated in these seminars and attempts to elucidate the role technology plays in international trade and general economic development. The book should be of interest to policymakers and academic economists concerned with the long-term issues of the revival and sustainability of economic growth in an increasingly global environment.

Vinod Thomas, Director
Economic Development Institute

Acknowledgments

This book owes a great deal of debt to the many people who helped to bring it to publication, in particular to my fellow authors: Martin Bell, Carl Dahlman, Sanjaya Lall, Keith Pavitt and Kenji Takeuchi. The production of a multiauthor volume, I have learned, is not a simple task, especially when the authors are separated by large geographical distances. I am grateful to my coauthors for collaborating in this effort and for their consideration and promptness in responding to my many requests.

This book could not have come into being without the moral support and encouragement of Peter Knight during the organization of the seminars dealing with the issues of trade, technology, and international competitiveness and, later, during the actual preparation of the volume. Isabel Guerrero, who succeeded Peter as Chief of the National Economic Management Division in the EDI, was equally generous in her support and encouragement during the book's final stages.

The debt to Michael Scherer is enormous. He reviewed drafts of the volume with interest and care and raised important questions of reasoning, presentation, and factual accuracy. Richard Nelson, who read an earlier version of the volume, served as both critic and guide. Bruce Scott reviewed the penultimate version of the book; his insights into industrial development strategy helped to sharpen the volume's reasoning. Sikander Rahim offered valuable advice on clarifying concepts and improving style. Naturally, none of these readers can be held accountable for the errors and weaknesses that remain in the work.

Manjula Maudgal and Andrew Mountford provided research assistance, compiling the background data and running the regressions for Chapter 2.

Emily Chalmers provided editorial assistance and advice, and Carmen Alvarado prepared the manuscript. Dulce Afzal processed the earlier drafts of the chapters, and provided general secretarial support. Thanks are also due to David Davies and John Didier for their help and sound advice during the long process of review and publication.

Finally, I would like to thank the participants in the seminars on trade, technology, and international competitiveness, who provided both the reason and stimulus for this book. Interacting with public officials and private sector representatives of such high caliber was a learning experience for those of us who served as resource persons. The participants made sure that the discussion of issues remained firmly anchored in the everyday reality that confronts them in their work. This book, I hope, will serve as a useful memento of their contribution to our collective learning.

Irfan ul Haque
Washington DC

Contributors

Martin Bell	Senior Fellow, Science Policy Research Unit, University of Sussex
Carl Dahlman	Resident Representative in Mexico, the World Bank
Irfan ul Haque	Principal Economist, Economic Development Institute, the World Bank
Sanjaya Lall	University Lecturer in Development Economics, University of Oxford
Keith Pavitt	R. M. Philips-Professor of Science and Technological Policy, Science Policy Research Unit, University of Sussex
Kenji Takeuchi	Professor of Economics, Keiai University, Japan

. . . three centuries ago, around the year 1660, two of the greatest monuments of modern history were erected, one in the West and one in the East: St. Paul's Cathedral in London and the Taj Mahal in Agra. Between them, the two symbolize . . . the comparative level of architectural technology, the comparative level of craftsmanship and the comparative level of affluence and sophistication the two cultures had attained at that epoch of history. But at about the same time there was also created—and this time only in the West—a third monument, a monument still greater in its eventual import for humanity. This was Newton's *Principia*, published in 1687.

Ideals and Reality

Abdus Salam, Nobel Laureate in Physics

1

Introduction

Irfan ul Haque

The ability to compete in the world market is a major concern today in the industrial countries, a concern that is debated in the mass media as well as in academic research. In the United States, as a result of the persistent and large trade deficit and the displacement of domestic industry by imports, the issue has figured prominently in recent election campaigns. Western Europe is worried about slow economic growth and high unemployment, which many attribute to competition from low-wage countries. Japan's preoccupation with competitiveness is generally regarded as the key to both its phenomenal export success and its "catch-up" with the United States in terms of per capita income, but its industry is also facing serious adjustment problems, not the least because of the appreciated yen.

The debate on international competitiveness—which Paul Krugman (1994) has called a "dangerous obsession"—has often been emotional. It has centered around two questions: whether a country's competitiveness has a clear meaning, and whether anything can or should be done about it. Indeed, some of the measures proposed for promoting competitiveness are liable to result in retaliatory actions by other countries that could end up causing a great deal of harm to the global economy. At issue is the state's role in promoting domestic industries and the relative merits of the various market systems found in industrial countries.

The developing countries have by and large been left out of this debate, even though the spectacular success of some in international trade is often cited as part of the problem. This is rather curious, since the current in the developing world is running in the direction of greater engagement in world trade. An increasing number of countries have moved to open up their economies and have embarked on trade policy reforms. Concerns over the unreliability of the world market and what are deemed to be unfair trading relations remain, but the demand for a "new international economic order" that favors the developing world is now a matter of the distant past. Nevertheless, while exposure to foreign competition has necessitated major industrial restructuring, it has also underscored the wide differences in the ability of economies to compete in the world market. Trade liberalization and other structural reforms have stimulated exports, but the performance across countries has varied considerably. There is some question as to whether rapid export growth can be sustained in the long term. In countries where economic performance has been less than satisfactory, already instituted policy reforms are in danger of being reversed.

Notwithstanding the various disagreements, the competitiveness debate has had one important outcome: there is now a much greater appreciation of the critical role innovation and technological improvements play in the relative economic performance of countries. Although it is ultimately how individual firms perform in the marketplace that determines a country's overall economic strength, certain national characteristics—how human capital is used, the technical skills of the labor force, managerial practices, and government policies—do seem to influence firms' ability to compete. But these ideas have only recently begun to be incorporated into the analyses of problems facing developing countries. The role of technology has been stressed in the development literature, but mostly in the context of minimizing the use of capital and adopting appropriate technologies in an environment where labor is relatively cheap. All too often the case for acquiring new technology has been confused with the advocacy of "high-tech" industry. The contemporary literature goes much further in clarifying the nature of technology and impediments to its transfer across countries, with profound implications for economic policy.

This volume is intended to elucidate the concept of international competitiveness. It attempts to apply recent advances in thinking on the issues of trade, technology, and competitiveness to the conditions generally found in developing economies. These countries stand to learn a great deal from the current debate, particularly those that are in the process of opening up their markets to foreign competition. The benefits such countries can derive from their integration into the world economy will depend largely on their competitive strength, which in turn depends on a host of factors, notably their technological prowess. The chapters that follow put forward the view that international competitiveness is a legitimate national concern and, provided it is defined with due care, a worthwhile objective for the design of policy and institutions in both industrial and developing countries. Although the common image of competitive struggle is one of winners and losers, the pursuit of international competitiveness need not be a zero-sum game, at least not in the long term. Few economists would, for example, argue that the success of Japan or Germany in the postwar period, or the dramatic growth of some East Asian economies more recently, was achieved at the expense of other countries or that this rapid economic growth harmed the world economy. Quite the contrary: it stimulated world commerce and economic growth. The question of whether competitiveness is a "dangerous obsession" depends on how the concept is defined and on the kind of measures adopted in its pursuit.

Defining International Competitiveness

A firm is considered competitive if it is able to sustain its earnings over time and can be viewed as a strong competitor if it is able to increase both its market share and its earnings. Competitive strength is less certain if a firm expands its market share by reducing prices and taking losses, notwithstanding the strategic reasons that might lie behind such moves. Similarly, an economy may be regarded as competitive if it is able to grow without being constrained by balance of payments difficulties and is judged as doing particularly well if it grows faster than other countries.[1] There are, however, some obvious and significant differences between the competitiveness of a firm and that of a country. As Krugman (1994) has stressed, competition among firms, which is usually oligopolistic, implies winners and losers, but the success of one country in the world market need not be at the expense of other countries, because higher exports can also mean higher imports. Also, countries produce and trade a wide variety of products and thus may be competitive in some areas and not in others. The point need not be overdrawn. Strictly speaking, a firm that expands its sales also increases its purchases, while countries (to the extent that they compete in similar markets) often behave like individual firms, in that the gains of one can imply losses for the others, especially when demand is stagnant.

---

1. The imperative of economic growth differs widely among countries. In general, countries with low per capita incomes can be expected to aim for higher growth than richer countries.

A country's competitiveness is, however, complicated by two distinct notions of productive efficiency: its *relative* efficiency (or comparative advantage) in producing tradable products; and the *absolute* level of production costs relative to other countries. While the concept of relative efficiency helps to explain the pattern of international specialization in production, it provides no indication of the overall competitiveness of countries. And while the comparisons of absolute production costs (converted into a common currency unit) may help to explain the success (or failure) of countries in world markets for individual products, such comparisons are easily distorted by exchange rate changes and are hard to aggregate economywide.

Export growth and/or the magnitude of the trade balance are popularly viewed as signs of a country's general economic strength and competitiveness. But these indicators, when seen in isolation from their causes, also suffer from serious shortcomings. Exports may rise on account of some transitory factor (such as an unexpected rise in prices), or because a devaluation makes exports attractive, much as reduced prices increase demand. Devaluation may be necessary to restore a country's competitive position if the country has suffered from relatively high inflation, but by itself such a step has no effect on a country's productive efficiency. The same is true of the size or sign of the trade balance, which can also be affected by factors that have nothing to do with a country's competitive strength. For example, the Republic of Korea, a highly successful exporter, ran substantial trade deficits for many years because it borrowed abroad to finance its heavy investments and imports of capital goods and technology. An opposite example is provided by several heavily indebted Latin American countries, which had to compress domestic demand and cut imports during the early 1980s in order to create trade surpluses to service their external debt. These trade surpluses had little to do with the countries' ability to compete; in fact, the sharp decline in investment directly impinged on the expansion and upgrading of productive capacity and therefore weakened the competitive position of these economies in the long term. In short, a country's ability to compete is affected by macroeconomic policies, but it is not entirely a macroeconomic phenomenon (Blecker 1992).

A practical and widely used definition of competitiveness has been put forward by the U.S. Commission on Industrial Competitiveness, according to which international competitiveness is the ability of a country to produce goods and services that meet the test of international markets and simultaneously to maintain and expand the real income of its citizens (Tyson 1992; Ostry 1991). The definition is understandably vague about the rate at which incomes should expand, for the requirements of growth obviously differ across countries and over time. There is likely to be little disagreement that, at a minimum, income growth should keep up with population growth to prevent living standards from declining. In a world of widely different income levels, poor countries may strive for faster growth than rich economies, not just in order to "catch up" but because rapid growth is essential to alleviating poverty and reducing unemployment. At the same time, rich countries must also seek growth, for they too must meet domestic demands for better health care, housing, schooling, and the like that are more easily met when incomes are rising.

These considerations suggest that a country's competitiveness must be judged not only against its performance in the world market but also in terms of its capacity to sustain economic growth over a period of time. It is in this light that such countries as Germany, Japan, Korea, and several other East Asian economies appear as strong competitors. Their rapid export growth has been accompanied by rising incomes, and their economic performance has been maintained over a long period. The analysis and discussion of issues in this volume have been informed by this notion of international competitiveness.

Why International Competitiveness?

To some degree, the debate on international competitiveness is simply the revisiting of traditional issues under new names, but there are several reasons why the subject has come to be regarded as "new" and and why it has recently attracted a great deal of attention. These include the increasing weight of international trade in the world economy, a phenomenal increase in the mobility of capital across countries, and the sharply divergent performances of countries in terms of trade and economic growth.

Developments in International Trade

One remarkable feature of economic development since the Industrial Revolution has been that world trade has grown much faster than output, so that exports today account for roughly one-fifth of world output. According to the data for one group of industrial countries, the growth of exports has exceeded GDP growth by a considerable margin since the eighteenth century (World Bank 1987). The only exception is the period between 1913 and 1950, when two world wars and the Great Depression disrupted trade channels and protectionism among the industrial countries was rampant.

This phenomenon characterizes virtually all countries. In only a few cases did the share of exports in GDP fail to rise over time, and where this happened, the countries suffered from economic stagnation. The export share rose from 7 percent in 1960 to 18 percent in 1990 in low-income countries; from 16 to 28 percent in middle-income countries; and from 12 to 20 percent in industrial countries. At the broad sectoral level, the proportion of output traded internationally has also generally risen.

The growth in exports has been accompanied by a major shift in the structure of international trade in favor of manufactures, which now account for about 80 percent of world merchandise exports. The shift has been dramatic in a handful of developing countries, where the share of manufactured exports rose from 15 percent in 1965 to 66 percent in 1990. International trade no longer seems to follow the traditional pattern, according to which developing countries supplied primary products to industrial countries in exchange for manufactures. In fact, countries now trade increasingly in similar products, as is evidenced by the growing number of countries that produce and export manufactures ranging from garments to automobiles. At the same time, trade among industrial countries (mostly intraindustrial trade) has risen more rapidly than trade between developing and industrial countries over the last three decades.

The jump in manufactured exports has had a profound impact on the pattern of specialization as well as on trading relationships. The growth in intraindustry trade has manifested itself in increasing product differentiation, so that apart from the costs of production, other considerations—such as design, quality, and reliability—have become increasingly important to consumers. But there is also increased specialization at lower levels of production—that is, production of a single good is now often spread over a number of countries. The nature of world competition has been colored by the mushrooming of so-called "strategic alliances" among firms. These alliances govern inter- and intrafirm marketing relationships across countries. The increasing prominence of "sourcing," or the purchasing of inputs from preselected overseas suppliers, is part of this phenomenon. In short, the character of international trade has changed profoundly over time in terms of both its content and its institutional linkages, and a fairly sizable proportion of world trade is now conducted in other than free, arm's-length marketing arrangements.[2]

---

2. The data on intrafirm purchases are scarce, but according to recent estimates, close to 30 percent of U.S. exports fall into this category (OECD 1993).

At the same time, there has been a significant shift in accepted development strategy from import substitution to export promotion. The dominant view among development economists in the early years of the postwar period was that, given an environment in which exports from developing countries could be expected to fare poorly, only import substitution would allow the affected economies to overcome their balance of payments difficulties. Import substitution was also advocated on the grounds that it promoted the skills and capabilities necessary to develop domestic industry. However, subsequent events showed that import substitution had definite limits and could not be relied on to remove trade deficits in the long term. The dramatic growth in manufactured exports from a few developing countries belied the predictions of the "export pessimists." The result has been that today most countries accept the imperative of export promotion and the need to compete in the world market.

Capital Mobility

Capital movements are intimately tied up with the question of international competitiveness, whether through their impact on exchange rates or their effect on a country's productive capacity. The rapidly increasing mobility of capital in recent years has been viewed as a positive development because it has helped to equilibrate the demand for and supply of capital among countries. Developing countries short on capital are held to benefit from both the inflow of financial resources and the transfer of new technology. In reality, however, capital mobility has proved to be a mixed blessing. The movement of short-term capital (by far the dominant form) is not driven by countries' need for resources but is basically speculative.[3] Capital flows are highly sensitive to monetary and exchange rate policies and more often than not determine whether such policies are viable. This may be helpful when policies need to be reversed, but it also makes macroeconomic management more difficult, especially in situations where economic stability is fragile—in some Latin American countries, for example. Short-term capital movements directly affect a country's ability to compete in the world market through changes (and increased instability) in the exchange rate. To the extent that the increased exchange rate instability makes investment

---

3. Judging from the recent experiences of the Latin American countries, the movement of capital seems to bear an inverse relation to a country's need for finance—that is, it flees when economies are weak and vulnerable and flows in when they are strong and growing.

decisions shortsighted, such movements also impinge on a country's capacity for economic growth.

There is also considerable, and rapidly rising, direct foreign investment, which to a large extent is driven by long-term economic returns and countries' growth prospects. While direct investment is on the whole beneficial to both investors and recipient countries, it tends to excite anxieties among all parties. Many countries view foreign investment with distrust for reasons that are basically nationalistic, such as concern over the sale of national assets to foreign investors (who are not thought to have the nation's interest at heart) or the introduction of foreign management practices and values that threaten established local institutions. Such fears, which were in the past identified with the developing countries, are now becoming pervasive in industrial countries—notably the United States—where they have surfaced with force in recent election campaigns.

The concerns of capital-exporting countries are also significant. First, the outflow of capital is a resource transfer, requiring some element of sacrifice on the part of the nationals of the exporting countries. In addition, capital transfers augment the productive capacities of other countries at the expense of the exporters of capital. Generally speaking, while the well-being of capital-exporting countries may not suffer because of capital outflows, these transfers, which reduce domestic investment, do send jobs overseas and can depress wages. Here the interests of the owners and managers of capital (which moves relatively freely) diverge from those of labor (which continues to face enormous hurdles to international movement). The tension between the two appears to be heightened by the economic stagnation and high unemployment in many industrial countries today.

Capital mobility poses a problem for all countries where high wages are not matched by high productivity. Such an imbalance is often the result of a misalignment of exchange rates caused by expansionary fiscal and monetary policies. But when the problem of competitiveness arises out of differences in long-term productivity performance, foreign investment can aggravate the situation if capital moves from countries that are performing poorly to those that are performing well. For this reason, many countries have become acutely aware of their competitive position and are placing greater emphasis on designing public policy that attracts foreign capital.

Variations in Country Performance

Hidden behind the overall picture of the world economy are the enormous differences in output and export growth among individual economies.

Among the industrial countries, Japan and Germany made a dramatic recovery after World War II, and their per capita incomes grew rapidly until they more or less caught up with the per capita income in the United States, the postwar world economic leader. The performance over the last three decades of the so-called East Asian Tigers—Hong Kong, Korea, Singapore, and Taiwan, China—has been even more impressive, as these economies have sustained an unprecedented pace of economic expansion combined with fairly stable macroeconomic management. They have recently been joined by the other "high-performance Asian economies"—China, Indonesia, Malaysia, and Thailand—which have been growing rapidly for two decades and have developed some highly competitive industries. The most striking feature of all these economies is the rapid growth of exports produced by robust and dynamic manufacturing sectors.

The experience of these countries has attracted the interest of both industrial and developing countries and has stimulated a great deal of research into the causes of this success. While creating strong industries and expanding manufactured exports are prominent goals in developing countries, the great majority of these economies are still a long way from realizing them. These countries are eagerly searching for replicable lessons in the experience of East Asia. In the industrial countries, however, the concerns are rather different. Not only do these countries see East Asia's success as a serious threat to their economies, but they also tend to believe that the East Asians have gained the advantage through unfair trading practices ranging from hidden or overt government support and lax environmental and labor laws to dumping of one kind or another. Complaints about the need to establish a "level playing field" are today more often heard in industrial than in developing countries.

For these and other reasons, the international trading system has come under considerable strain, as was demonstrated by the protracted and difficult negotiations during the Uruguay Round of multilateral trade negotiations and by the problems the World Trade Organization (WTO) legislation encountered in the U.S. Congress. Currently, one group of countries has large trade surpluses and the others equally large deficits, but this state of affairs is sustainable only as long as the countries with surpluses are willing to finance the deficits. The current situation is therefore highly susceptible to both short- and long-term investor activity. There is also some evidence that countries are "getting tough" in trade negotiations, a trend that could result in a return to the beggar-thy-neighbor policies of the interwar period, an era marked by declining productivity and rising unemployment. A key question here is whether the slowdown in economic expansion and the high unemployment in industrial countries today are transitory phenomena that can be corrected by sensible economic policies and institutional changes, or whether they reflect barriers to technological progress and competition from low-wage countries. The issue of international competitiveness is central to this debate.

Organization of Chapters

The relationship between technology, economic growth, and international competitiveness is clarified in chapter 2, which argues that policymakers need to devote much closer attention to the behavior of labor productivity, elevating it to the level of such policy objectives as controlling inflation, balancing the current account, and increasing the rate of economic expansion. This analysis identifies the need for government action in three areas: (i) the promotion of a macroeconomic environment favorable to investment and growth; (ii) the implementation of policies and the promotion of institutions that enhance domestic technological capabilities; and (iii) the creation of competitive advantage in new, dynamic lines of production, a task that requires an articulated industrial policy. The succeeding chapters (chapters 3 through 6) cover each of these subjects.

Chapter 7 argues that national economic policies must be tempered by the international trading environment, which has been undergoing some profound changes and has, in turn, brought about significant changes in the nature of international competition. Institutional changes (such as the role of the "global" firm), as well as the technological revolution in information processing, are not only unifying and integrating the world market but also causing considerable tension in world trading relations.

The final chapter pulls together the discussion in the preceding chapters and offers a few broad conclusions for public policy and institutional change that may help to strengthen a country's performance in the world market and improve its prospects for economic growth. The chapter does not prescribe a set of rigid rules for countries to follow but instead argues for pragmatism in policies designed to restore macroeconomic stability, develop technological capabilities, and promote industrial development. It also attempts to bring out the importance of the context—defined largely by the way governments and businesses interact with each other—in which policy is made and implemented.

2

Technology and Competitiveness

Irfan ul Haque

The ever-increasing quantity, quality, and variety of goods and the general decline in the physical arduousness of work are nothing but the result of technological change. By increasing the range of choices in respect of new products and production processes, technological progress raises the potential for economic expansion and, in general, brings about human and economic development. Put obversely, technological backwardness to a large extent explains the low incomes in developing countries. Differences in living standards across countries were rather small until the eighteenth century. According to one estimate, the ratio of the per capita incomes of the poorest and richest countries around that time was less than 2:1, compared with more than 100:1 today (Dosi, Fabiani, and Freeman 1993). It was only during the eighteenth and nineteenth centuries—a period characterized by a spurt of technological breakthroughs—that the rates of economic growth across countries started to diverge significantly, leading to today's wide income disparities.

This chapter explores the intimate relationship between technology and international competitiveness by looking at the nature of technology and technological change and the ways in which the latter impinges on an economy's capacity to grow. The discussion begins with an examination of the treatment of technology and competitiveness in the mainstream or neoclassical theory of international trade. This is followed by an attempt to frame the definition of international competitiveness offered in the previous chapter in terms amenable to policy interventions and to clarify the ways in which productive efficiency and the ability to compete are closely linked. The discussion then turns to the role technological progress plays in economic development, bringing out the central role of productivity growth in the interaction of trade, technology, and international competitiveness. The chapter argues that countries intent on improving their competitive strength need not only to respect their existing comparative advantage but also to focus on enhancing their *absolute* advantage (defined as the ability to get more out of available inputs) if they are to grow rapidly, thus meeting the basic test of competitive strength. The chapter concludes with a discussion of the differences in technological capabilities and competitive strengths among countries and the reasons these differences persist over time.

Technology and Competitiveness in the Traditional Framework

The traditional theory of international trade and specialization among countries rests on the doctrine of comparative costs originally articulated by David Ricardo and subsequently developed by Heckscher, Ohlin, and neoclassical economists over the years. According to this doctrine, the pattern of specialization and trade depends not on the absolute but on the relative costs of production, which are determined—under certain rigorously specified conditions—by factor endowments. These conditions typically include identical tastes and production conditions across countries, nonincreasing returns to factor use, substitutability among the factors of production, competitive markets, and profit maximization. On the basis of its factor endowments, each country can then find at least one product in which it can specialize and which it can trade to its advantage, thereby improving real income (compared with what would occur in a closed economy). Specialization on the basis of comparative costs can be shown to be inherently efficient, and engaging in international trade is of mutual benefit to all countries, especially when no single country is in a position to affect the terms of international exchange. If a country is able to influence international prices, it may be able to improve its terms of trade (and hence increase its real income) by curtailing the supply of its exports or the demand for its imports with taxes and quotas. However, if other countries are also similarly placed, they can retaliate, initiating a mutually destructive trend toward autarky.

The Traditional Model's Policy Implications

The main message of the international trade model is one of optimism: free trade brings about efficiency and prosperity. One of its most powerful conclusions is that international trade can be a substitute for factor movement, provided countries are not completely specialized in production—that is, if some of the imported goods are produced domestically. Trade tends to equalize factor rewards across national frontiers by raising the price of the relatively abundant factor and lowering it for the relatively scarce. This message offers hope for developing countries, for it implies that by engaging in international trade in an otherwise static world, a low-income country with abundant labor will witness a rise in real wages, while the opposite will happen in a rich country where labor is scarce. Thus, the traditional theory offers a route to the convergence of living standards across countries. In short, under free trade, and given the assumption of full employment, factor substitutability, and perfect competition, the terms of trade can never be unfair, countries cannot exploit each other economically, and there cannot be immiserization of a country arising out of international trade. Nevertheless, these issues have remained prominent in trade policy debates and international relations among nations.

The doctrine of comparative advantage has been one of the most powerful influences on economic policy in recent history. As Krugman (1987) puts it:

> For one hundred seventy years, the appreciation that international trade benefits a country whether it is "fair" or not has been one of the touchstones of professionalism in economics. Comparative advantage is not just an idea both simple and profound; it is an idea that conflicts directly with both stubborn popular prejudices and powerful interests. This combination makes the defense of free trade as close to a sacred tenet as any idea in economics (p.131).

The reasons for the evident appeal and influence of the comparative costs theory are both theoretical and empirical. Theoretically, international trade expands a country's range of choices and, in a sense, straightens out the product transformation curve. Instead of being limited to domestic production possibilities, a country can exchange (transform) one good for another at the externally given terms of trade. As long as international prices differ from the prices that would prevail if the economy were closed, engaging in international trade can be shown to raise a country's economic welfare.

A country's specialization, of course, changes with the terms of trade: a country can start exporting what it once imported if the terms of trade shift sufficiently. Government intervention is not only unnecessary but liable to do harm by shifting production away from the country's comparative advantage. Although the literature gives considerable attention to the conditions under which trade interventions may be advantageous to a country, the neoclassical economists remain by and large agnostic. They believe that only when world prices can be influenced will trade policy unambiguously improve a country's welfare. Trade policy is ill-suited to the task of dealing with market failures that arise out of domestic causes, such as external economies or diseconomies, and mainstream economists tend to view the "infant industry" argument with suspicion (Bhagwati 1989).

Few countries engage in truly free trade, and there is little firm empirical evidence on its benefits. But there is considerable empirical evidence on the harm done by trade policy interventions and protection. There is also a great deal of data showing that factor endowments are important in determining trade patterns and that countries with relatively abundant labor generally tend to export labor-intensive products (conversely, countries with abundant capital tend to export capital-intensive products). However, a major embarrassment to the traditional theory was caused by "Leontief's paradox," a finding based on 1947 data showing that exports from the United States—a capital-abundant country—were relatively more labor intensive than its imports. Although later work attempted to restore the validity of the traditional theory by reinterpreting the data and modifying the methodology, the Leontief paradox nevertheless had a profound influence on subsequent thinking on the subject (Leamer 1987). One area that received particular attention as a result of this development was the role of human capital and technical progress in international trade (Scherer 1992).

Another perhaps more serious problem with the traditional model is its inadequacy in explaining the industrial development experience of Japan and the other newly industrializing economies (NIEs) of East Asia. These countries grew rapidly over a prolonged period of time, and they did so by dramatically and systematically altering their productive structures and creating competitive advantages in new industries. The phenomenal success of these industries in penetrating the world market has contributed to the displacement of the established patterns of trade specialization. Remarkably, this success, which appears now to be "market conforming," could not have been predicted from the countries' factor endowments at the start of the rapid development phase. Indeed, the economic (and political) outlook for Taiwan (China), the Republic of Korea, and other economies in East Asia around the early 1960s, and for

Japan somewhat earlier, was generally poor.[1] The consensus now is that the East Asian economic "miracle," far from being an outcome of free trade, was brought about by all manner of policy interventions (Amsden 1994; Wade 1990, 1994; Blinder 1990; World Bank 1993a).

Recent Theoretical Advances

Within the traditional model of international trade, neither competitiveness nor technology is presented as an independent issue, since countries with identical technologies specialize on the basis of their factor endowments. Competitiveness is not a problem because there is always something each country can profitably produce and trade (as long as markets are open and exchange rates realistic). Given identical production conditions, the question of differences in technological capability among countries is excluded from the discussion of comparative advantage. Significantly, however, Ricardo, who relies on the labor theory of value, explains comparative advantage in terms of the differences in labor productivity among countries (presumably a result of different technological capabilities). The traditional model focuses on the question of *efficiency* in resource allocation, but in strictly static terms, holding everything that matters constant and making any discussion of international competitiveness rather sterile. The questions of how "endowments" can be changed, and what principles should guide these changes, remain unanswered.

The stringency of the assumptions of the traditional model of international trade has troubled many economists, eliciting two basic types of responses. On one side, there has been a search for an alternative theory of international trade. Despite many attempts to construct such a theory— ranging from the exotic to the banal—no single, integrated explanation has

---

1. As the World Bank's *World Development Report* (1991) observed: "Forty-three years ago an influential government report in an important developing country observed that labor today shunned hard, productive jobs and sought easy, merchant-like work. The report showed that workers' productivity had fallen, wages were too high, and enterprises were inefficient and heavily subsidized. The country had virtually priced itself out of international markets and faced a severe competitive threat from newly industrializing China and India. It was overpopulated and becoming more so. This would be the last opportunity, concluded the prime minister in July 1947, to discover whether his country would be able to stand on its own two feet or become a permanent burden for the rest of the world. That country was Japan" (pp. 13–14).

so far emerged to displace the traditional model. (For a review of these "heretical" departures, see Dosi, Pavitt, and Soete 1990.)

On the other side, attempts have been made within the neoclassical analytical framework, which assumes the existence of competitive markets, factor substitutability and mobility, and profit maximization, to relax some of the most restrictive assumptions. The development of the so-called New Trade Theory represents the culmination of these efforts. The new theory seeks to extend and develop the traditional framework and provides, with the help of sophisticated analytical techniques, rigorous answers to questions that have preoccupied economists for some time, including the treatment of economies of scale, externalities, technical progress, product differentiation, and monopolistic and oligopolistic situations. This theory does not provide any startling new revelations but rather lends precision to the intuitions contained in the earlier analyses (Bhagwati 1989; Scherer 1992). In explaining the patterns of trade, the neoclassicists remain wedded to the traditional view of comparative advantage arising out of specified country differences and tend to display considerable caution in, if not ambivalence about, the policy conclusions of their analysis, which are suggestive of departures from free trade (see, for example, Krugman 1987).

A parallel development has occurred in the theory of economic growth that increasingly stresses the importance of human resource development and technological accumulation.[2] Rather than taking technical progress as a given exogenous factor, as in the original neoclassical model of economic growth (Solow 1956), the "new growth theory" views it as an endogenous result of capital accumulation and investment in human resource development. One significant conclusion of this theory is that a country's pattern of development and trade in the long run may reflect, among other things, the resources that are devoted to industrial research and assimilation. The treatment of technological accumulation in the models, however, remains highly formal, with research and development (R&D) viewed much like any other economic activity (that is, subject to the rule of profit maximization). Indeed, in some works, the decision to specialize in research and development activities is shown to depend on factor endowments, and the allocation of resources to such activities is seen as best governed by the market. Government promotion of research activities, according to this view, is likely to diminish global welfare if research is relocated in countries lacking

---

2. The literature here is expanding rapidly, but among the pioneers are Romer (1986), Lucas (1988), and Grossman and Helpman (1991).

in comparative advantage. As Grossman and Helpman (1992, pp. 340–41) note:

> It may seem at first glance that [subsidized R&D] would be desirable because it generates national productivity growth, where otherwise there would be none. But in fact, *the policy induces a waste of world resources during (at least) the period of technological catch up. The inefficiency in world research implies a loss of world output, and in general every country finds itself sharing in the loss* (emphasis added).

The reality is that any research activity, the outcome of which is necessarily uncertain, cannot be evaluated strictly in terms of the standard laws of economics governing cost minimization, even though profit provides the main motivation for researchers, at least in industry. Apart from a desire to catch up with technology leaders, a strong motivation for R&D is to be the first to develop new products and processes and thus to reap monopoly rents, but success is hard to predict. This uncertainty may deter some firms from pursuing R&D but is generally not an overwhelming factor. In any case, an important function of the R&D establishments is to keep up with technical developments in order to be ready to exploit opportunities as they arise. Research also begets research, and it seems unlikely that promoting it in countries that have no comparative advantage will necessarily reduce research activities in countries that do. Indeed, the meaning of comparative advantage in this context is far from clear: research activities cannot be allocated on the basis of *relative* abilities, however these abilities are defined. It is hardly rational to allocate research funds on the basis of a firm or country's inability to do anything else worthwhile. R&D abilities often have to be created, promoted, and fostered ("learning to learn" as Stiglitz [1987] puts it), a process in which public policy has traditionally played an important role. The question of how these abilities may be applied to different activities and the role of "localized learning" are explored in chapter 4.

The above critique of the neoclassical theory does not imply that economic theory offers little or no guidance on policy. What follows is an attempt to show how basic economic concepts can still usefully be applied to elucidate the interaction of trade, technology, and international competitiveness, and how they can help in determining the policies and institutions required to promote competitiveness.

Living Standards, Productivity, and Competitiveness

International competitiveness has been defined as an economy's ability to grow and to raise the general living standards of its population in a reasonably open trading environment without being constrained by balance of payments difficulties. Because imports tend to rise with national output, exports must grow at a commensurate rate if the balance of payments is to remain manageable. Apart from balance of payments considerations, export promotion has also been part of some countries' development strategies (notably in East Asia), as a way of removing the so-called X-inefficiency, developing technological skills, and injecting dynamism into the economy. Thus, international competitiveness implies economic growth accompanied by the development and expansion of internationally competitive tradable sectors. Productivity growth is essential to this process, for it is the basis for raising living standards and strengthening the competitiveness of the tradable sectors.

Labor Productivity and Living Standards

A country's per capita income, taken as a measure of the standard of living, can be expressed as the product of labor productivity, the proportion of the labor force that is employed, the labor force participation rate, and the country's terms of trade with respect to the rest of the world. The exact relationship can be described as follows:

(2-1) $$w = \frac{Y \cdot P}{L} \cdot \frac{1}{d} \cdot \frac{L}{N^*} \cdot \frac{N^*}{N} .$$

In this case, real per capita income (w) is equal to the value of output per employed person (YP/L), deflated by the cost of living index (d), and multiplied by the product of the rate of employment (L/N^*) and the labor force participation rate (N^*/N). Y is total output or GDP in a given period, P the price of output, L the number of persons employed, N^* the size of the labor force, and N the size of the population.

Let the cost of living index (d) be measured by the geometric mean of domestic and foreign prices (P and P^*, respectively) with proportional weights (that is, $d = P^b \cdot P^{*(1-b)}$), where b is the proportion of income spent on domestic goods. Then equation 2-1 can be rewritten as:

(2-2) $$w = \frac{Y}{L} \cdot \left(\frac{P}{P^*}\right)^{(1-b)} \cdot \frac{L}{N^*} \cdot \frac{N^*}{N}$$

where (Y/L) is output per employed worker, or labor productivity, and P/P^* represents the ratio of domestic to foreign prices, or the terms of trade. It is clear that in the case of a closed economy ($b = 1$), equation 2-2 amounts to a tautology. When differentiated with respect to time, it can be rewritten in terms of growth rates:

(2-3)
$$\frac{\Delta w}{w} = \frac{\Delta y}{y} + (1 - b)\frac{\Delta p}{p} + \frac{\Delta l}{l} + \frac{\Delta n^*}{n^*}$$

where $y = Y/L$, $p = P/p^*$, $l = L/N^*$, and $n^* = N^*/N$. In other words, the growth of per capita income (w) is simply the sum of the rates of change of labor productivity (y), the terms of trade (p) weighted by the share of imports in GDP ($1-b$), the employment rate (l), and the labor force participation rate (n^*). Of the factors influencing the growth of per capita income in equation 2-3, the labor force participation rate (N^*/N) remains reasonably stable over time, dependent as it is on such cultural and institutional factors as female labor force participation rates, child labor, and the country's demographic profile (for instance, the proportion of working-age population). None of these factors normally changes abruptly. Furthermore, many of the changes that occur over time tend to offset each other; for example, as societies develop, the use of child labor tends to decrease and the number of women in the work force to increase.

The employment rate (L/N^*), however, is dependent on economic activity, which can fluctuate considerably in the short run on account of changes in the external environment, and, importantly, in macroeconomic policy. Income and employment levels are closely correlated, and per capita income is sensitive to the unemployment rate in the short run, since productivity rises quickly during periods of economic recovery and falls during slowdowns. The recent restructuring of industry in several industrial and developing countries has increased labor productivity, but there is some evidence that this increase has occurred at the expense of employment. Although this outcome suggests a positive association between productivity growth and unemployment (that is, rapid productivity growth spells unemployment), there is little evidence of such an association over the long term (Baumol, Blackman, and Wolff 1989). Over time, economies tend to adjust to a certain rather stable rate of unemployment that is variously called natural, frictional, or structural. Thus, while changes in emloyment rates do affect the level of output, and the proportion of the labor force actually employed fluctuates considerably in the short term, the long-term rate of change in this ratio is likely to be small and may not have a significant trend.

The terms of trade (P/P^*) can also change abruptly and, depending on the importance of foreign trade, can have an enormous impact on a country's real income. The terms of trade can also follow an unfavorable secular trend, though this may not imply a real loss if the declining trend is the result of improvements in the productive efficiency of the export sector. In this case, a country does not expend additional real resources for a given amount of imports and is therefore not worse off because of the deteriorating terms of trade. All the same, a country normally has little influence over its terms of trade, especially in the case of manufactures, since production is typically dispersed over several countries. This does not of course mean that individual firms do not seek and exploit opportunities to move prices in their favor.

These considerations suggest that over a period of years, the collective influence of changes in employment rates, labor force participation, and the terms of trade may not be systematic or very large and that the growth of per capita income will be closely correlated with productivity growth. In other words, the key to raising per capita income over the long term is productivity growth, notwithstanding the influence of other factors. This supposition is supported by considerable empirical evidence, especially for industrial countries (see, for example, Baumol, Blackman, and Wolff 1989). It is in fact often the case that the two are taken as substitutable in empirical studies. For developing countries, the data on employment are generally unsatisfactory and the measures of economywide productivity even less so. However, for a cross-section of fifteen industrializing developing countries, a close and statistically significant positive correlation was found between the growth of productivity in manufacturing (as a substitute for overall productivity growth) and the growth of per capita income over the 1979–89 period.[3] The regression result is given below:

(2-4)   GDP (per capita) growth = $-.027 + 0.410$ *PDTY growth*

$$(2.24)$$

$$R^2 = 0.31.$$

_____

3. See the appendix to this chapter for data sources. Countries include Argentina, Brazil, Chile, Colombia, Hong Kong, India, the Republic of Korea, Malaysia, Mauritius, Mexico, Pakistan, the Philippines, Singapore, Thailand, and Turkey.

Sectoral Composition and Labor Productivity

Overall labor productivity is the average of sectoral productivity rates weighted by the proportion of the labor force engaged in each sector. That is:

$$(2\text{-}5) \qquad \frac{Y}{L} = Y = \Sigma l_i \cdot y_i$$

where l_i and y_i are, respectively, the proportion of the labor force employed and labor productivity in sector i, and $\Sigma l_i = 1$.

The rate of growth of productivity then can be derived as follows:

$$(2\text{-}6) \qquad \frac{\Delta y}{y} = \Sigma v_i \cdot \frac{\Delta y_i}{y_i} + \Sigma v_i \cdot \frac{\Delta l_i}{l_i}$$

where $v_i = V_i/Y_i$, or the share of i sector's value added (V_i) in GDP. The first half of the right-hand side of equation 2-6 is simply the weighted average of sectoral productivity growth; the second half is the weighted average of the proportional shifts in the distribution of labor (some positive and some negative) among different sectors. Thus, the overall productivity level depends on the sectoral composition of output (the extent to which the output structure leans toward higher productivity sectors). The growth rate of productivity depends on productivity growth in individual sectors according to their weight in the economy (the share of value added in GDP), as well as on sectoral shifts in employment. Productivity rises as the structure of output shifts in favor of high-productivity sectors and as progressively more efficient production methods are adopted. However, output structures in fact are rather slow to change, and since the contribution of each sector to overall growth depends on the sector's share in the economy, the move toward the more dynamic sectors initially makes only a small difference to the overall growth.[4] The corollary is that a search for productivity improvement needs to begin in the traditional sectors because of their large weight

---

4. Suppose agriculture and manufacturing have shares in GDP of 60 percent and 15 percent, respectively, at the start of a period. If the productivity in these sectors grows at rates of 2 percent and 10 percent a year, it will take close to twenty years for the two sectors to have matching output levels.

in the economy and also, as in the case of agriculture, to release labor for other sectors.

Nevertheless, there are systematic differences in both productivity levels and growth potential across sectors. Because a country's long-term income growth depends on the lines of production it chooses to specialize in, living standards will not rise if production is concentrated in low-productivity sectors with little growth potential. The case for the industrialization of primary producing countries and for increasingly sophisticated manufacturing in the NIEs turns essentially on this point. As is frequently observed, it matters a great deal today whether a country specializes in the production of potato chips or micro chips. According to conventional trade theory, however, this choice does not really matter.

In the push to develop high-productivity, high-growth sectors, existing relative strengths and comparative advantage should not be disregarded; rather, areas of specialization need to be reevaluated regularly so that comparative advantage can be created in sectors with high income elasticity of demand. This was the basic thrust of the industrial strategy pursued in the East Asian economies and Japan, as described by an ex-Vice Minister of the Japanese Ministry of International Trade and Industry (MITI):

> The Ministry of International Trade and Industry decided to establish in Japan industries which required intensive employment of capital and technology, industries that in consideration of comparative cost of production should be most inappropriate for Japan, industries such as steel, oil refining, petrochemicals, automobiles, aircraft, industrial machinery of all sorts, and later electronics, including electronic computers. From a short-term, static viewpoint, encouragement of such industries would seem to conflict with economic rationalism. But, from a long-range point of view, these are precisely the industries where income elasticity of demand is high, technological progress is rapid, and labor productivity rises fast. It was clear that without these industries it would be difficult to employ a population of 100 million and raise their standard of living to that of Europe and America with light industries alone; whether right or wrong, Japan had to have these heavy and chemical industries (Scott 1985, p. 97).

Should the sectoral shift in production remain an autonomous, market-driven process, as the flow of new products and processes renders certain activities obsolete and opens up new possibilities for specialization, or should public policy attempt to influence the direction and pace of the shift? This has been the major area of debate in development economics, for it concerns new investment in plants and equipment, the promotion of technology, and the development of needed skills. These issues are examined in some depth in later chapters.

Productivity, Trade, and Technology

Economic growth cannot be sustained if it gives rise to trade deficits that cannot be financed, or, more broadly, if a country is unable to meet its foreign debt obligations. From the viewpoint of sustainability, then, the *quality* of economic growth cannot be separated from the rate at which the economy expands. Apart from determining the level of income, productivity growth is a major determinant of a country's ability to buy and sell goods in the international market. Productivity growth, in short, is twice blessed: it ensures a rise in incomes, and it helps to sustain that rise by keeping a country competitive in the world market.

Productive Efficiency and Competitiveness

No matter what a country chooses to produce, it must keep its production costs in line with those of other producers in order to stay competitive, and it must see real costs (measured in terms of physical inputs) decline in order for living standards to rise. In fact, the faster costs decline, the greater becomes the possibility that living standards will increase. Comparative advantage indicates what should be produced, but there will still be competition for a product, whether it is West African cocoa or South Asian textiles. Real costs can be lowered either by reducing the earnings of domestic factors (for example, by devaluing the currency) or by improving productive efficiency. The trick to becoming internationally competitive is to succeed in the world market not by pushing down real incomes but by raising them. Put differently, one way of differentiating competitively strong and weak countries is by the methods they adopt to gain the competitive edge—productivity increases or reduced wages.

There are, in short, two distinct issues involved in increasing a country's well-being and competitiveness: the *level* of real costs and their *decline* over time. The first (productive efficiency) determines the relative level of real income across countries and the latter the rate at which real income rises. Because catching up with the industrial economies is a major goal of developing countries, it is the rate of improvement in productive efficiency over time that must be of primary concern. The efficiency with which factor inputs are used—that is, their productivity—depends on the intrinsic quality of the inputs and the way they are put to work on the basis of known technologies. This process is inherently dynamic. In today's competitive world, products and production methods are constantly being improved, and achieving success in a competitive market requires that a country stay abreast, if not ahead of, new developments in at least some lines of production. If it fails, it risks stagnant or declining incomes. This is a case of having to run to stay in one place while the world around is progressing, and it is as true of primary products as of manufactures. In agriculture, for instance, technical progress has been sustained and rapid, and developments in genetic engineering and biotechnology hold the key to future sectoral growth.

Inputs are of two varieties: those that are normally traded internationally (such as raw materials and machinery) and those that are not. It is the purely domestic inputs—management and worker skills and physical infrastructure—that ultimately determine a country's ability to compete in the world market. The price and quality of traded inputs can, in principle, be kept more or less comparable across countries, but the efficiency with which imported inputs are used depends on purely domestic factors. A key feature of industrial policy in Korea and other East Asian economies has been that the exporters of manufactured goods are given easy access to imported inputs at prevailing international prices. In the case of nontradable inputs, however, countries wishing to stay competitive have only one option: to improve both availability and quality. The need to upgrade domestic inputs is particularly strong if new areas of competence are to be created, whether in sophisticated industries or in traditional sectors.

Measuring Productive Efficiency

Assessing competitiveness requires a measure of productive efficiency that can be used to compare producers across countries and over time. This measure should give an approximate sense both of a plant's or an industry's "distance" from optimum productive efficiency and of the evolution of improvements over time. If there were only one homogeneous input and one output, or if homogeneous inputs were combined in strictly fixed proportions to produce an output, productive efficiency could be unambiguously measured and compared. However, the multiplicity and varying quality of inputs and outputs make comparisons of efficiency across producers enormously difficult, and when comparisons relate to countries, differences in price and quality among inputs and outputs make the task virtually impossible. The measurement of capital poses other serious conceptual issues, especially when technology is embodied in the equipment. As Salter, who pioneered work in this area some three decades ago, notes: "The difficulty is . . . that the interpretation of even the simplest measures of productivity raises a host of very complex problems. For behind productivity lie all the dynamic forces of economic life: technical progress, accumulation, enterprise and the institutional pattern of society" (1966, p.1). If the problems of comparing productive efficiency across different producers are somehow overcome, measuring change over time is a relatively simple matter.

Different methods have been proposed to get around the difficulties of aggregating outputs and inputs in order to measure efficiency and its changes over time. Of these, the measure of total (or multi-) factor productivity (TFP) is perhaps the most widely used. The concept of TFP itself has several variants but in essence amounts to aggregating multiple inputs and outputs into one measure on the basis of a set of weights (see Baumol, Blackman, and Wolff 1989 for an overview of TFP). One straightforward method is to use the share of different inputs and outputs in the total value of production as weights, as is commonly done in constructing index numbers for quantities. A crude measure of TFP at time (t) would then be $Y(t)/X(t)$, where $Y(t)$ and $X(t)$ are, respectively, weighted aggregate output and input. Thus, growth in TFP is represented simply by:

(2-7) $$[Y(t+1)/X(t+1)]/[Y(t)/X(t)] - 1 .$$

The most popular variant of the TFP measure, which has been applied to both economywide and sectoral data, relates to the estimation of the shifts in a hypothetical production function. This method, which was originally introduced by Solow (1957), relies on standard neoclassical assumptions—that is, that there exist a well-behaved, differentiable, constant returns-to-scale production function; competitive markets; and profit maximization, with factors earning rewards equal to the value of their marginal products. Technical progress is assumed to be "Hicks neutral": for any given combination of inputs, the rise in output due to technical improvements is equiproportional, leaving marginal factor productivities unchanged. Given these conditions, the growth of TFP is estimated as the difference between growth in output and in the use of inputs, each input being weighted by the share of its earnings in output (usually assumed to be constant). That is:

(2-8) $$\text{TFP (growth)} = dY/Y - \sum_i B_i \cdot dK_i / K_i$$

where Y is output, K_i is input of factor i (including labor), and B_i represents the share of that factor's earnings in the output. Since the production function is constant returns to scale, $\sum B_i = 1$, and equation 2-8 can be rewritten in terms of output and inputs per unit of labor employed as:

(2-9) $\qquad\qquad$ TFP (growth) $= dy/y - \sum B_i \cdot dk_i/k_i$.

Lower-case letters denote different variables per unit of labor—$y = Y/L$, $k_i = K_i/L_i$, and so forth. Equation 2-9 shows that the growth of TFP is in the nature of a *residual* left after the weighted change in the input use per unit of labor is subtracted from the growth of labor productivity.

The biggest problem with this measure of TFP growth is the extreme restrictiveness of the assumptions employed, which presuppose the existence of a production function that has little intuitive appeal, even if markets are held to be perfectly competitive. The measure implicitly assumes that all producers operate on an identical production function, with no efficiency differences among them.[5] Indeed, it can be shown that this method, far from estimating technological progress, yields only the weighted average of the increase in factor rewards (Sheikh 1987; Hsing 1992).[6] Furthermore, equations 2-8 and 2-9 measure only disembodied technical progress, ignoring that substantial portion of improvements which is embodied in plants and equipment. Finally, as a residual, TFP growth is liable to contain all the measurement errors and may not in fact be a measure of technical progress. It has been aptly called "a measure of our ignorance."

Another widely used measure of efficiency in factor use is the estimate of "domestic resource costs" (DRCs), or the ratio of value added in a sector (with factor inputs valued at their shadow prices) to the estimate of value added derived by applying international border prices to output and inputs. Because this measure requires a great deal of detailed data that are not usually available, it must often rely on a great deal of guesswork. How-

---

5. Further simplifying assumptions have been used in an effort to separate the efficiency among producers from technical progress (Nishimizu and Page 1982).

6. National income is composed of wages and profits and can be written as $Y = wL + rK$, where Y, L, and K refer to income, labor, and capital, and w and r are wages and profit rate, respectively. The equation can also be written in terms of units of labor as $y = w + rk$. When differentiated with respect to time, the equation becomes:

$$\frac{\dot{y}}{y} = \beta\frac{\dot{w}}{w} + (1-\beta)\frac{\dot{r}}{r} + (1-\beta)\frac{\dot{k}}{k}$$

where β is the share of wages in the national income. Then:

$$\text{TFP (growth)} = \frac{\dot{y}}{y} - (1-\beta)\frac{\dot{k}}{k} = \beta\frac{\dot{w}}{w} + (1-\beta)\frac{\dot{r}}{r}.$$

ever, when carefully calculated, this ratio can provide, for a given country at any given time, an indication of the efficiency of resource use in different sectors in relation to the alternative of importing. Pack (1993), for example, uses the concept to analyze the problems of industrialization in Africa. However, the DRC measure is unusable for international comparisons or even temporal comparisons within the same country. It therefore cannot serve as a basis for measuring the relative competitive strengths of different countries or the changes in these strengths over time.

This leads to the consideration of labor productivity as an indicator of productive efficiency and competitiveness. The growth of labor productivity, as shown earlier, is correlated with growth in per capita income, and the factors that stimulate productivity also help to raise income. But growth in labor productivity can also be taken as representative of a general improvement in productive efficiency and hence can serve as a reasonably reliable indicator of the competitiveness of the tradable sectors. However, even if the significant differences of quality within labor itself are ignored, labor productivity as a measure disregards the contribution of other inputs, notably capital equipment, and therefore cannot in itself indicate whether factors of production are being optimally combined and used. Thus, differences in labor productivity, especially when comparisons are made across countries, may reflect different factor combinations rather than relative productive efficiency. Specifically, producers using capital-intensive techniques will normally have higher labor productivity than other producers, but this difference does not imply that capital-intensive producers are necessarily more efficient in the use of resources.

Two points, however, can be made in favor of labor productivity as a measure of efficiency. First, there is considerable empirical evidence showing that labor and capital are complementary because their contributions to output cannot be separated, except possibly at the margin. Nelson (1981) offers the analogy of a cake: the effect of an ingredient can be appreciated at the margin (that is, a little more sugar means a sweeter cake), but this does not mean that one ingredient can substitute for another. The second point is that the range of factor combination possibilities in industry is often much narrower than it is in the textbook case of a smooth production isoquant. At the same time, productivity improvements take place at the point of actual practice, reflecting what has been called "localized learning" (Atkinson and Stiglitz 1969). Thus, producers look for ways to cut costs that save on at least one input, rather than testing the cost differences of various factor combinations along a given production isoquant. This is more true of manufacturing than of agriculture, where there is usually greater scope for capital/labor substitutability. Producers also tend to respond to changes in the prices of factors or products by looking for techniques that are absolutely superior rather than by exploring other points on a given production isoquant. It seems reasonable to conclude that at least in manufacturing, differences in labor productivity are more likely to reflect a ranking of the superiority of techniques than of differences in factor combinations.

Whether or not the absolute level of labor productivity can be taken to represent overall productive efficiency, the rate of increase in productivity over time can be taken as revealing the increasing sophistication of production methods and processes. Producers in two countries with very different labor productivities can still be competitive, provided the one with the lower productivity also has lower wages. But if the low-productivity country wants to raise its wages and living standards in order to catch up with the high-productivity country, it will have to speed up improvements in production methods. These improvements are likely to be in the general direction of the techniques being used in the high-productivity country.

However, complex phenomena other than technological advances underlie the behavior of labor productivity. Productivity may be improved in three ways: (i) by reorganizing production processes to achieve the "rated" capacity of a given plant (that is, by getting rid of X-inefficiency); (ii) by making marginal improvements in plants and production practices over time; and (iii) by tapping the available best-practice technology. In real life, as chapter 4 shows, these three contributors to productive efficiency need not be adopted in any particular order and may be difficult to distinguish from each other. The notion of "best practice" is not unambiguous, and producers may abandon one technology for another without removing plant-level inefficiencies, or they may be technological leaders during one period but not in another.

At the level of industry, productivity changes are the combined result of improvements in the "best practice" and of the speed with which producers lagging behind catch up, but in reality the two are hard to differentiate. In other words, changes in productivity in an industry over a period of time are the result both of technological changes and management decisions at the level of individual plants and of the weight of those improvements in the aggregate.

The Empirical Evidence

There is evidence from both industrial and developing countries that labor productivity and its growth tend to be associated with the efficient use of capital. Countries with high absolute levels of labor productivity and rapid growth also tend to have high capital productivity. Dosi, Pavitt, and Soete (1990) found a negative correlation between labor productivity in manufacturing and estimated capital-output ratios across a group of developed countries and a few relatively industrially advanced developing countries. In other words, the countries with more efficient labor were also, generally speaking, more efficient users of capital. The researchers conclude: "Higher degrees of development are . . . associated with both higher labor productivity and higher capital productivity" (p. 57). This finding seems to be consistent with Salter's observation that technical advances leading to "absolute savings in labor unaccompanied by absolute saving in capital (both measured per unit of output)" are the exception, and that the "more usual case is that of advances which involve some absolute saving of both factors" (1966, p. 45).

The relationship between growth in manufacturing productivity and the economywide incremental capital-output ratio (ICOR) was examined for the group of developing countries included in the regression results reported in equation 2-4. The period covered was the 1970s.[7] As noted earlier, the economywide productivity measures for developing countries tend to be unreliable, but productivity growth in the manufacturing sector may be an adequate indicator of the general technological dynamism of a country. The Spearman rank correlation between labor productivity growth and the ICORs for the group in question was found to be –0.53, and the simple linear regression result is given below:

(2-10) $ICOR = 4.713 - 0.167 \, PDTY \; growth$
                           (1.878)
                           $R^2 = 0.28.$

This result, which is significant only at the 90 percent level, suggests that countries with a productivity growth rate of 10 percent a year would have, on average, an ICOR that is 35 percent lower than the ICOR for those with no productivity growth. Along with the findings of Dosi, Pavitt, and Soete (1990), this finding suggests that countries face varying production conditions and do not have identical production functions. The result also hints at the existence of increasing returns to capital use, in that high investment

---

7. The 1980s data were not used because of the serious macroeconomic imbalances and recessionary conditions that prevailed in a number of countries in the group during this period. These data would have distorted ICOR estimates.

may not be associated with diminishing returns, a point that is explored further in the next chapter.

The suggestion that labor productivity growth captures broader efficiency gains—what Salter (1966) called "growth in depth"—and reduces the real costs of production can also be viewed in terms of the impact on the export performance and competitive strength of individual countries. Baumol, Blackman, and Wolff (1989) quote the results of a study of six industrial countries showing that Japan, Italy, and Germany, all of which have good or outstanding records of productivity growth, increased their shares of manufactured exports in world trade substantially between 1881 and 1973. However, in the United States and United Kingdom, where productivity growth lagged, these shares decreased. The data from the group of fifteen developing countries mentioned earlier tend to corroborate this finding. Table 2.1 reports the results of a series of regressions in which the dependent variable is the change in a country's share in the total of manufactured exports from the developing countries over a ten-year period (using trend values) and the independent variable is growth in productivity in manufacturing over the same period (also taken as the trend value). The two periods examined were 1970–79 and 1980–89.

The regression coefficient of productivity growth is significant at the 95 percent level for both periods for the entire group of countries. Although the intercepts are strikingly different, the regression coefficients are rather close (within one standard error of estimate). However, the results are highly sensitive to the inclusion of Korea, which had a large increase in productivity as well as in shares of exports in both periods. If Korea is excluded from the observations, the results cease to be statistically significant, although the sign of the regression coefficient remains positive. However, an examination of the scatter diagrams (Figs. 2.1 and 2.2) suggests the presence of a cluster of ten countries, eight of them overlapping in both periods, that display a close relationship between productivity growth and the changes in the share of exports. Korea is not in either cluster, but its position lies close to the extended regression line. The other five countries display no distinct pattern.

Several observations can be made about these results. First, a significant improvement in productivity performance appears to have taken place between the 1970s and 1980s among roughly the same group of countries (as suggested by the rightward shift in the regression line). This improvement can be viewed as the result of the extensive economic reforms and liberalization that these countries embarked on in the 1980s. But it also appears that productivity growth has come to matter more than before in determining export performance, given the large negative intercept and the steeper slope of the regression line for the 1980s. The fact that the intercepts for both the entire sample and the cluster are positive for the 1970s but negative for the 1980s suggests that, in the earlier period, some countries were able to increase their market shares despite low productivity growth. But during the 1980s, the competition facing exports from these countries intensified, and the countries needed to achieve a certain level of productivity growth before they could expect to see their market shares rise. Finally, the importance of productivity in export performance suggests that countries may exploit their relative strengths (as reflected in their factor endowments) in determining what to produce but still need to develop an "absolute advantage"—that is, to improve their overall productive efficiency—in order to compete with other producers and raise their incomes while doing so, a point stressed by Dosi, Pavitt, and Soete (1990).

Table 2.1. Export Performance and Productivity Growth

(Selected sample of developing countries)

Countries covered		Intercept	Productivity growth
Entire Group			
1970s		0.683	0.468
		(0.82)	(2.25)
	$R^2 = 0.28$		
1980s		–0.954	0.565
		(0.86)	(2.29)
	$R^2 = 0.29$		
"Clustered" Countries[a]			
1970s		0.793	0.734
		(0.94)	(2.13)
	$R^2 = 0.36$		
1980s		–6.334	31
		(3.30)	(3.77)
	$R^2 = 0.64$		

Note: See appendix to this chapter for data sources. The dependent variable is the absolute change in the share of a country's manufactured exports in the total of developing country manufactured exports, derived on the basis of trend values at the beginning and end-year of the period.

a. The cluster included Brazil, Chile, Colombia, India, Malaysia, Mexico, Pakistan, Singapore, Thailand, and Turkey for the 1970s; and for the 1980s, Brazil, Colombia, Hong Kong, India, Malaysia, Mexico, Pakistan, the Philippines, Singapore, and Turkey. Besides Korea, the countries not included are Argentina and Mauritius.

Figure 2.1 Export Performance and Productivity Growth: Entire Sample

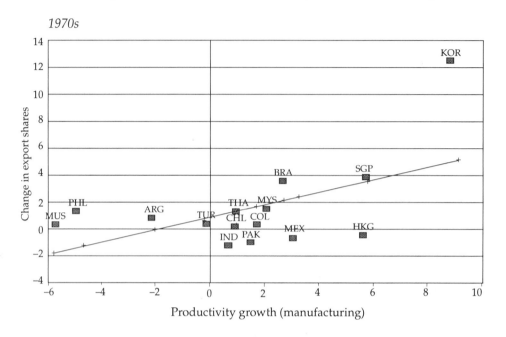

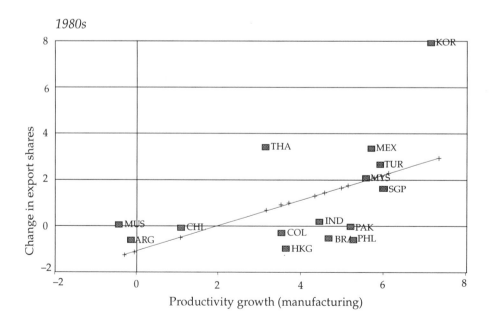

Figure 2.2 Export Performance and Productivity Growth: "Clustered" Countries

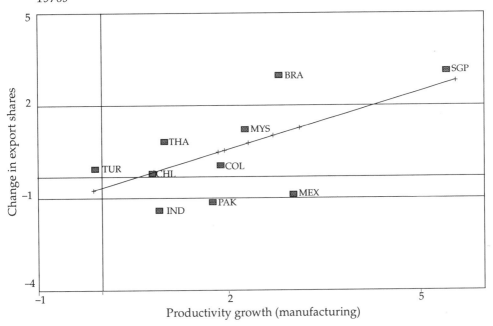

1970s

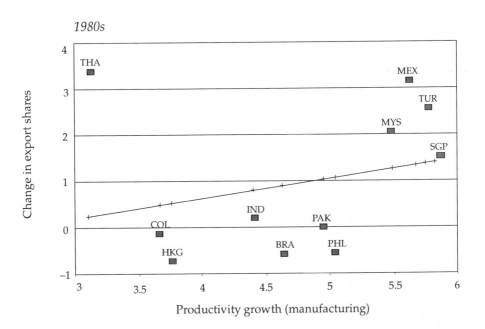

1980s

What Explains the Differences in Competitive Strength?

Until the 1980s, a large number of developing economies managed to maintain high growth rates. During the period 1965–80, some forty developing countries achieved an annual average GDP growth rate of 5 percent or more, with almost half recording growth of more than 6.5 percent (World Bank 1992). Although the Asian NIEs were among the leaders in this latter group, it was in the 1980s that their economic performance became a subject of growing interest. The ability of the Asian NIEs to sustain high growth stood in sharp contrast to the economic stagnation and decline in output most other developing countries were experiencing. During this period, the participation of these high-performance economies in international trade increased, and their manufactured products penetrated world markets and displaced traditional suppliers. Thanks to rapid productivity growth, these economies have demonstrated their capacity to compete in the world market and raise their living standards rapidly at the same time (World Bank 1993a).

Although productivity growth has a significant influence on export performance, it is clearly not the whole story. Other factors, such as quality, design, delivery time, and customer service, also play an important part in determining the performance of exports. Nevertheless, productivity behavior and production costs are fundamental to a producer's ability to compete, in the sense that success in marketing ultimately depends on productive efficiency. To the extent that products of high quality or design command higher prices, the distinction between competition based on price and competition based on quality becomes virtually immaterial: the products may be seen either to differ in quality at a given price or to differ in price at the same level of quality. Generally speaking, therefore, international comparisons of productivity do provide an approximate notion of countries' ability to compete in the world market, rather like a thermometer that can indicate the presence of fever but not diagnose the malady.

For this reason, one approach to weighing countries' competitive strengths is to compare productivity ratios in individual sectors and in aggregate over time. Basically, this approach involves cross-country comparisons of three kinds: (i) labor productivity in a given tradable sector; (ii) labor productivity adjusted for wages; and (iii) the rate of productivity growth over a period of time. The first comparison gives an idea of the approximate distance between, say, the world's leading producer of a traded good and the country being assessed, as superior production techniques imply higher productivity. Since the productivity level by itself gives no indication of a country's competitive strength (rich countries are not necessarily more competitive than poor), the second comparison provides an idea of the extent to which wage differences compensate for productivity differences across countries. Finally, the last comparison gives an indication of whether the country in question is catching up with or lagging behind its competitors, according to whether its productivity in a given sector (or in aggregate) is rising relatively quickly or relatively slowly. The productivity performance of technologically dynamic, rapidly growing sectors is of special interest in the long term, for it provides an indication of how well a country's competitive advantage is evolving in relation to other countries.

When an economy is generally competitive, its performance, in terms of these comparisons, is likely to be superior in some sectors and inferior in others, depending essentially on the economy's comparative advantage. But when the economy lags behind others in a whole range of industries, the problem can be defined as one of competitiveness. To the extent that the wage level is simply out of line with the productivity level, the country's competitive position can be improved by means of macroeconomic policy, notably a devaluation. When productivity growth is low, however, and remains low over a long period, then a country's ability to compete in the world market is fundamentally constrained and the underlying causes must be addressed.

The issue of what determines productivity growth has been widely debated in the economics profession, even though it is generally agreed that technological progress is a central driving force (Nelson 1981). There is also little question that productivity growth is affected by the quality of labor and by investment in new plants and equipment, although management, with its awareness of and ability to implement technological improvements, plays a decisive role in the final outcome. Some researchers concerned with the issue of international competitiveness have emphasized the influence of institutions, corporate organization, and finance. Porter (1990), for example, has stressed the importance of the national environment in which companies are born and compete. This environment is determined by what he calls "the diamond of national advantage"—that is, the interaction of the supply of factors (notably skilled labor); domestic demand and competition; the presence of supplier industries; and the conditions governing the creation, organization, and management of firms. It is not necessary to accept Porter's framework to recognize that all these factors affect a nation's technological performance and dynamism as well as the competitive climate for firms. (These considerations are discussed later in this volume, particularly in chapter 4.) This section focuses on identifying the key factors that influence the behavior of productivity over time, abstracting from institutional and organizational factors.

Determinants of Productivity Differences

A great deal of theoretical and empirical research has been done to explain the diversity of the growth experience, particularly the success of the East Asian NIEs. According to the standard neoclassical growth model, labor productivity rises with capital accumulation, and low-income countries employing low-capital intensive techniques of production can be expected to grow faster than rich countries (at similar rates of savings) and eventually to catch up with them. Taking this notion as the point of departure, recent theoretical work shows that technological differences are the main explanation for variations in growth experiences (see, for example, Lucas 1988; Romer 1986). Technology in these analyses is equated with knowledge, which is held to be more or less universally available.[8] For this reason, emphasis is placed on the human capital that makes the access to and use of this knowledge possible. Such analyses generally ignore the role of technical progress embodied in new plants and equipment, although recent empirical studies (see, for instance, De Long and Summers 1993) show that the impact of investment in machinery on productivity growth is statistically highly significant, an issue discussed in chapter 3. Furthermore, investment in human capital is regarded in the same way as any other investment that is associated with current sacrifices and future returns.

The empirical estimates of the impact of human capital on productivity are impressive and more or less consistent across different studies. Barro (1991) demonstrates that when human capital (as measured by primary and secondary school enrollment rates) is taken into account, there is a statistically significant tendency toward convergence, and low-income countries grow faster than those with higher incomes. In other words, poor countries with high levels of human capital will catch up with the rich, but not otherwise. A recent World Bank study of the East Asian miracle reports similar findings (World Bank 1993a). Taking a somewhat different approach, Baumol, Blackman, and Wolff (1989) find evidence of convergence among groups of rich, "intermediate," and centrally planned economies but not among the developing countries in the sample. However, when education

---

8. For example, Lucas (1988, p. 15) takes technology "to refer to something common to all countries, something 'pure' or disembodied . . ."

indices are included in the regressions, the convergence phenomenon appears among countries with similar education levels.

For the group of developing countries for which regression results have already been reported (Table 2.1), the behavior of productivity growth in manufacturing—taken to represent a country's competitive strength—has been examined in relation to education indicators as well as to investment (Table 2.2). (A few countries from the original group of fifteen had to be excluded for want of comparable data.) However, for this set of regressions, the cross-country data on the trend values for the two periods (1970–79 and 1980–89) were not regressed separately, as in Table 2.1, but taken as panels of two observations for each country. This approach has the advantage of doubling the total number of observations for an otherwise rather small sample. Following the approach adopted by Kaldor (1967), productivity growth was first regressed on output growth in manufacturing in acknowl-edgment of the so-called Verdoorn Law, according to which the close rela-tionship between these two variables is based on increasing returns to scale as well as on technological progress. The principal concern, then, is with explaining the differences between the observed and the estimated values of productivity growth from this regression equation in terms of school enrollment and investment across countries.

While the data for developing countries tend to confirm the Verdoorn Law (line 1, Table 2.2), the result is not as robust as it is for Kaldor's indus-trial countries. The residuals of productivity growth, however, are rather better explained by the secondary school enrollment rate than by invest-ment (lines 2 and 3). Because of some collinearity between secondary school enrollment and investment, the quality of the regression fails to improve when these two variables are taken together (line 4). On the other hand, the impact of primary school enrollment on productivity growth is statistically insignificant, probably because of the rather small variation in this rate across countries in the sample and because secondary school education is likely to be more relevant to the manufacturing sector.

As proxies for human capital, however, school enrollment rates do not quite capture technological sophistication and dynamism—that is, the pace at which technologies are improved and put to work—which are what must ultimately determine productivity growth. There are many examples of countries whose educated citizens remain unemployed or migrate to other countries. Education is a key factor in determining the quality of labor and thus a country's ability to tap new technologies, but it does not by itself ensure that a country will achieve technological mastery. For one thing, the type of education that is emphasized matters, in particular the distribution of students among the arts and sciences and engineering. The East Asian economies, which have a high proportion of students continuing on to secondary and tertiary schools, also have a relatively high proportion studying sciences and engineering—much higher than in other countries, including some industrial countries. However, developing and improving a country's technological base requires more than just investment in education. It also requires overcoming the impediments to the transfer of technology from one firm to another and from one country to another, as chapter 4 discusses. Technology cannot be equated with "information" or "ideas," as it is in much of the recent literature on the subject (for example, in Romer 1992). It cannot be easily passed from those who have it to those who do not. In fact, the transfer of technology is not easy, smooth, or without costs, for several reasons.

Table 2.2. Determinants of Manufacturing Productivity Growth

Dependent variable	Intercept	Manufacturing output growth	Secondary school enrollment	Investment rate
1. Productivity Growth	0.681 $R^2 = 0.21$	0.329 (2.93)		
2. Productivity Residual [a]	−1.988 $R^2 = 0.14$		0.050 (2.31)	
3. Productivity Residual	1.830 $R^2 = 0.06$			7.758 (2.08)
4. Productivity Residual	−2.702 $R^2 = 0.16$		0.044 (1.79)	3.693 (0.81)

Note: Data are from Argentina, Chile, Colombia, India, Korea, Malaysia, Mexico, Pakistan, Singapore, Thailand, and Turkey. See the appendix to this chapter for data sources.

a. The residuals of the observed from the estimated productivity growth are derived from the regression result (1) reported in this table.

The first is the proprietary nature of technology: firms that invest in technology development like to protect their results through patents and secrecy. Second, even if technology could be seen as a book of blueprints and therefore easily transferable, a certain expertise is required to interpret and apply the engineering principles to a real-life situation. Firms or countries often lack this capability. Third, only a portion of technological knowledge is codified in the form of basic principles; a good proportion is tacit or unwritten. Thus, some skills take time to learn—in some cases, considerable time. For example, shoe manufacturing techniques are fairly straightforward, but the secrets of making top-quality shoes are not easily transferable. And, finally, even if engineering and scientific principles are well-established and can be learned (as they are, for example, in the techniques of automobile manufacturing), applying them requires heavy capital investment in order to develop effective prototypes and a long period of learning to get the technology right.

There are also problems for recipients of new technologies. Firms or countries may be unable to adopt these technologies because of difficulties in breaking away from the inherited technological base—that is, technology that is embodied in physical capital, the institutions that govern it, and the standards that are used to evaluate it. Technological knowledge is cumulative and builds on itself, and the adoption of even simple techniques is conditioned by the existing knowledge base. In general, firms find it easier to improve on what they are used to doing and often harbor the expectation that there will be a technological breakthrough within their adopted system. In addition, national safety standards differ, and regulations are often instituted with the tacit objective of protecting domestic industry from foreign competition. It is for these reasons that electrical and communication systems vary across countries, for example, and that appliances such as video recorders and televisions often operate with different systems in various parts of the world.

Technological dynamism, however, involves more than acquiring technological know-how. It requires a culture of intellectual curiosity, a drive to innovate, and a certain motivation for making small improvements within individual firms (what the Japanese call *kaizen*). Considerable empirical work, inspired by the Schumpeterian notion of "creative destruction," has been done in recent years on the role of innovation in a country's competitive strength and general economic performance (Dosi, Pavitt, and Soete 1990; Fagerberg 1988). According to these studies, the gaps in productivity levels across countries are largely the result of technological differences, and productivity growth depends on the pace of technological improvements. Besides the more conventional factors such as investment rates and initial income levels, R&D expenditures and the number of patents issued, as proxies for the innovative effort, are seen as significant determinants of productivity growth and economic performance. Fagerberg, for example, concludes that ". . . to catch up with the developed countries . . . semi-industrialized countries cannot rely only on a combination of technology import and investments, but have to increase their national technological activities as well" (1988, p. 451). This viewpoint is a significant departure from the conventional view, which posits technological leaders that are on the technology "frontier" and are the main source of innovation, and followers (developing countries) that simply attempt to catch up through imitation. As chapter 4 shows, the distinction between innovation and diffusion/imitation is in reality far from sharp: both require efforts to build up technological capabilities, and even the simplest techniques of production require considerable adaptation to local conditions and innovative skills.

Figure 2.3 traces the sequence that has been discussed in this chapter. Productivity growth occurs as productive efficiency in existing industries improves and as productive structures shift in favor of high-value-added activities. But this change requires investment in plants and equipment, the development of worker skills, and a general increase in a nation's ability to generate and manage change. However, this sequence is not rigid, for there are strong feedbacks, and the direction of causation (as discussed below)

Figure 2.3. A Framework for Trade, Technology and International Competitiveness

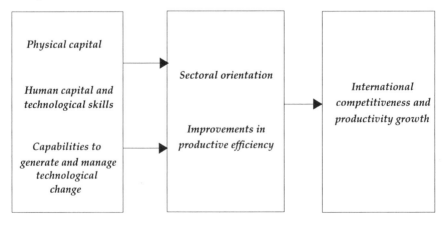

can easily go the other way. It should be also noted that the actual outcome is conditioned by the institutional setup as well as by the general economic and political environment.

Toward a Virtuous Circle

While evidence supporting the importance of human capital and innovative effort to productivity growth is strong, it does not convincingly establish a cause-and-effect relationship. It can be argued, in fact, that as countries become richer, education is increasingly valued and more is spent on schooling and research. Similar reverse causation is possible with regard to the links between productivity and savings or productivity and trade. For example, the high savings rates in the East Asian NIEs may be the result of consumption lagging behind rapidly rising income levels. Similarly, competing in the world market itself often brings about improvements in productive efficiency and strengthens a country's ability to compete.

What the empirical results do suggest is that countries with low incomes are more liable to get caught in a low-income/low-growth trap, with little prospect of catching up with wealthier economies. In the rapidly growing economies, success seems to feed on success. The growth phenomenon seems to be characterized by what Nurkse some decades ago called "virtuous" circles. The original idea was that low incomes result in low savings and investment rates, which in turn result in low growth. Technological know-how and dynamism add new elements to the circle, stimulating productivity growth and strengthening a country's ability to compete in the world market. It can be argued that a self-reinforcing connection exists between the accumulation of human and physical capital and technological progress, which stimulate each other in a dynamic setting. As Nelson notes: "Just as a high rate of capital formation and a well-educated work force stimulate technological advance, so technological advance stimulates a high rate of capital formation and motivates young people to acquire formal education" (1981, p. 1055).

Competition in the world market feeds technological dynamism by exposing producers to different products and approaches to production, by improving the skills of workers who use imported goods that embody new technology (such as computers), and particularly by establishing buyer-seller contacts that often result in technological improvements in products and processes. John Stuart Mill noted the importance of this last factor over a hundred years ago:

It is hardly possible to overrate the value in the present low state of human improvement, of placing human beings in contact with persons dissimilar to themselves, and with which they are familiar. Such communication has always been, particularly in the present age, one of the primary sources of progress (quoted in Dornbusch 1992, p. 75).

As has been noted, competing in the world market requires exploiting a country's existing strengths (comparative advantage), while searching for new areas of competence. The latter cannot be a passive pursuit; it requires a deliberate strategy to keep abreast, if not ahead, of technological developments elsewhere.

Figure 2.4 illustrates the interaction of trade, technology, and international competitiveness, which together affect overall economic growth. Economic success depends on the dynamism and self-reinforcing tendencies of this interaction. The rapidly growing East Asian economies appear to have overcome the barriers to the virtuous circle of trade, technology, and competitiveness and have started to catch up with the industrial countries. While views differ on how these countries entered this virtuous circle—in part because the approaches used differ in significant respects from each other—two characteristics stand out: a national commitment to economic development (the basis of a "developmental state," as it has sometimes been called), and pragmatism in government policies and national strategies. These countries took a series of complementary, sensible, and practical measures without paying obeisance to any particular ideology or economic model. The Republic of Korea and Taiwan, China, followed this course thirty years ago, and China and Viet Nam are pursuing it today, especially with regard to technology and trade. Aggressive export promotion, protection for domestic industry, and deliberate efforts to build the domestic technological capabilities needed for new, more advanced industries are the hallmarks of these countries' development strategies.

It does not seem possible to break into the virtuous circle simply by relying on international trade as an engine of growth (through, for example, blanket trade liberalization), or on investment in education and infrastructure as a means of promoting technological advances that will spur industrial development. International trade promotes technological improvements through increased competition, in turn stimulating the search for improvements in processes and products and facilitating the flow of information. This, however, is not enough. For one thing, world trade is not characterized by atomistic competition, with small individual sellers facing perfectly elastic demand. In fact, the world market has come to resemble a battleground where economic survival depends on producers' ability to

Figure 2.4 The Interaction of Trade, Technology, and International Competitiveness

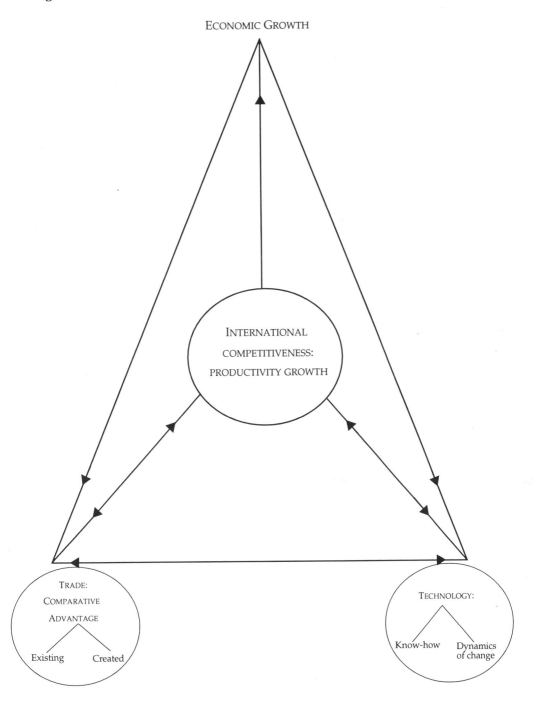

adapt to changing market conditions and anticipate future technological and economic trends as well as on short-term marketing tactics and long-term production strategies. Countries need to promote capabilities for searching out, evaluating, adapting, and developing technologies that will enhance competitiveness. At least during the early stages of industrial development, this requires a great deal of government involvement, be it to promote investment, regulate economic and financial rules, or redistribute wealth across classes and time periods.

It was argued earlier that in order to gain competitive strength, countries need to focus on enhancing their absolute advantage by positioning themselves to catch up with or do better than other countries; a principal determinant of their ability to do so is the technological base. As long as markets are reasonably free, a country's trade orientation can be expected to follow the principle of comparative advantage, but it is absolute advantage that determines whether a country has successfully entered a virtuous circle. Relying on the market alone may not be enough to enhance absolute advantage and become competitive in new, more dynamic activities; active public policy interventions may be required. Three areas have been identified in which government leadership has a critically important role to play in helping a country enter the virtuous circle: creating a favorable macroeconomic environment, building up national technological capabilities, and implementating industrial strategies to develop new areas of competence. The following chapters discuss these activities and the government's role in each.

Appendix: Sources of Data

The data sample included the following countries: Argentina, Brazil, Chile, Colombia, Hong Kong, India, Indonesia, Korea, Malaysia, Mexico, the Philippines, Pakistan, Singapore, Thailand, and Turkey. However, due to incomplete or nonexistent time series for some variables in certain countries, the sample size had to be smaller for some of the regressions. The period covered was 1970–89. In order to abstract from short-term fluctuations in such variables as productivity change, output growth, and incremental capital-output ratios (ICORs), trend values were taken for ten-year periods. In other words, the data sets for most variables were broken into two periods: 1970–79 and 1980–89 (Tables A2.1, A2.2). This approach also allowed for treating the two periods separately in order to take into account the rather sharp differences in the overall macroeconomic environment.

For Table A2.3, the index of productivity in manufacturing was computed by dividing the constant-price value-added index in manufacturing by the index of employment in manufacturing. The growth in productivity was then calculated as the simple annual average trend rate of growth in the productivity index. The data on value added were obtained from the World Bank National Accounts file in the Basic Economic and Social Data (BESD). Employment figures were obtained from the United Nations Industrial Development Organization (UNIDO) files.

The export shares in manufacturing were derived by dividing the exports of manufactures in current dollars by the total of developing country exports. The changes in these shares were calculated for each of the two periods—1970–79 and 1980–89—by taking the trend values at the beginning and end of each period. The data on exports were obtained from the World Bank Foreign Trade Statistics files. The data on total developing countries manufactured exports were obtained from the World Bank's *World Tables* (various years).

ICORs were calculated using the data on gross fixed capital formation and GDP at factor cost (both in constant prices), available from the IMF National Accounts files.

Table A2.1. Variables used in the Regressions (1970–79)

	Productivity growth (percent change per year)[a]	Change in export shares, absolute change (percent)[a,b]	ICORS
Argentina	−2.1	0.49	—
Brazil	2.7	3.39	3.76
Chile	0.8	0.13	—
Colombia	1.7	0.28	3.75
Hong Kong	5.6	−0.65	3.11
India	0.9	−1.38	6.61
Korea, Rep. of	8.5	12.43	3.25
Malaysia	2.1	1.30	—
Mauritius	−5.8	0.16	—
Mexico	3.2	−0.85	3.66
Pakistan	1.5	−1.12	4.15
Phillippines	−5.0	1.22	3.95
Singapore	5.7	3.83	4.45
Thailand	0.9	0.97	4.30
Turkey	−0.1	0.32	5.37

— Missing ICORS indicate lack of comparable data on changes in capital stock.

a. Export shares and productivity growth are for the manufacturing sector in each country and are fitted values from the trend.

b. Export shares are calculated as a percent of developing country exports.

Source: World Bank, BESD.

Table A2.2. Variables Used in Regressions (1980-89)

	Productivity growth (percent change per year)[a]	Change in export shares, absolute change (percent)[a,b]
Argentina	−0.2	−0.42
Brazil	4.6	−0.45
Chile	1.0	−0.00
Colombia	3.6	−0.16
HongKong	3.7	−0.78
India	4.4	0.27
Korea, Rep. of	7.0	7.99
Malaysia	5.4	2.11
Mauritius	−0.4	0.06
Mexico	5.6	3.22
Pakistan	4.9	0.08
Philippines	5.0	−0.42
Singapore	5.8	1.71
Thailand	3.1	3.32
Turkey	5.7	2.64

a. Both variables reported here are for the manufacturing sector in each country and are fitted values from the trend.

b. Export shares relate to manufacturing products and are calculated as a percent of developing country exports of manufactures.

Source: World Bank, BESD.

Table A2.3. The Impact of Education and Investment: Variables Used in the Regressions Reported in Table 2.2

	Growth in productivity	Growth in manufacturing (percent value added)	Estimated residuals	Secondary school enrollment (percent)	Investment ratio (percent)
Argentina	2.41	−2.1	−3.57	50.0	0.25
	−1.36	−0.2	−0.43	65.0	0.19
Chile	1.30	0.8	−0.31	47.0	0.19
	3.18	1.0	−0.72	64.0	0.22
Colombia	6.58	1.7	−1.14	36.5	0.20
	2.83	3.6	1.98	46.5	0.22
India	4.80	0.9	−1.36	28.0	0.20
	6.74	4.4	1.49	37.5	0.23
Korea, Rep. of	17.85	8.5	1.94	58.5	0.25
	12.43	7.0	2.22	81.0	0.33
Malaysia	12.22	2.1	−2.60	42.5	0.25
	9.48	5.4	1.59	49.5	0.31
Mexico	7.17	3.2	0.11	33.0	0.25
	2.58	5.6	4.07	49.5	0.24
Pakistan	6.67	1.5	−1.36	13.5	0.20
	7.58	4.9	1.72	17.0	0.19
Singapore	11.18	5.7	1.29	52.5	0.40
	7.43	5.8	2.67	63.5	0.45
Thailand	10.96	0.9	−3.34	22.5	0.28
	9.43	3.1	−0.68	28.5	0.30
Turkey	6.07	−0.1	−2.76	32.0	0.29
	5.9	5.7	3.07	43.0	0.25

Source: The World Bank, BESD; and *World Development Report* (various issues).

3

The Macroeconomic Environment and Competitiveness

Irfan ul Haque

The macroeconomic environment occupies a central place in the discussion of international competitiveness because of its impact on an economy's capacity to grow, the health of the tradable sectors, and the balance of payments. There are two distinct but not mutually exclusive ways to define the macroeconomic environment: it can be taken to refer to the state of the economy—that is, stable or unstable—or to a set of policies. This distinction is useful in discussing the prospects for economic growth, for policies needed to bring about economic stability may conflict with those needed to stimulate growth. In other words, the state of the economy may be stable, but the policies that are in place may not be conducive to growth. The predominant view is that unless an economy has been stabilized, efforts to stimulate growth are futile (see, for example, Corden 1990). It is argued that policy reforms must first be aimed at achieving economic stability; only later should long-term problems of growth and competitiveness be tackled. A complementary view holds that in getting the fundamentals right—that is, reducing budget and trade deficits to manageable levels, maintaining competitive exchange rates, and eliminating distortions in the financial sector—an economy will have made the necessary adjustments, and no specific growth enhancing policies will be needed. This argument also holds that it is not usually possible to target specific discretionary policies at the determinants of economic growth.

The positive effects of a stable economic environment, and the role macroeconomic policy plays in creating it, are widely recognized. There is little support today for large budget deficits or overvalued exchange rates, for instance. But questions have been raised about the relationship between economic stability and growth and about the ability of macroeconomic policy to stimulate economic growth and create competitive productive structures. Many developing countries that have adopted macroeconomic adjustment programs over the past decade have failed to achieve sustained rapid growth, including those (such as Mexico) that were particularly successful in bringing down inflation. In many other economies—ranging from Sub-Saharan African countries to the states of the former Soviet Union—output remains low, unemployment high, and economic stability elusive. An issue of special interest for these countries, which are caught in a cycle of inflationary decline, is whether economic expansion should or can be included as an essential component of stabilization programs. At the same time, persistent trade imbalances in industrial countries (notably the United States) have given rise to the question of whether such imbalances are purely macroeconomic and therefore correctable by means of suitable fiscal, monetary, and exchange rate policies, or whether they are the result of some fundamental weakness in the productive structure (Blecker 1992).

This chapter underscores the importance of both economic stability and appropriate macroeconomic policies and attempts to give some precision to the role they play in economic growth. Strictly speaking, economic stability is a relative state, and it is worth exploring how much importance should be attached to this goal in macroeconomic policy. Macroeconomic policy instruments, however, affect growth and competitiveness in different and often conflicting ways, and it is important to distinguish the positive from the negative influences. However, whether macroeconomic policy first creates the appropriate environment or acts directly on growth, the most important factor is the behavior of investment—its pattern, magnitude, and efficiency. According to the MIT Commission on Industrial Productivity, "Investment, in its broadest sense, is crucial for productivity, and the macroeconomic environment largely determines the level of investment" (Dertouzos, Lester, and Solow 1989, p. 35). Before exploring the impact of the macro-economic environment, therefore, it is necessary to clarify the link between investment and growth and its implications for an economy open to international trade.

Investment and Economic Growth

In the earlier economic development literature, investment and economic growth were held to have a very close relationship and early strategies of economic development focused on raising savings and investment in developing countries. This view, however, came under sharp scrutiny during the 1980s. It was noted that a number of developing countries and centrally planned economies had managed over the years to achieve high rates of investment, but with meager economic growth. This evidence led to the view that the policy and institutional context—which bears on the efficiency of resource use—was at least as important as investment in determining economic growth outcomes. This section first examines the theoretical link between investment and growth and then reviews the available empirical evidence.

Two Approaches

One way to see how investment affects economic growth is to take investment as an increase in capital stock—a factor of production—that increases output. If this relationship is expressed in the form of a production function, then economic growth can be shown to equal the sum of growth rates of individual inputs, each weighted by its respective share of earnings in output, assuming that there are constant returns to scale and that the factors earn rewards equal to the value of their marginal products. That is:

$$(3\text{-}1) \qquad \frac{dY}{Y} = \Sigma \beta_i \frac{dK_i}{K_i}$$

where Y represents output, K_i represents input (i), and B_i the share of input's earnings in total output. Thus, the contribution of capital accumulation to economic growth equals the share of profits and interest earnings in output. Since this share is typically between 25 and 35 percent, capital accumulation alone will account for no more than around one-third of total economic growth. The outcome suggests that other factors have been left out, including technical progress, which taken together are much more important than capital accumulation as determinants of economic growth. This method of attributing a certain share of growth to different factors has some serious flaws that were discussed in the context of total factor productivity growth in chapter 2.

Another method of describing the link between investment and growth is in terms of the so-called Harrod-Domar equation, which is derived from the national income identity of savings and investment. The growth of national output here equals the ratio of the savings rate (s) and the incremental capital-output ratio (v), thus:

(3-2)
$$\frac{dY}{Y} = \frac{s}{v}$$

This relationship, which featured prominently in discussion of development policy during the postwar period, is quintessentially macroeconomic and sends the message that good economic policies are those that raise both the savings rate and the productivity of capital. The emphasis on raising the savings rate has been called "the traditional wisdom of development economics" (Sen 1983, p. 750). This basic framework was later refined by the inclusion of the effects of international trade, leading to the birth of the so-called two-gap models of economic growth. These models recognize that balance of payment difficulties can constrain growth and that countries able to acquire foreign financing to support trade deficits will have higher rates of investment and hence growth (conversely, countries with trade surpluses will have higher savings and lower growth rates). Issues such as the competitiveness of the productive structure and the significance of the patterns of growth in these models, which are usually highly aggregative, are by and large suppressed. International trade serves basically as a constraint to the pace of economic expansion.

There is no inconsistency between the production function formulation (equation 3-1) and the Harrod-Domar equation (3-2), except that the first describes the supply-side and the second the demand-side conditions. In practice, the capital output ratio in the first formulation is assumed to vary according to production conditions and factor prices, while in the Harrod-Domar equation it is taken as a parameter that reflects productive efficiency. However, neither expression captures the full dynamics of capital accumulation—that is, the benefits from increasing returns to scale, growth and absorption of technology, and upgraded worker skills.

Evidence on the Investment-Growth Link

In general, economic growth models do not discuss international competitiveness, and when they do, the main concern is the appropriateness of the exchange rate, which determines the relative profitability of producing tradable goods. However, industrial countries have given considerable attention to the determinants of productivity growth, especially in the manufacturing sector, which holds the key to international competitiveness (see chapter 2).

Studies tend to confirm, for instance, that investment has an important influence on productivity growth. It has been almost thirty years since Kaldor (1967) showed, in the context of explaining slow growth in Great Britain, that there exist in the industrial countries close relationships between overall economic growth and the growth of manufacturing, and between the latter and productivity growth in the manufacturing sector. However, one significant result of his regressions demonstrated that the *deviations* from the regression line were highly correlated with the rate of investment. Countries with productivity growth rates significantly higher than those on the trend line (that is, those lying well above the regression line) tended to devote a higher proportion of their income to investment and to have higher incremental capital-output ratios than countries whose growth rates lay below the line. In essence, Kaldor observed, "The countries which invested a great deal in relation to their growth rate were the good performers, whilst the countries whose investment was small in relation to their growth rate were poor performers" (1967, p. 15). This finding suggests that the good performers in terms of productivity growth rather paradoxically had lower-than-average capital productivity, resulting in a *lower* rate of economic growth for a given investment rate. The opposite seems to hold true for the poor performers, possibly because productivity growth is the result of the combined effects of the growth in output (which reflects increasing returns) and the increasing capital intensity of output. Importantly, Kaldor concluded that increasing returns were by far the most important reason for the differences in productivity growth rates and that differences in investment behavior were relatively less important.

A more recent study of the problem of U.S. competitiveness found a close relationship in industrial countries not only between productivity growth and the rate of increase in the capital-labor ratio but between productivity growth and the rate of national savings (Hatsopolous, Krugman, and Summers 1988). Using data from 1970–85, the researchers showed that countries where the capital-labor ratio rose rapidly (most notably Japan) also displayed rapid productivity growth. The study found that the contribution of capital accumulation to productivity growth was much greater than the estimates from the growth accounting exercises. This finding suggests a dynamic relationship between capital and output, displaying increasing returns to the use of capital rather than the diminishing returns that would prevail in a static production function, which takes no account of new technology embodied in capital. The fact that productivity growth was seen to be positively correlated with the savings rate indicates that domestic savings in industrial countries are the principal determinant of the investment rate.

The strong correlation between productivity growth in manufacturing and the capital/labor ratio was also observed by Dosi, Pavitt, and Soete (1990) and confirmed the evidence of increasing returns from capital accumulation (see chapter 2). However, unlike Kaldor, Dosi's group found that higher levels of manufacturing productivity were associated with lower capital/output ratios, or higher capital efficiency. In other words, the more successful countries (in terms of productivity growth) displayed greater efficiency in the use of both labor and capital, indicating that production functions may differ across countries.

On the basis of the data for developing as well as industrial countries, De Long and Summers (1993) found a close connection between investment in machinery and productivity growth. This relationship is statistically robust in a variety of circumstances, showing that machinery investment accounts for around one-fourth to one-third of the variation in the growth rate. According to one of these calculations, an increase of one percentage point in the machinery investment rate can raise the productivity growth rate by 0.25–0.33 percentage points. According to De Long and Summers, "The strong association means that differences in machinery investment account in a statistical sense for essentially all of the extraordinary growth performance of many fast-growing nations—for example, Japan, relative to the sample as a whole" (1993, p.7). Furthermore, investment in machinery is also strongly correlated with total factor productivity growth, or the residual left after the growth in individual factors of production, including capital, has been accounted for.

The point of these findings is that investment plays a role in stimulating output growth, which is inherently dynamic and transcends the simple productivity–capital intensity relationship that results from a "well-behaved" production function. Investment does not just augment a factor of production but is the means by which new technologies are put into practice.

This relationship has important ramifications. First, there are the benefits of learning-by-doing and learning-by-using, which stimulate further technological progress, raise workers' skills, and increase human capital. As De Long and Summers point out, "A given investment in machinery can have large external benefits if learning-by-using helps to create a work force experienced and competent at handling modern technologies, and helps organizations to develop the rules of thumb and standard operating procedures necessary to produce efficiently that other firms can imitate" (1993, p. 51). These are the supply-side benefits. However, demand-side benefits are no less important. Investment in one sector stimulates investment in the others and encourages technical progress. Unless investors purchase machinery of the current year's vintage, for instance, there is little incentive to produce the next vintage. Thus, capital accumulation tends to display increasing returns, implying that the private return to investment may not reflect the social return. There may therefore be a tendency in a market economy for private agents to underinvest, and public policy may be required to offset this shortage. As Serven and Solimano (1992) note,

> Since each individual firm is likely to view its own contribution to aggregate investment as negligible, the social and private returns to investment diverge, with the former exceeding the latter. Under certain conditions, the economy may get stuck in an insufficient investment equilibrium, in which individual firms invest too little . . . precisely because each firm expects aggregate investment to be low (p. 99).

Economic Stability and Growth

A distinguishing feature of those economies that are able to maintain rapid growth and manageable current account balances is economic stability reflected in a low rate of inflation. On the basis of cross-section and panel data covering some thirty-two developing countries, Fischer (1993) found that economic growth is negatively correlated with inflation, a relationship that remains statistically significant in a variety of circumstances. This finding corroborates the results of several earlier studies.

The Dynamics of Inflation

If money is taken simply as the numerator in terms of which all prices are expressed, and institutional arrangements are such that all prices adjust instantly to higher levels, there is no apparent reason for inflation to affect the real economy and economic expansion. At relatively low inflation rates, economic growth may be relatively insensitive to upward pressure on prices, and it may be possible to stabilize the rate of price increase, but the situation is entirely different when inflation is high. As inflation accelerates, the time period within which price adjustments must be made in order to avoid big shifts in relative prices gets shorter and shorter; eventually, established wage-price contracts and other indexing mechanisms break down. In the absence of government action to bring the situation under control, the inflationary spiral will continue unabated, culminating in hyperinflation. Thus, low- and high-inflation situations differ not just in magnitude but also in their innate dynamics.

The first explanation, therefore, for the negative inflation-growth link is increased uncertainty about the absolute and relative movements of prices and the potential government response to what is usually a deteriorating situation. Private investors react adversely to this situation. High inflation rates may or may not affect the behavior of savings, depending on the strength of the real balance effect (Corden 1990). However, domestic investment can decline in cases of capital flight, even when savings do not fall. Fischer's regression results confirm the negative relation between inflation and capital accumulation and also show a negative impact on total factor productivity growth. One reason for this negative effect is that inflation is a kind of tax that tends to change relative prices and make the productive sectors (which are exposed to international competition) less attractive for investors than purely domestic sectors such as real estate. Thus, even if the overall investment rate does not decline, the orientation of investment changes, leading to slow growth and a decline in competitiveness. Uncertainty also reduces the efficiency of the price mechanism, causing productivity growth to decline (Lucas 1973).

It is, however, the loss of competitiveness and the emergence of balance of payments difficulties that interrupt economic growth in high-inflation situations. Rising public expenditures and the consequent budget deficits are often a principal cause of inflation. Expansionary public policies may initially stimulate economic expansion, but as capacity limits and full employment are reached, output fails to keep up with rising expenditures, a situation that sooner or later results in rising trade deficits. This situation cannot be sustained for long because of the increasing difficulty of financing the deficits. The shift in relative prices in favor of nontradable sectors does not help the situation. Indeed, in this situation it is difficult to avoid an overvalued exchange rate, since the usual adjustment mechanisms, such as a crawling peg or a float, are effective only when inflation is moderate and reasonably predictable. In fact, governments often rely on the exchange rate as a nominal anchor to stabilize inflation, since a deteriorating exchange rate can be a source of instability.

The Nonlinearity of the Inflation-Growth Link

There are, however, some important qualifications attached to the negative link between inflation and growth. A number of countries have maintained relatively low inflation rates but have failed to achieve high rates of growth (for example, the African franc zone countries during the 1980s), while some others have experienced high inflation accompanied by high economic growth and a strong foreign trade performance (notably Brazil during the 1970s). Table 3.1, which gives data on inflation, GDP growth, and export growth for different regions of the world from 1965–80 and from 1980–90, shows that accelerated inflation was associated with a slowdown in growth in Sub-Saharan Africa and Latin America, while accelerating growth was accompanied by declining inflation in southeast Asia. However, this relationship did not hold in the Middle Eastern, North African, and industrial (Organization for Economic Cooperation and Development [OECD]) countries; in these cases, the decline in inflation was associated with a slowdown in GDP growth. The Republic of Korea and Japan showed a similar trend: both registered a reduction in inflation and in growth over the two periods.

Table 3.1. GDP, Inflation and Export Growth in Selected Regions

Region/Country	GDP growth		Inflation		Export growth	
	1965–80	1980–90	1965–80	1980–90	1965–80	1980–90
Sub-Saharan Africa	4.2	2.1	11.4	20.0	6.1	0.2
East Asia/Pacific	7.3	7.8	9.3	6.0	8.5	9.8
Korea, Rep. of	9.9	9.7	18.4	5.1	27.2	12.8
South Asia	3.6	5.2	8.3	8.0	1.8	6.8
Middle East/North Africa	6.7	0.5	13.6	7.5	5.7	-1.1
Latin America/ Caribbean	6.0	1.6	31.8	192.1	-1.0	3.0
OECD	3.7	3.1	7.6	4.2	7.2	4.1
Japan	6.4	4.1	7.7	1.5	11.4	4.2

Source: World Bank 1992.

The negative relationship between inflation and growth appears even weaker if comparisons are made across regions during the same time periods. Particularly noteworthy is the fact that inflation was much higher in Latin America than in East Asia during the 1965–80 period and growth only slightly lower. Indeed, GDP growth was considerably higher when compared with South Asia or Sub-Saharan Africa. The same is true for the Middle East and North Africa. However, Korea maintained a high inflation rate (18 percent) and high GDP growth (10 percent) for fifteen years (1965–80), and Japan had only slightly higher inflation but considerably faster growth than the OECD countries. The negative inflation-growth link seems to be stronger during the 1980s, but in this period some regions (notably Latin America and Sub-Saharan Africa) experienced high inflation and depressed output that were exacerbated by attempts to cope with the external debt crisis.

The impact of inflation on export growth is even less clear. In a few striking cases, the relationship seems to have been reversed, as in Korea during the 1965–80 period, when exports increased dramatically in a situation of high inflation. Similarly, during the 1980s, Latin America managed to achieve a significant increase in exports (compared with its performance during the 1965–80 period), despite very high inflation. Some countries, notably the Middle Eastern economies during the 1970s, experienced terms of trade shocks that unleashed inflationary pressures but maintained rapid growth in export earnings.

From the above comparisons, it is possible to conclude that although economic stability, economic growth, and international competitiveness are mutually reinforcing, the relationship is far from straightforward. It seems possible for countries to combine very high rates of inflation (exceeding, say, 50 percent a year) with high growth for short periods (two or three years), as Brazil and Peru did during the mid-1980s. (Fischer 1993, Table 11, gives examples of several countries that experienced episodes of high inflation and high growth). At moderate levels of inflation, rapid economic growth may be sustained for a relatively long period, provided inflation remains reasonably stable, as it did in some Latin American countries and Korea during 1965–80.

There is also some evidence that the relationship between inflation and growth is nonlinear, since both very high and very low inflation rates may be incompatible with rapid growth—very low rates because the costs of reducing inflation below a certain floor may be too great in terms of employment, output, and growth. The countries that successfully disinflated to low inflation—such as Ireland, Korea, and Spain—did so at significant cost to output (Dornbusch and Fischer 1993). Aggressive stabilization measures also tend to dampen what Keynes called "animal spirits," or a sense of optimism about the future that is essential to increasing investment. There is also an indication that expectations and institutions seem to adjust to a certain rate of inflation that varies across countries. For these reasons, the Latin American countries have tended to have considerably higher rates of inflation than the East Asian countries.

In short, a stable functional relation between inflation and growth does not seem to exist for individual countries, and there is little evidence that exports are sensitive to moderate levels of inflation. This means that there is no powerful reason why inflation must always be brought down before economic growth can resume. Fischer (1993) concludes that ". . . the statement that macroeconomic stability is necessary for sustainable growth is too strong, but . . . the statement that macroeconomic stability is conducive to sustained growth remains accurate" (p. 3). Low inflation is an important macroeconomic policy objective, but in some circumstances—especially in cases of moderate inflation—declines in inflation may entail high costs in terms of declines in output and growth. At the same time, it is easier to achieve fiscal stability in a growing economy (because the tax base expands, while expenditures may not actually be reduced), and more difficult when output and employment decline. Thus, it may make sense, when output is declining and unemployment is high, to attempt to establish economic stability through economic expansion rather than through the compression of demand alone.

Macroeconomic Policy and Growth

Apart from its role in creating a propitious and stable economic and financial environment, macroeconomic policy has a role in promoting economic growth and international competitiveness through its impact on investment, savings, and the performance of the tradable sectors. How policies actually impinge on the determinants of growth has been extensively debated, and theory has oscillated between the state activism that followed the Keynesian revolution—which assigned a key role to discretionary public policy in smoothing out business cycles and stimulating growth—and "state minimalism" (Streeten 1993). The current orthodoxy, which has been enormously influential during the past decade and has colored economic reforms in both developing and industrial countries, approaches minimalism, emphasizing fiscal discipline, deregulation, market liberalization, and the privatization of public enterprises.

This view holds that a combination of conservative fiscal policy (which will promote a stable economic environment) and freely functioning markets unfettered by government interference and regulation will bolster investor confidence and encourage entrepreneurial drive, stimulating economic growth. Liberalizing financial and credit markets can, in turn, facilitate the mobilization of domestic savings and encourage efficient investment by eliminating distortions from the capital market. A combination of trade liberalization and exchange rate adjustment will strengthen the balance of payments and improve international competitiveness as relative prices shift in favor of the tradable sectors. In these sectors, reduced import barriers and a favorable exchange rate will stimulate exports by removing the bias in favor of domestically produced import substitutes.

In short, the government needs to concentrate basically on getting the "fundamentals" straight: managing its own finances and eliminating the budget deficit (or at least bringing it down to a level consistent with economic stability), while steering away from market interventions. Trade deficits and competitiveness problems, according to this view, are not caused by any inherent weaknesses in the productive structure but are the result of expansionary public policies, overvalued exchange rates, and other systemic distortions.

Few economies have tested this orthodox prescription in its pure form. The two countries where the orthodoxy was particularly dominant—the United Kingdom and the United States—displayed a rather mixed overall economic performance during the 1980s. While there was a remarkable reduction in inflation, their competitive strengths remain a matter of some debate, even with the recent improvements in plant-level efficiency, at least in the United States. During the 1980s, a large number of developing countries embarked on structural adjustment programs, which were often modified to include sectoral (generally liberalizing) policies and interventions to protect the poor. Those countries that persevered with reforms achieved reduced budget deficits, lower inflation, higher exports (in many cases dramatically higher), more competitive exchange rates, and a generally liberalized economic environment. However, economic growth in these countries remained generally modest, falling well short of the high rates observed prior to 1980, even though in a large number of cases either the rate of expansion rose or the rate of decline fell in comparison with the prereform period. In short, many adjusting countries have not yet found the road to economic prosperity (Dornbusch 1990; Mosley and Weeks 1993).

Policies That Stimulate Investment

Different considerations apply to public and private investment. Public investment, which constitutes a fairly large portion of total investment in most developing countries, is constrained primarily by the availability of resources, although a government may, as a matter of policy, limit its involvement to a few selected areas. However, there is no satisfactory theory to explain the behavior of private investment. The ambiguity surrounding the determinants of private investment arises from the problem of measuring the cost of capital in a situation where the future plays a key role and where investment decisions are sensitive to other investors' actions. The investment climate seems to play a significant role, and there is considerable evidence that output growth itself induces a rise in investment (Blomström and others 1993). Despite this ambiguity, however, three types of public policy are held to have a significant influence on private investment: fiscal policy, interest rate and credit policy, and exchange rate policy.

Public deficits, with their inflationary impact and claim on private savings, are believed to discourage private investment, although they may (as many Keynesian economists believe) also boost effective demand in recessionary situations and help to improve the investment climate. If public deficits are financed through money creation, they contribute to inflation and can discourage private investment. Alternatively, if they are financed through public borrowing, they cause interest rates to rise, discouraging or crowding out private investment in the credit market. But the impact of inflation and interest rates on private investment is difficult to predict, as it depends largely on how these factors influence investors' expectations. The evidence is also rather mixed on whether public investment, on balance, "crowds in" or "crowds out" private investment. On the basis of data from a group of developing countries, Easterly and Schmidt-Hebbel (1993) conclude that increasing public investment reduced private investment in some countries and raised it in others. An explanation for these varied experiences could lie in the orientation of public investment—that is, whether it supplements or substitutes for private investment (Chhibber, Dailami, and Shafik 1992). Public investment in social and physical infrastructure may improve the efficiency of investment in productive sectors, raising the return to private capital. There is evidence that depressed public investment in the 1980s caused the physical infrastructure to deteriorate in a number of African and Latin American countries, a development that has often been cited as a principal reason for the limited supply response. Public investment in industry may also preempt investment opportunities and displace private investment, yet there are numerous examples of successful public investment in industry made because the private sector lacked the interest or ability to invest. Public investment in industry was far from inconsequential in most East Asian NIEs, for example. In short, no firm evidence exists to indicate whether public investment discourages or encourages private investment.

Persistently negative returns to financial assets and unrealistically low interest rates reduce savings and cause misallocation of resources. As Chhibber and others (1992) note, "Subsidized interest rates, while often justified as a policy to promote private investment, actually have had negative consequences for private capital formation. The rationing that characterizes repressed financial systems tends to result in a misallocation of investment resources" (p. 14). Unrealistically low interest rates are also often a principal cause of capital flight. Conversely, positive real interest rates may help to mobilize domestic savings and, by increasing the supply of available credit, to encourage private investment. By screening out low-yield investments, positive rates also tend to improve the overall quality of investments. Thus, it can be argued that positive real interest rates and financial sector liberalization induce economic growth, especially because a positive and statistically significant relationship seems to exist between positive real interest rates and GDP growth (World Bank 1989).

However, as Dornbusch (1990) points out, most evidence on the adverse effects of poor financial policies arises out of the disproportionate influence of countries where strongly negative interest rates prevailed over a prolonged period. He observes, "The evidence does not support the view that positive real interest rates promote savings or that a linkage between real interest rates and investment raises the growth rate" (p. 41). Barring cases of extreme forms of financial repression (that is, negative real interest rates), private savings are not very sensitive to interest rates. Indeed, the extensive use of credit subsidies and rationing in several of the East Asian economies seems to suggest that a moderate amount of financial repression, accompanied by complementary policies, can stimulate private investment and help develop selected industries (World Bank 1993a).

Devaluation may also affect private investment. The effect tends to be unfavorable in the short term, raising the cost of imported machinery and intermediate goods, but favorable in the long term, stimulating expansion in the tradable sectors (Chhibber, Dailami, and Shakif 1992). Real devaluation, which causes the relative prices of tradables to rise, also reduces real wages and increases the expected return on investment. But this effect can be offset if inflationary pressures build up and concerns that the government will react to curb them emerge to create a climate of uncertainty. If individual firms have heavy foreign debts, a devaluation also raises the debt servicing burden and tends to depress private investment (Serven and Solimano 1992). The effect of exchange rate changes on investment therefore remains unclear but can be only incidental, as the exchange rate is not a policy instrument that can be used to promote investment.

In the end, it is easier to identify the factors that inhibit investment than those that stimulate it. By far the most influential factor is uncertainty about the economic environment and the government's policy stance. As Pindyck and Solimano (1993) observe, "If a goal of macroeconomic policy is to stimulate investment . . . stability and credibility may be much more important than particular levels of tax rates or interest rates" (p. 2). Countries where the economy is uncertain, especially those with high inflation and declining output, can find themselves caught in a "Catch-22" situation: investors will not invest unless the economic environment becomes less uncertain, but the prolongation of the period of economic stagnation or decline makes uncertainty worse. This situation characterized Latin America in the 1980s, and, more recently, has developed in the former Soviet Union.

Promotion of the Tradable Sectors

As has been noted, the orthodox view on promoting the tradable sectors holds that free trade, or a close approximation of it, is the most effective means of exploiting a country's comparative advantage. This view presumes that the price system works well (that is, market prices reflect social costs) and that the world market is by and large uninfluenced by an individual country's actions (Bhagwati 1989). Given these conditions, trade liberalization, accompanied by a suitable adjustment in the exchange rate, stimulates economic growth and relieves the balance of payments constraint. Trade policy interventions create a wedge between the domestic and international prices of traded products, resulting in suboptimal patterns of specialization. Among the available means of restricting imports, quantitative restrictions (such as quotas and licenses) are considered more harmful than tariffs, as the latter are less distortionary because they are either proportionate to price (in the case of ad valorem duties) or a fixed amount (in the case of specific duties).

All trade barriers affect the exchange rate, raising it above the levels that would prevail under a free trade regime. In this situation, a country's exports are hampered both by the protection afforded to import substitutes (which makes them more profitable) and by the artificially elevated exchange rate. For these reasons, trade liberalization has been a major component of recent policy reform programs in an increasing number of countries. While trade liberalization, strictly speaking, need not shut out support for infant industries, the effect is to do just that. Since the rationale for protection is primarily domestic market failures, it can be argued that domestic policies (such as subsidies), rather than tariffs or other restrictions on foreign trade, are more appropriate to remedy the situation. As Bhagwati (1989) notes, "Domestic market failures are best dealt with, not by trade policy interventions, but by choosing domestic policies tailor-made to assist and counteract the market failure at its source" (p. 27). As a practical matter, countries normally find it easier to impose import duties than to raise other taxes to pay for subsidies to infant industries. In any case, the General Agreement on Tariffs and Trade (GATT) restricts the use of subsidies in the production of exports.

In their pursuit of trade liberalization, developing countries have undertaken reforms both with and without exchange rate adjustment, with mixed results (see chapter 6 for some specific country examples). Exports have generally responded well to the more favorable exchange rates, and formerly protected industries subjected to restructuring and rationalization have become more efficient and competitive. However, the impact on productive efficiency has been hard to measure, because in countries like Mexico, where trade liberalization has been vigorously pursued, the rate of plant closings has been high and manufacturing productivity seems to have declined (Table 3.2). Export expansion, where it has occurred, appears to be largely the result of depressed wages rather than of productivity growth; in fact, far from catching up with the world's most competitive suppliers, these countries seem to be falling behind. A large number of countries with

Table 3.2. Productivity Growth in Manufacturing
(percent per annum)

	1970–75	*1975–80*	*1980–85*	*1985–latest year*
Korea, Rep. of	12.2	6.8	7.0	8.4 ('89)
Turkey	1.6	–4.7	6.8	7.3 ('88)
Mexico	3.9	1.4	2.8	–0.6 ('88)
India	1.1	2.6	8.6	7.1 ('87)

Source: World Bank 1992.

rising import levels and falling public revenues now face both balance of payment and fiscal difficulties that make macroeconomic management more difficult. However, in countries where trade reforms have been moderate and have brought about the rationalization of production and government regulations—for example, in Turkey and India—productivity gains during the 1980s have been impressive.

For most developing countries, some degree of trade policy reform was essential and long overdue. These economies had suffered from overprotection (in terms of level as well as length of time), redundant controls that combined high tariffs with quotas, and policy conflicts between import restriction and industry promotion. Rationalizing those policies helped to unshackle many economies (including Ghana and India) and to stimulate economic expansion. Nevertheless, it seems that the expected benefits of trade liberalization may have been exaggerated (Dornbusch 1992; Havrylyshyn 1990). As Dornbusch notes, "Although the discussion of trade policy at times gives the impression that a liberal trade regime can do wonders for a country's economy, and most observers believe firmly that trade reform is beneficial, yet systematic attempts at quantification fail to single out trade policy as a major factor in economic growth" (p. 73).

At the practical level, it is doubtful that trade policy interventions can or will be completely abandoned. They have been used successfully in industrial development in the East Asian and other NIEs and are employed extensively to protect domestic industry in industrial countries. They also constitute an important tool for macroeconomic management in situations that call for reduced imports but preclude the use of the exchange rate, either because it is not overvalued or because it must be maintained to support domestic economic stability.

Conclusions

Macroeconomic policy clearly plays an important role in achieving satisfactory economic growth and strengthening the tradable sectors, but its focus has been primarily on short-term economic management. While it is easy enough to see the adverse consequences of "wrong" policies, it is much harder to define macroeconomic policies that stimulate investment, growth, and competitiveness. "Luck" seems to play a significant role in determining economic outcomes, increasing the already considerable difficulty of correlating policies with economic growth (Easterly and others 1993). For one thing, too many noneconomic variables—weather, civil strife, and exogenous shocks—can ultimately affect a country's economic situation, though good policy may mitigate some of the adverse effects. For another, the consequences of what may generally be regarded as bad policies are often modified by economic growth or decline. Thus, for example, Malaysia and Thailand (among other countries) maintained large budget deficits during the 1980s without inciting inflation because of rapid growth. Deficit financing has a less inflationary impact when economies grow than when they decline. And finally, most problems of slow growth and competitiveness in fact lie outside the domain of macroeconomic policy: poor infrastructure, a weak human resource and technological base, and deficiencies in industrial management, for example, can hardly be remedied by macroeconomic policy.

Although there is broad consensus on the general direction institutional and policy reforms should take, the poor economic recovery in many adjusting countries has raised the possibility that an "additional ingredient" may be necessary in macroeconomic reform packages to stimulate economic growth and promote international competitiveness (Williamson 1990). In this respect as in others, the experience of the East Asian NIEs, with their success in combining economic stability and growth, holds several important lessons for other developing countries.

First, in general these countries did not allow their macroeconomic fundamentals to get seriously out of line. When a problem developed, the governments acted promptly to bring the situation under control. Korea, Thailand, and Indonesia in the early 1980s are particularly apposite examples (World Bank 1993a).

Second, economic growth remained a central concern in the design of economic reforms. Particularly interesting is the case of Japan, which after the war resembled the present-day economies in transition in some important respects. Its physical infrastructure had badly deteriorated; it had serious macroeconomic imbalances; its industrial structure was ill-suited to growth in a time of peace; its political institutions were in disarray; and public morale and confidence were low. The stabilization program the Japanese Government adopted after the war was perhaps the first example of a heterodox approach to economic reform. The program envisaged economic stability and economic growth not just as compatible goals but as mutually supportive and interdependent objectives (Teranishi 1992). In particular, economic growth was seen as the best way to make public deficits easier to reduce and less harmful to economic stability.

A related feature of the East Asian NIEs was their commitment to export expansion rather than import substitution as a means of relieving balance of payments constraints. This commitment did not mean that import substitution was not pursued—in fact, it was pursued quite aggressively. But there was a basic difference between the strategies of these countries and the strategies used by countries that relied more or less exclusively on import substitution. In countries that relied on export expansion, trade policy was generally not made to serve two objectives at the same time—that is, it was not used to try to relieve balance of payments constraints as well as to direct investment into strategic industries. These two goals often conflict, for the first is strictly a short-term concern, while the other involves long-term development. Given the uncertainties of external financing, in practice managing the balance of payments tends to take precedence. Countries that relied on export promotion were more successful in avoiding these conflicts, were able to pursue industrialization strategically, and were not burdened by the need to restrict trade in order to maintain a reasonable current account balance.

In all of these countries, macroeconomic policies were supplemented by other policies—the "additional ingredient"—designed to encourage real investment, promote industry, and develop human resources, an approach that caused some countries to be labelled "developmental states." As the recent World Bank Study of the East Asian "miracle" (1993a) notes, these economies "maintained macroeconomic stability *and* accomplished three functions of growth: accumulation, efficient allocation, and rapid technological catch-up. They did this with combinations of policies, ranging from market oriented to state led, that varied both across economies and over time" (p. 10). The policies included measures designed to achieve macroeconomic stability, promote investment, and increase openness to foreign technology, as well as selective interventions such as directed credit, subsidized interest rates, and trade policy reforms to promote targeted industries. How this was done and what role it played is discussed in chapter 6.

However, the most important lesson may lie in these countries' ability to avoid excesses in macroeconomic policy. They ran budget deficits, subsidized interest rates, and maintained trade barriers, but their policies remained, on the whole, moderate and pragmatic. Their experience also shows that the pursuit of macroeconomic stability need not always take precedence over economic growth. Clearly, when economies overheat—that is, when full employment is reached and supply bottlenecks start to appear—restoring economic stability requires sacrificing growth and introducing such deflationary measures as tax and interest rate increases and reductions in domestic expenditures. But the situation is rather different when economies are caught in a spiral of accelerating inflation and declining output. In these situations, reducing expenditures and raising taxes may not yield economic stability if such steps lead only to further declines in output. Thus, there may be a case for including in reform programs for such countries explicit growth-enhancing measures targeted at capital accumulation and growth in output and productivity.

4

The Development of Technological Capabilities

Martin Bell and Keith Pavitt

The acquisition of technology has long been seen in all economies as central to the process of raising productivity and otherwise improving competitiveness. In general, it has been assumed that industries in developing countries can aquire new technology fairly easily. For while the problems of transferring agricultural technologies among countries have been widely recognized, the difficulties of transferring industrial technology have not. Industrial technology is widely viewed as being much less dependent on local factors than agricultural technology and therefore as much more accessible. More specifically, it has been assumed that developing countries can achieve high rates of growth of labor productivity—and probably also of total factor productivity—by investing in the physical capital embodying new industrial technologies and training workers in the necessary operating skills.

These assumptions, however, are generally misplaced. Although developing countries have expanded their industrial production capacities rapidly over the last forty years, correspondingly raising and diversifying their shares of world manufacturing output and exports, a growing body of evidence shows considerable variations in the efficiency with which that industrial expansion has been achieved. Low levels of *static efficiency* in a wide range of industries are evident in numerous sectoral studies of domestic resource costs and effective rates of protection. More detailed studies of specific industries have also shown considerable variations in efficiency in the use of technologies. Pack (1987) indicates that textile producers in Kenya in the 1980s operated at lower levels of productivity than those in industrial countries, despite the presence of similar spinning and weaving technologies—and that textile producers in the Philippines with the same types of equipment had not even reached Kenya's productivity levels.

Similar variability is evident in *dynamic efficiency* in the use of technology. In only a few cases have high rates of productivity growth been achieved through the transfer of technology from industrial countries. For instance, in the Republic of Korea, the annual rates of growth of labor productivity in manufacturing have typically exceeded 10 percent since the 1960s, and the growth rates of total factor productivity in manufacturing have been substantially higher than those in the advanced industrial countries (Dollar and Sokoloff 1990). In many other developing countries, however, rates of growth of total factor productivity in industry (or, more narrowly, in manufacturing) have been a fraction of Korea's and have tended either to be lower than those in most of the advanced industrial countries or to remain negative for long periods (see Nishimizu and Page 1989; Pack 1988, 1992). Even labor productivity seems to have grown more slowly in manufacturing in most of the developing world (UNIDO 1992).

The effectiveness with which countries have created new areas of comparative advantage in increasingly technology-intensive industries also varies widely. Particularly striking has been the limited technological development in countries where significant industrial growth began in the early decades of this century or even before. In the early 1980s, Poznanski (1984) pointed to the poor performance of the (then) centrally planned economies in industries involving sophisticated technologies, especially compared with the newly industrializing economies (NIEs)—a weakness confirmed in more recent comparisons by Ray (1991).

Latin American countries have performed even more poorly than other NIEs, particularly in electronics production (Riedel 1988; Freeman 1991). In fact, structural change has been constrained in Latin American industry for decades. For example, by the 1950s Brazil had developed a substantial capital goods sector, but the development of industries such as steel was not followed by the emergence of internationally competitive production in more complex and specialized areas, such as machinery and instrumentation, or in science-based sectors like electronics. Typically, Latin American economies began producing simple machinery and then moved to limited production of more complex machinery, but these economies were rarely able to remain internationally competitive (Scott-Kemmis 1988). Similarly, the automobile industry grew rapidly in Argentina during the 1950s and 1960s, and a nascent structure of specialized supplier industries emerged, but little or no effort was made to develop new models or to keep up with technological improvements elsewhere (Katz and Bercovich 1993).

In contrast, some of the Asian NIEs have changed the structures of industrial production rapidly to keep up with new technologies. Korea, for example, moved rapidly from labor-intensive to scale-intensive industries (automobiles, steel, consumer durables, and chemicals) and later to industries supplying specialized production equipment. Similarly, large firms in the Korean electronics industry have been shifting from labor-intensive assembly production to technology-intensive processes. Singapore simply bypassed the heavy, scale-intensive industries, moving instead from labor-intensive production to engineering-intensive segments of the electronics industry and information-intensive service industries. Other countries in Southeast Asia (including Indonesia, Malaysia, and Thailand) are poised between Latin America and the East Asian NIEs. It remains to be seen whether these economies will shift rapidly to technology-intensive industries or remain locked into areas in which competitiveness rests primarily on relatively low wages and abundant natural resources.

The conventional wisdom is that these variations in the dynamic efficiency of industry can be explained largely by differences in policies that have little direct impact on technology—in particular, macroeconomic and trade policies that distort prices and patterns of comparative advantage, and policies that affect the level and structure of investment in education (see, for example, World Bank 1993a). But this view, while it captures important parts of the story, overlooks key issues in technology and technology-related policy that strongly affect dynamic efficiency and competitiveness.

The central argument of this chapter is that dynamic efficiency does not follow automatically from the acquisition of foreign machinery embodying new technology and the accumulation of related operating know-how. Sustained dynamic efficiency depends heavily on domestic capabilities to generate and manage change in technologies used in production, and these capabilities are based largely on specialized resources (such as a highly skilled labor force) that are neither incorporated in, nor automatically derived from, capital goods and technological know-how. Like other productive industrial assets, they need to be accumulated through deliberate investment—a management problem. But market mechanisms alone are unlikely to ensure socially efficient rates of investment in these assets—a policy problem. Thus, countries concerned with improving their international competitiveness need to address shortcomings in both management and policy design.

The assumption that industrializing countries can generate technical change simply by choosing and adopting technologies from industrial countries has often obscured the importance of accumulating pertinent domestic assets. The next section discusses the prevailing views on technology transfer and acquisition, along with alternative viewpoints that give much greater prominence to the local accumulation of capabilities for generating and managing technical change. This is followed by sections that explain how the sources of technical change differ across industries and define the various types of technological capabilities that play different roles in developing industrial competitiveness. Finally, the role of businesses, which make key contributions to the accumulation of national technological capabilities, is discussed.

Technical Change and Technological Capabilities

The importance of accumulating technological capabilities to the process of industrialization has frequently been obscured by a number of influential ideas about the nature of technology and the role of technical change in late-industrializing countries. These ideas must be examined critically in order to provide a clearer basis for understanding the development of technological capabilities and competitiveness.

The Traditional Model of Technical Change

At the heart of the prevailing ideas about technical change is the notion that technology takes two main forms: codified information (or disembodied technology), and capital goods (embodied technology).[1] The essential characteristics of these forms of technology are that the technology is readily transferable among organizations and locations and that transfers can be readily effected through market-mediated mechanisms.[2] From this point of view, there is little need for industrializing countries to develop their own

---

1. For some, technology is expressed simply as a ratio between the inputs and outputs of a production system, but this ratio is seen as largely determined by the inherent productivity of the inputs of capital goods, which may or may not be used with the skills required to achieve the latent level of efficiency.

2. Although market imperfections may exist, especially for technology as information (Arrow 1962), these are usually seen as affecting the likely price in commercial transactions, not transferability.

resources for generating and managing technical change. This theory rests on several contingent assumptions.

- First, a sharp distinction can be drawn between technological innovation and the subsequent diffusion of technology. With minor exceptions, industrializing countries should concentrate on exploiting already existing technologies rather than expending resources on efforts to generate innovation and technical change.[3]

- Second, there is a corresponding distinction between those sectors of the economy producing innovative technology (the capital goods sectors) and those using it (the others).[4] With minor exceptions, efficient industrialization involves concentrating on the latter and leaving the development of capital goods sectors until later.

- Third, industrial technologies tend to be transferred to developing countries at late stages in the product or technology cycle; by that time, the technology is mature and stable, requiring only the appropriate know-how and competitive wage levels.

- Fourth, economies can increase efficiency levels in a relatively short period in ways that have little to do with innovation and technical change. Provided that workers have been sufficiently trained in basic operating skills, efficiency can be improved through the accumulation of production experience, or "learning by doing."

- Finally, technological change occurs only intermittently, and efficiency tends to move forward in distinct "steps" as a result of innovation in industrial countries. Developing countries can take advantage of the relatively slow pace of change by acquiring the latest vintage of capital that embodies new technologies or licensing new product designs.

As noted earlier, these ideas are fundamentally misleading. In reality, technology is so complex that it can be only partially encompassed by either codified information or physical capital. Innovation requires more than codified knowledge, because scientific laws and models cannot fully predict the performance of new products and processes. Both the operation of existing technologies and innovation require tacit knowledge that is

---

3. This argument is sometimes supported by the assertion that the most successful industrializing economies, like Korea and Taiwan, China, have adopted existing technologies and given very little attention to innovation.

4. This distinction leaves aside product innovation in the final goods sectors, which is in any case seen as largely irrelevant in late-industrializing countries that adopt already developed product technologies.

highly specific to particular products, processes, firms, and markets and can therefore be acquired only through trial and error and the accumulation of experience in particular contexts. Futher, capital goods in themselves cannot constitute technology, for while much technology is embodied in plants and equipment, operational technologies also encompass complex relationships involving equipment, process characteristics, product specifications, and work organization.

The Generation and Management of Technical Change

If technology were simply a matter of information, competitiveness would be relatively easy to achieve and sustain, and catching up economically would be much less difficult than it has been. But in fact technology consists of complex "bundles" of information—both codified and tacit—as well as physical capital. Because tacit information is not readily transferable among firms and countries, technological blueprints do not contain inherent performance characteristics (such as set productivity levels). Instead, these blueprints have to be translated into specifications and procedures that are specific to particular applications—an uncertain creative process that can result in highly variable levels of performance. Moreover, even when such bundles have been created and molded into the configurations required for applications to specific firms, they must be continually remolded if the firms are to remain competitive in a world where the benchmarks for competitive efficiency are constantly rising. Thus, technological capabilities must include capacities for generating and managing such change. In late-industrializing countries, the acquisition of capabilities to generate and manage change is governed by four considerations.

(I) IN PRACTICE, THE PROCESSES OF "INNOVATION" AND "DIFFUSION" ARE HARD TO DISTINGUISH. All too often, the common distinction between these two processes carries with it a corresponding notion about the international division of labor. Innovation—the development and initial commercialization of new technology—is assumed to be heavily concentrated in the industrial countries. According to this thinking, it becomes significant in developing economies only as they catch up technologically. In the meantime, these economies are expected to concentrate on diffusion—the application of readily available and transferable technologies. Because diffusion is seen basically as a process of choosing, acquiring, and adapting existing technologies, this assumption precludes the need for developing countries to accumulate capabilities for innovation. From this perspective, therefore, technological accumulation in developing countries is seen as consisting simply of the accumulation of technology embodied in capital goods (and product specifications) and the acquisition of the needed operating know-how.

In fact, diffusion involves more. It also incorporates a process of continuing, often incremental technical change that molds technology for use in a range of specific situations and modifies it to improve on the original performance standards. The importance of building on acquired technology during the diffusion process has long been emphasized by more perceptive observers (Rosenberg 1972, 1986; Metcalf 1988). In addition, many of the improvements are localized and specific to firms, products, and markets, because acquired technology is adapted and improved on in two stages: first, during the investment phase, when the technology is initially brought into use; and second, during the operational lifetime of each project, when a stream of incremental improvements is incorporated into the system.

Although the providers of technology can make important contributions to localized processes of technical change, recipient firms and countries must develop their own capabilities in order to stay internationally competitive. Incremental improvements must continue throughout the operational lifetime of projects, since it is difficult and costly to draw continuously on new capital goods and inputs to facilitate change. Thus, late-industrializing countries may adopt and use technology, but they also need to contribute to its ongoing development. However, it is not necessary for each country to develop a domestic capital goods sector.

(II) TECHNICAL PROGRESS IS GENERATED BY BOTH THE PRODUCERS AND USERS OF TECHNOLOGY EMBODIED IN CAPITAL. As noted above, firms making capital goods are not the sole creators and sources of new processes. In fact, the users of capital inputs often play active and creative roles in changing the technology they use. Some play dominant or even exclusive roles in developing new machines, and many more interact with machinery producers and engineering companies in making incremental modifications and improvements to production technologies. Again, these changes continue throughout the operating lifetime of a project.

This involvement in innovation has been an important feature of Japanese firms' strategies for improving competitiveness. The Japanese did not invent the technique, however: it has also been common among firms in North America and Europe. For example, DuPont, a late entrant to the international rayon market, acquired the technology to manufacture rayon from European sources in the 1920s. The firm then built up the technological capabilities it needed to build new plants and improve efficiency (Hollander 1965). Similarly, in the 1970s European oil companies acquired from the United States the technology needed for offshore exploration and production in the North Sea. They rapidly built up their capabilities to generate and manage improvements in much of the equipment-embodied technology that they used (Bell and Oldham 1988).

In industrializing countries, firms that use acquired technology and become competitive have also found the ability to generate change to be important in maintaining competitiveness. For example, petrochemical and steel companies in Korea rapidly built up their capabilities to design and construct plants and then increased efficiency by incorporating engineering improvements into the plants (Enos and Park 1988). And Korean automobile companies have made substantial efforts to develop and build their own machine tools (Lee 1993).

(III) "LEARNING BY DOING" ALONE WILL NOT KEEP TECHNOLOGY-IMPORTING FIRMS COMPETITIVE. The notion that certain techniques must be learned is inherent in most discussions about the competitiveness of infant firms and industries. It is suggested that infant firms, having chosen such techniques, may still be inefficient relative to established firms simply because the new firms lack the production experience necessary to use the techniques at optimum efficiency. Once the firms acquire that experience, they will be able to achieve the levels of efficiency inherent in the chosen techniques; if the firms fail, it is because of market distortions and limited incentives that give rise to various forms of X-inefficiency.

This perspective is mistaken because it suggests that competitiveness involves reaching a particular level of, rather than a particular rate of improvement in, efficiency. It implies that a distinction can be drawn between two types of improvements: improvements in using the given techniques based on experience (or higher utilization rates of the inherent full capacity of capital equipment), and the intermittent introduction of new vintages of physical capital that embodies technology. However, the localized and continuous nature of technical change means that competitiveness is not simply a level that can be reached by combining greater experience with an initial level of skills and a given stock of physical capital. It is a constantly changing state achieved and sustained by rates of technical change that surpass or at least match the rates being generated elsewhere.[5] Accumulating the capabilities to generate these changes is therefore a necessary condition for competitiveness.

The central feature of this analysis is the distinction between production capacity and technological capabilities shown in Figure 4.1. This distinction reflects an important change over the last century in the processes of technological accumulation in industry—namely, the increasing specialization and professionalization of the activities involved in generating and managing technical change. In the early stages of industrialization in today's technologically advanced countries, the resources needed to undertake these activities were accumulated alongside (and through interaction with) expanding production capacity and output. The knowledge and skills required to generate technical change were relatively close to those needed for production and were frequently developed largely on the basis of cumulated production experience. Both typically existed in the same organizational location—not just in the same firms, but often within the same parts of firms (such as the machine shops of textile factories).

However, across a range of industries and technologies, increasing specialization has widened the gap between the kinds of knowledge and skills required to use given technologies and those required to create and change technology. Skills based only on cumulative operational experience have become progressively inadequate as a basis for generating change, and this differentiation in the knowledge base for industrial activity has been reinforced by increasing organizational differentiation. Some of this differentiation has involved the emergence of distinct engineering departments, design units, and research and development (R&D) centers within firms.

Sectors have also emerged that are devoted exclusively to the design and manufacture of capital goods and the provision of other inputs to technical change in production—what is called "vertical disintegration." In the industrial economies, this distinction between creating and operating industrial technologies has developed within institutional arrangements that have kept the two kinds of capabilities closely linked. However, for newly industrializing countries, these two sets of capabilities are not necessarily so closely and effectively linked. Industrial output can grow and production capacity can be expanded and diversified without automatically giving rise to the development of effective capabilities for generating and managing technical change. Hence the distinction in Figure 4.1 between

---

5. This holds true unless continuing exchange rate devaluation and the consequent steady erosion of real incomes are used to overcome (probably only temporarily) any shortfall in the real technological base of competitiveness.

Figure 4.1. Technological Accumulation: Basic Concepts and Terms

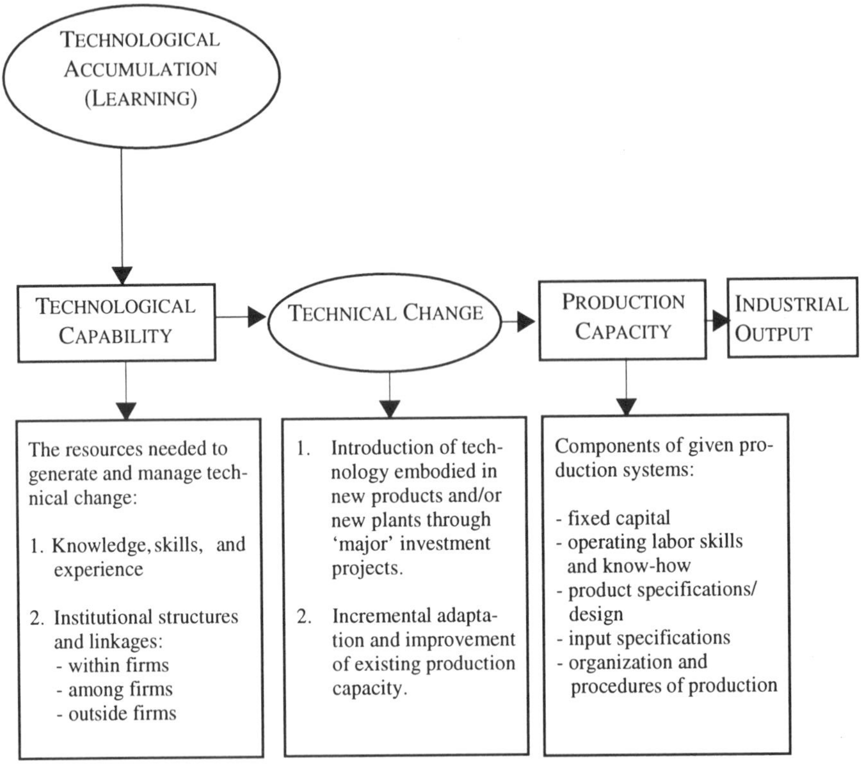

two kinds of resources: *production capacity* and *technological capabilities*. The former incorporates the resources used to produce industrial goods at given levels of efficiency and given input combinations: equipment that embodies technology, operational and managerial know-how and experience, product and input specifications, and organizational methods and systems. The technological capabilities needed to generate and manage technical change include skills, knowledge, and experience that often (but not always) differ substantially from those needed to operate existing technical systems, as well as the particular kinds of institutional structures and linkages necessary to produce inputs for technical change.

(IV) THERE IS OFTEN LITTLE TECHNOLOGICAL STABILITY IN THE LATER STAGES OF THE PRODUCT LIFE CYCLE. It cannot be assumed that technologies become stable in the later stages of product or industry life cycles and that it is consequently unnecessary for firms acquiring foreign technology to develop their own capabilities for generating and managing technical change. There are often periods when technological innovation proceeds relatively slowly, and, as has already been mentioned, much of the technology developing countries initially acquire is at relatively late stages in its life cycle. However, it is not the case that phases of technological stability coincide with late stages in product/industry life cycles. Industries and products frequently pass through such periods of stability into phases of renewed and rapid change. The cotton textile industry, for instance, has gone through several such cycles.

Consequently, developing country firms in supposedly mature industries may need to develop substantial capabilities for generating change in order to achieve or sustain competitiveness, especially when new countries with lower labor costs are entering the industries. Developing these capabilities requires constantly improving techniques through actively engineered technical and organizational change, not just the kind of passive "learning by doing" that yields increased proficiency in operating given techniques as a result of increased production experience.

Sources of Technical Change in Industry

One reason it is difficult to make useful generalizations about the correct sequencing involved in the accumulation of technological capabilities is that the nature and sources of technological knowledge differ across industries. In the industrial countries, categories of terms can be distinguished, each with its distinctive sources and directions of technological change (Table 4.1). In *supplier-dominated firms* (primarily in agriculture and textiles), technical change comes almost exclusively from suppliers of machinery and other production inputs. Technical choices reflect relative factor costs, and technological accumulation is focused on improving and modifying production methods and associated inputs, and occasionally on product design. International technology transfers are relatively easy, as technology is embodied mostly in capital goods and other inputs; in the agricultural sector, extension efforts can help to disseminate new knowledge and practices. As such, the choice of technology in supplier-dominated firms bears some resemblance to the substitution possibilities reflected in the conventional production function.

In *scale-intensive firms* (in the steel and automobile industries, for instance), technological accumulation is generated by the design, creation, and operation of complex production systems and products. The main sources of technological improvements are design and production engi-

Table 4.1. A Technology-Based Classification of Business Firms

Characteristics	Category of Firm				
	Supplier Dominated	*Scale Intensive*	*Information Intensive*	*Science Based*	*Specialized Supplier*
Typical Core Sector	Agriculture, housing, private services, traditional manufacturing.	Bulk materials (steel, glass), consumer durables, automobiles, civil engineering.	Finance, retailing, publishing, travel.	Electrical, electronics, chemicals.	Capital goods, instruments, software.
Size of firm	Small	Large	Large	Large	Small
Type of user	Price sensitive	Mixed	Mixed	Mixed	Performance sensitive
Main focus of technological activities	Cost reduction	Mixed	Mixed	Mixed	Product improvement
Main sources of technological accumulation	*Suppliers* Production learning, advisory services.	*Production engineering* production learning, suppliers, design.	*Corporate software and systems engineering* Equipment and software suppliers.	*Corporate R&D* Basic research, production, engineering, design.	*Design and development (advanced users)*
Main direction of technological accumulation	Process technology and related equipment.	Process technology and related equipment.	Process technology and related software	Technology-related products	Products improvement
	[Upstream]	[Upstream]	[Mixed]	[Concentric]	[Concentric]
Main channels of imitation and technological transfer	Purchase of equipment and related services.	Purchase of equipment, know-how, licensing and related training, reverse engineering.	Purchase of equipment and software, reverse engineering.	Reserve engineering, R&D hiring of experienced engineers and scientists.	Reverse engineering, learning from advanced users.
Main methods of protection against imitation	Nontechnical (marketing, trademarks).	Process secrecy, design and operating know-how.	Copyright, design and operating know-how.	R&D know-how, patents, design, and operating know-how.	Design know-how, patents, knowledge of users' needs.
Main strategic management tasks	Use technology generated elsewhere to reinforce other competitive advantages.	Incremental integration of new technology in complex systems, improvement and diffusion of best practice, exploitation of process technology advantages.	Design and operation of complex information-processing systems, development of related products.	Development of related products, exploitation of basic science, complementary assets, reconfiguration of divisional responsibilities.	Monitoring of advanced users needs, integration of new technology in products.

Source: Based on Pavitt 1984.

neering, operating experience, and suppliers of equipment and components. Given the potential economic advantages of increased scale, and the complexity of products and production systems, the risks of failure associated with radical change are potentially very high. Process and product technologies therefore develop incrementally. International technology transfer requires the licensing of production and design know-how and related training, in addition to trade in machinery and other inputs.

In *information-intensive* firms (in finance and retailing, for instance), a major new form of technological accumulation has emerged, the result of revolutionary improvements over the last forty years in the capacity to store, process, and transfer information. Technological accumulation comprises the design, construction, operation, and improvement of complex systems for the storage and processing of information. The improvements themselves tend to be incremental, and the main sources are operating experience—the so-called systems departments in large user firms—and suppliers of systems and applications software. Although comprehensive data are scarce, surveys suggest that large firms in the service industries (such as banking and retailing) have become major centers for the accumulation of information technology.

In *science-based firms* in industries such as chemicals and electronics, technology is accumulated mainly by corporate R&D laboratories and is heavily dependent on the knowledge, skills, and techniques emerging from academic research. Technological accumulation focuses primarily on a horizontal search for new and technologically related product markets. International technology transfers require a strong capability for reverse engineering (that is, disassembling competitors' products to see how they work), which itself requires a capacity for R&D and design activities. These transfers also require trained research scientists and engineers with foreign contacts. This style of technical change is best exemplified by the innovative firm described and analyzed in the writings of Schumpeter (1934, 1942).

Specialized supplier firms (for example, in machinery and control instrumentation) provide high-performance inputs into complex systems of production in the form of machinery, components, instruments, and software. Technological accumulation takes place through the design, construction, and use of these production inputs. Specialized supplier firms accumulate the skills necessary to match the advances in machine design, which—given the complexity and interdependency of production processes—put a premium on reliability and performance rather than on price. International technology transfers take place through the purchasing activities of advanced user firms and through reverse engineering. This type of technical change is noted in the writings of Stigler (1956) and Rosenberg (1976) on vertical disintegration and technological convergence.

Thus, each category in Table 4.1 represents a different style of technological learning and a different organizational location for specialized learning activities:

- production operations (quality control, production planning) in supplier-dominated firms;
- process and product improvements (production engineering, design) in scale-intensive firms;
- exploitation of basic research for product and associated process developments (R&D) in science-based firms; and
- equipment and component development (design) in specialized supplier firms.

Over time, learning processes within sectors have become the basis for local production in other sectors—for example, through the vertical disintegration of production activities developed in one type of firm, the transfer of accumulated knowledge and expertise to other types of firms (such as specialized suppliers), the migration of skilled people from firms in one category to firms in another, and the development of new areas of knowledge and new skills among local firms and technological institutions. More generally, learning-based structural change has involved the emergence of technologically sophisticated sectors that have their roots in technological accumulation in less complex industries, including:

- the U.S. textile machinery industry, which became a specialized supplier sector in the nineteenth century on the basis of technological accumulation in textile firms (which became supplier dominated);
- specialized suppliers of production equipment, which are built on the technology accumulated in scale-intensive sectors (such as consumer durables, automobiles, and process industries); and
- science-based industries that have adopted technology used in other industries—electronics, for instance, which drew on specialized supplier sectors, and science-based chemicals, which evolved from less complex process industries.

Such trajectories of technological learning and progress are not preordained. Nonetheless, three mechanisms seem to have been particularly influential in the past and will undoubtedly continue to influence strategies for technological accumulation and industrial development: factor endowments; directions of persistent investment, especially those with strong intersectoral linkages; and the cumulative mastery of core technologies and their underlying knowledge bases. The relative significance of these mechanisms changes during the process of industrialization. In the early stages, the directions of technical change in a country or region are strongly influenced by the availability of factors of production, domestic market conditions, and local investment opportunities. At higher levels of development, however, the local accumulation of specific technological skills itself becomes a means of focusing technical change.

Different Types of Technological Capabilities

Several studies have distinguished between different types of technological capabilities (for example, Dahlman, Ross-Larsen, and Westphal 1987). Table 4.2, which is based on the framework developed by Lall (1992), emphasizes the difference between basic production capabilities (elements of what were described earlier as "production capacity") and technological capabilities. It also distinguishes between what can loosely be described "depths" of technological capabilities. A basic level of capabilities may permit only relatively minor and incremental contributions to change, but at the intermediate and advanced levels, technological capabilities may result in more substantial, novel, and ambitious contributions to change. Finally, the table distinguishes between six different functions for which firms may develop technological capabilities (the columns in the table). The first two columns may be described as *primary functions*: generating technical change and managing its implementation during relatively large investment projects to create major new production systems, such as new plants or production lines, additions to existing plant's capacity, and distinct new product lines; and generating and managing technical change during production activities undertaken in the postinvestment lifetime of production facitilities. The last two columns of the table may be considered *supporting functions* that consist of developing change-centered links and interactions with other firms and institutions and producing the capital goods that embody elements of locally created new technology. Over the long term, the capabilities for carrying out these functions help to strengthen the sequences of accumulating technological capabilities and create the basis for diversifying into new products and industries. These functions deserve some elaboration.

Table 4.2. Industrial Technological Capabilities: An Illustrative Framework

| | Primary Activities | | | | Supporting Activities | |
| | Investment | | Production | | | |
	Facility user's decision-making and control	Project preparation and implementation	Process and production organization	Product centered	Developing linkages	Capital goods supply
Basic production capabilities Capacities to use existing production techniques	Engaging primary contractor. Securing and disbursing finance. Officiating at opening ceremony.	Preparation of initial project outline. Construction of basic civil works. Simple plant erection.	Routine operation and basic maintenance of 'given' facilities. Efficiency improvement from experience in existing tasks.	Replication of fixed specification and designs. Routing QC to maintain existing standards and specifications.	Procurement of available inputs from existing suppliers. Sale of 'given' products to existing and new customers.	Replication of unchanging items of plants and machinery.
TECHNOLOGICAL CAPABILITIES (CAPABILITIES TO GENERATE AND MANAGE TECHNICAL CHANGE)						
BASIC	Active monitoring and control of feasibility studies, technology choice/sourcing, and project scheduling.	Feasibility studies. Outline planning. Standard equipment procurement. Simple ancillaries engineering.	Commissioning and debugging. Improved layout, scheduling, and maintenance. Minor adaptation.	Minor adaptation to market needs, and incremental improvement in product quality.	Searching and absorbing new information from suppliers, customers, and local institutions.	Copying new types of plants and machinery. Simple adaptation of existing designs and specifications.
INTERMEDIATE	Search, evaluation and selection of technology/sources. Tenders/negotiation. Overall project management.	Detailed engineering. Plant procurement. Environment assessment. Project scheduling and management. Commissioning. Training/recruitment.	Process improvement. Licensing new technology. Introducing organizational changes.	Licensing new product technology and/or reverse engineering. Incremental new product design.	Technology transfer to suppliers and customers to raise efficiency, quality, and local sourcing.	Incrementally innovative reverse engineering and original design of plant and machinery.
ADVANCED	Developing new production systems and components.	Basic process design and related R&D.	Process innovation and related R&D. Radical innovation in organization.	Product innovation and related R&D.	Collaboration in technology development.	R&D for specifications and designs of new plant and machinery.

Source: Lall 1992.

Technological Capabilities and Investment

Basic elements of existing technology that are incorporated into new production facilities are frequently improved or adapted to specific situations. Typically, making these changes is a complex and creative process, the importance of which is widely acknowledged. Voss (1988) discusses the process in terms of the adoption of advanced manufacturing technology in industrial countries; Amsalem (1983) shows the complexity and creativity of the engineering activities involved in acquiring technology during the investment phase for new textile and paper plants in developing countries. Thus, even with apparently established technologies, the initial productivity of new plants will be highly variable, depending on the strength of available capabilities for managing and generating a process of technical change. And, when more novel elements of technology are incorporated into investment projects alongside established technology, the necessary capabilities may require more sophisticated engineering and R&D.

Creativity on the part of the recipients of technology is important to investment projects. Investment in new production facilities obviously draws on a range of suppliers for capital goods, engineering services, project management services, and so forth, but technologically dynamic firms rarely play a purely passive role during the acquisition of technology. They can control key decisions about the choice of technology and its implementation; interact with their suppliers in developing designs and specifications; and generate a significant part of the technology themselves, perhaps also incorporating it into the design of the capital goods that will be used in production. Developing the capabilities needed to perform these functions can have a significant effect on the efficiency of investment. For example, Korean firms have made substantial efforts to build up these capabilities, ultimately speeding up implementation of low-cost industrial investment projects (Amsden 1989; Enos and Park 1988).[6]

---

6. This contribution to Korea's high rates of productivity growth has sometimes been hidden behind explanations that see alternative investment projects as having *inherent* levels of productivity. According to this argument, efficiency in investment is simply a matter of choosing the most productive alternatives and allocating the necessary resources accordingly. For example, the World Bank (1993a) study of high-productivity growth in the East Asian economies suggests that the region's remarkable productivity performance stemmed from the efficient allocation of capital to high-yielding investments, among other things.

Technological Capabilities and Postinvestment Production

As emphasized earlier, sustaining competitiveness requires that technical change continue through the postinvestment operational lifetime of production facilities. The abundant literature on learning curves (the reduction of unit production costs as a function of cumulative production experience) highlights the significance of the economic gains that result from continuing improvements in technologies. Much of this literature obscures the process, however, for improved performance is not the result simply of experience in operating new technologies but is generated by the continuing pursuit of creative technical change (incremental innovation).[7] Firms can generate change by:

- incorporating incremental improvements in existing process technology that can be introduced into new facilities during subsequent investment projects;
- modifying and improving existing products that can subsequently be incorporated into imitative products; and
- improving or adapting existing materials and components, or developing substitutes for those already in use.

The continuing cost reductions achieved in the DuPont rayon plants after the acquisition of European technology illustrate the importance of these types of changes (Hollander 1965). Continuous technological improvements are widely held to have contributed to the competitive success of Japanese firms (Imai 1986). The significance of such technological dynamism has also been observed in developing countries—for example, in the steel industry in Brazil and the petrochemical industry in Korea (Dahlman and Fonseca 1987; Enos and Park 1988). More recent studies have emphasized the importance of ongoing change to the organizational dimension of production technology (Hoffman 1989; Meyer-Stamer and others 1991; and Mody, Suri, and Sanders 1992).

These contributions to sustained competitiveness require the users of acquired technology to contribute actively to ongoing technical and organizational change. Technical changes in existing production systems will often draw on inputs from external suppliers, but the firms using the technology must themselves play a significant role, both independently and in

---

7. See, for example, the review of the frequently cited evidence about learning curves in aircraft and ship production during World War II in Bell and Scott-Kemmis (1994).

conjunction with the external suppliers. As firms acquire deeper levels of capabilities, the functional distinctions may become increasingly blurred—for example, R&D capabilities for improving existing processes may become intermingled with engineering capabilities for incorporating new process technology into major investment projects.

Technological Capabilities and Interfirm Links

Although the technologically creative activities of individual firms often play a central role during both the investment and postinvestment phases of projects, interactions among firms also have a profound effect on the process of technological change. Some of these interactions involve informal collaboration between suppliers and customers in the exchange of knowledge, information, and skills accumulated during the design, production, and use of production inputs (Lundvall 1988; 1992; OECD 1992a). Others involve a wider range of collaborative arrangements—such as licensing, joint R&D programs, and technological exchange agreements—among competing as well as complementary firms (Chesnais 1988; Cainarca, Colombo, and Mariotti 1992; Kleinknecht and Reijnen 1992; Hagedoorn and Schakenraad 1992).

Thus, one important component of industrial technological change is the complex structure of interactions among firms. This structure relies on links connecting the *technological capabilities* of collaborating firms, which often depend heavily on the capabilities of leading firms within emerging networks. Users of components, material, or equipment, for instance, can actively induce their suppliers to make improvements in these inputs; they can use their own technological capabilities to generate those inputs; or they can transfer technical competencies to enable the suppliers to generate the changes. But these interactions will not take place unless significant technological capabilities exist in one or the other (or preferably both) of the firms. Otherwise, interactions will be limited to market transactions for already existing inputs and outputs.

Technological Capabilities and the Production of Capital Goods

Because much technological change is embodied in capital goods, the ability to produce machinery with new specifications (though not just to replicate existing specifications) is another important component of industrial technological capability. This ability can be developed in specialized machinery-producing firms, but, as emphasized earlier, the users of these machines can help develop new technologies and can even start producing machinery themselves. In many industries, this user-specific capability makes an important contribution to increased competitiveness (von Hippel 1988). Along with other technological capabilities, it contributes to the competitive strengths of new industries.

Accumulating Technological Capabilities

It has sometimes been suggested that firms in developing countries have accumulated technological capabilities in particular sequences, moving through definable stages (Dahlman, Ross-Larsen, and Westphal 1987). It has even been suggested that these sequences and stages can provide guidelines for both firm-level strategies and government policy (Kim 1980; Lee, Bae, and Choi 1988).

In a very general sense, such sequences do reflect realities. For example, firms and industries seeking to improve their technologies generally have to build on what already exists. Beyond such generalities, however, rigid ideas about sequences and stages may be misleading, especially at the firm level. The rate at which a firm should proceed in accumulating capabilities, and the level of sophistication it should aim for, seem likely to vary widely, as does the potential sequencing of accumulation among different functional areas. For example, in some industries, it may be important to develop investment-related capabilities rapidly and to considerable depths before, say, accumulating significant capabilities for improving product technology during the postinvestment production phase—and perhaps even before entering production in the first place. The Japanese synthetic fibre industry followed this path in the 1950s (Ozawa 1980). In other situations, precisely the reverse may be indicated, with competitiveness depending heavily on the rapid accumulation of capabilities for improving performance in the postinvestment phase, as the case of the small Jamaican firm described by Girvan and Marcelle (1990) illustrates.

In other firms and industries, competitiveness may depend heavily on moving quickly to sophisticated levels of capability in the design and development of products and in technological innovation. In such cases, investment-related capabilities may receive little attention, perhaps because few major investment projects are planned, or because the costs and risks of acquiring and using those capabilities are particularly high. Conversely, in some cases it may be especially important to develop substantial capabilities for improving processes (though perhaps not for more radical and comprehensive innovation) and for managing key technological aspects of investment projects. In these instances, product-related capabilities may be less important. This pattern seems to have prevailed in Korean petrochemical firms (Enos and Park 1988).

The variability of these patterns suggests the need for care and clarity in choosing specific strategies for accumulating technologies at the firm level. Although there is a growing body of knowledge concerning the technological strategies of firms in industrial countries that have already accumulated some advanced levels of capabilities, there are few guidelines for firms to follow in designing strategies to move from more basic levels to these advanced capabilities. Nor are there many guidelines for developing strategies of accumulation at the economywide level. A few economies have achieved considerable competitive success in the postwar period, in particular Korea and Taiwan, China, where firms across a wide range of sectors have developed strong capabilities for generating continuous change in technologies acquired from industrial countries; for synthesizing diverse elements of increasingly complex imported technology into new plants and products; for independently replicating technologies already developed elsewhere; and now for more sophisticated innovations. These accomplishments initially depended heavily on the accumulation of various engineering capabilities (Westphal, Kim, and Dahlman 1985; Enos and Park 1988; Amsden 1989). More recently, especially in the electronics industry (but not only there), these firms have drawn on the rapid growth of business-financed R&D, which has included the evolving mix of imitative and innovative technological activities common to countries in the early stages of industrialization (Ernst and O'Connor 1992; Bloom 1992).

In other developing countries (including China, India, and some in Latin America), the accumulation of these kinds of technological capabilities within industrial firms has been much more limited or more narrowly focused—for example, in the aircraft industry and selected informatics product groups in Brazil, and in the defense and space industries in India. In places such as Africa, the intrafirm accumulation of such capabilities has been virtually absent.

Diversification and Structural Change

The technological capabilities for carrying out the various functions outlined above have a major influence on the degree of industrial competitiveness that is based on established comparative advantages. But they also play another long-term role, creating a technological base for new areas of potential advantage by opening up opportunities for diversification into related products and new industries.

The historical experience of today's industrial countries shows that the paths they followed toward national technological development were based on cumulative knowledge and experience (see David 1975; and, in a different tradition, Porter 1990). In general terms, technological accumulation involved the progressive acquisition of largely country-specific and internationally immobile intangible capital in the form of personal and organizational skills and related institutional structures. This capital enabled countries gradually to adopt and develop process and product technologies of increasing complexity. Changing bases of international competitiveness evolved along with, and increasingly as a result of, these technological capabilities. Over time, the learning processes within sectors laid the groundwork for production in other sectors, as the following examples illustrate:

- the creation of capacities to design and develop capital goods outside established user industries through vertical disintegration;
- the transfer of accumulated knowledge and expertise to enhance the competitiveness of other types of firms; and
- the migration of skilled people from firms in one category to firms in another, in general stimulating awareness of new areas of knowledge and new skills among local firms and technological institutions.

However, opportunities for technology-based diversification in today's developing countries are not the same as they were in the past. For example, in the nineteenth century textile production was the basis for accumulating knowledge on the design and building of textile machinery and related capital goods. Today, the locus of accumulation has shifted to specialized suppliers of textile machinery. Nevertheless, the experience of large Korean *chaebols* (conglomerate firms) suggests that experience in one field of production (such as cement) can be an important input in the establishment of another (such as automobiles) (Amsden 1989). Furthermore, the production of automobiles and consumer durables has become important to technological accumulation in industries such as machine tools and related capital goods. For example, Japan's capability in computer-controlled machine tools in the 1970s grew out of pressure to improve production efficiency in automobiles and electronic products. Similar patterns seem to be evolving in these industries in Korea (Lee 1993).

Compared with the experience of earlier industrializing countries, however, there appears to be a much lower degree of automaticity in the diversification and shifting of sectoral structures of production. Accumulating experience in one line of production seems to have become progressively less adequate as the sole basis for diversification. High levels of explicit investment in technological capability are required today, since—as was emphasized earlier—the accumulation of these capabilities is not automatically linked to the expansion of production capacity or to the growth of output. In order to help industries break out of the constraints of past experience, policy mechanisms to induce shifts in sectoral patterns of investment in production capacity may also be necessary (see chapter 5).

The Role of Business Firms

Given the specific, localized, and partly tacit nature of technological knowledge and of the capabilities needed to use and build on it, the business firm is the central agent in creating and managing patterns of technological change. The behavior of firms in accumulating technology is determined in part by market signals and in part by government policy. Within a policy environment, however, firms differ in their responses to a complex present and an uncertain future, depending on the skills they have accumulated and the discretionary judgments their managers have made. Such judgments are particularly influential in deciding the level of intangible investment in training, R&D, and other activities related to change, the benefits of which are often not immediately obvious.

The increasingly global activities of large firms based in industrial countries are accelerating the growth of international production and the international diffusion of technology associated with such production. But the intangible resources for generating and managing change (such as R&D and production engineering) remain heavily concentrated in the industrially advanced countries (Patel 1994). The degree to which firms deploy these change-generating resources in a foreign country depends not only on competitive pressure but on the quality of local human resources (including worker skills and the number of qualified scientists and engineers) and the change-generating capabilities of local business firms. Thus, the design and strengthening of what can be called "national systems of innovation" are just as important for developing as for industrial countries.[8] The technological capabilities of local firms are the central features of these systems.

This section examines key features of these national systems of innovation: the characteristics of successful management, the complementary links between technology imports and local capabilities, training by business firms, and the contributions of R&D institutes.

Successful Management of Technological Change

There is a flourishing research-based literature on the firm-specific factors that affect the success and failure of innovation in advanced countries, but there is no literature of equivalent scope and depth for developing countries.[9] Nonetheless, existing studies do point to several important factors that can be influenced by effective management.

Technology acquired from firms in more advanced countries is obviously important to firms in industrializing countries that are trying to catch up technologically. But it is also true for firms in industrial countries. Much international trade in technology (either as disembodied knowledge or as technology embodied in capital goods and engineering services) takes place among advanced industrial countries, and a significant proportion of the innovations developed in these countries is based on imitations of existing technology (De Melto, McMullen, and Wills 1980; Smith and Vidvei 1992; Deiaco 1992). In addition, R&D in industrial countries is often undertaken in order to monitor, assimilate, and modify the technological advances of competitor firms in other countries (Levin and others 1987; Cohen and Levinthal 1989). There is therefore no clear-cut distinction between the kinds of activities and resources required for innovation and those required for imitation.

The level of technical competence in senior management is an important factor influencing a firm's commitment to change-generating activities. This finding is based on:

---

8. "National systems of innovation" can be defined as the intangible investments that accompany tangible investments as necessary inputs into economic growth. More specifically, they can be seen as the national institutions (including their incentive structures and their competencies) that determine the rate and direction of technological learning in a country (see Lundvall 1992; Nelson 1993; Patel and Pavitt 1994).

9. Notable exceptions include Kim and Kim (1985) and Gerstenfeld and Wortzel (1977).

- intercountry comparisons showing that strong commitments to industry-funded R&D and training activities are associated with high proportions of scientists and engineers in senior management (Lawrence 1980; Pavitt and Patel 1988);
- intracountry comparisons of firms' performance with the competencies of senior management (Scherer and Huh 1992); and
- the experiences of countries that have been successful in catching up technologically (Gerstenfeld and Wortzel 1977; Amsden 1989).

Technically competent senior managers are obviously necessary if firms are to choose and implement new technology effectively. Choosing the right technology requires the evaluation not only of any measurable economic benefits but also of the potential future benefits of technological learning along alternative and irreversible paths. Conventional project appraisal techniques such as discounted cash flow cannot (and should not) be used in the assessment of the option value of alternative technological paths (Myers 1984; Mitchell and Hamilton 1988). The judgment of experienced engineers may be the only realistic method of forming expectations about the likely benefits of alternative technological paths and policies.

Good communication and effective collaboration, both among internal departments and with sources of knowledge and potential customers, are important distinguishing features of successful innovation in industrially advanced countries (Rothwell 1977). The importance of intrafirm cooperation has also been identified as a significant factor in the successful accumulation of technological capabilities in Korean semiconductor firms (Choi 1993). However, there is some evidence that external linkages, although important for technological latecomer firms in developing countries, differ from those found in state-of-the-art firms in industrial countries. In latecomer firms attempting to catch up technologically, technical feasibility and market acceptance are already established. The main uncertainties and risks relate to the firms' capacity for learning and improvement (see Kim and Kim 1991). The most important external linkages are therefore to organizations able to help the learning process—suppliers, customers, licensers, businesses producing competitive products (for reverse engineering), and technical support institutions. In state-of-the-art firms, the main uncertainties and risks relate to technical feasibility and market acceptance of previously untried technology. Links with repositories of fundamental technical knowledge (such as universities) and with potential customers are therefore of particular importance.

Importing Foreign Technology

One common assumption that policymakers have made is that importing foreign technology and creating it locally are substitutable means of generating technical change in industrializing countries, even though there is enough evidence to suggest that imported technology and local technological accumulation are complementary. In other words, generating change requires considerable domestic innovative effort as well as the acquisition of imported technology. Even when technical change depends heavily on imported technology, new equipment and techniques may be complemented by intensive efforts to accumulate locally the capabilities for improving the acquired technology, generating new components, and promoting technological independence.[10] Investment in related technological capabilities can begin before technology is imported, providing the knowledge buyers need to make the best deal and speeding up the assimilation of new materials. Japan followed this path when it first undertook synthetic fibre production (Ozawa 1980). The exchange of information through educational and other formal or informal channels is also important to the acquisition of new technology and the development of local capabilities. Engineers and managers from developing countries who study and work in industrial countries not only are trained in technological problem-solving but also have access to the informal international networks that are so important in science-based technologies. For example, one study of Korea shows that experience acquired through overseas employment was much more important than the acquisition from abroad of basic process and production technology (Westphal, Rhee, and Purcell 1981).

Complementarity between imported and local technology is often less visible (but more intense) in commercial technology transactions among firms—for instance, when the licensing of process specifications is accompanied by access to design data; training in design routines or production engineering; or opportunities to acquire experience in design, engineering, and R&D activities. Firms in the East Asian NIEs have used international technology transfers as an active investment in learning. The training components of technology transfer agreements with foreign companies frequently cover much more than the acquisition of the skills necessary to operate and maintain new facilities. They also focus on acquiring various

10. See Hollander (1965) on the DuPont Corporation. On various aspects of Japanese technological accumulation, see Tanaka (1978, 1992); Fukasaku (1986); Nakaoka (1987); Odagiri and Goto (1992); and Ozawa (1974, 1985).

combinations of design, engineering, and project management skills that can be used to generate change (Enos and Park 1988; Hobday 1994a). Further, customers in industrial countries have been used as an important source of knowledge and expertise, especially in industries that rely primarily on assembly (Westphal, Rhee, and Purcell 1981).

This aspect of the East Asian experience suggests that successful firms go through what might be described as a "reverse product cycle" (Hobday 1994b). The firms begin with simple assembly processes but gradually and systematically accumulate the capacity to modify, design, and build their own product and process technologies. Customers play a major part in this cycle, which proceeds through successively higher value-added forms of production. Finally, some firms in the more knowledge-intensive segments of the electronics industry (especially Korean firms) have set up their own operations in the industrial countries to facilitate the acquisition of new information. They have started their own R&D centers (concentrating heavily on technological learning in advance of the acquisition of existing technology) or acquired established firms in those countries in order to gain access to particular skills, experience, and knowledge.

Again, there seem to be wide variations in the extent to which developing countries have been able to develop these two forms of complementarity. Firms in the East Asian NIEs have commonly entered new industries in much the same way as firms in other developing countries—by drawing very heavily on imported inputs of core technology, engineering services, equipment, and know-how. But as these industries expand, successive projects draw increasingly—though very seldom exclusively—on local sources. The East Asian NIEs have been massive importers of industrial technology through:

- direct foreign investment (largely as joint ventures in some countries);
- subcontracting and original equipment manufacturing agreements with foreign customers; and
- licensing and other contracts with unrelated suppliers of know-how, designs, equipment, and services (Hobday 1994b).

But these inflows of technology have been complemented by locally sourced technology, which emerged after intensive efforts to improve what was initially acquired. In other words, firms did not choose between imported and local technology as sources of technical change: instead, they chose both.

In other late industrializing countries, particularly the formerly centrally planned economies, international technology transfers have not been as

closely integrated into the process of domestic technological accumulation
(Girvan and Marcelle 1990). They have played a major role in the expansion
of production capacity but a minor role in building local technological capabilities. Commercial technology transfer arrangements have been used in
some industries (steel and petrochemicals, for instance) in the large Latin
American countries to augment technological capabilities as well as production capacity (Dahlman and Fonseca 1984; Sercovich, 1980). However,
such cases appear to have been relatively infrequent.[11]

The East Asian NIEs have also benefited from the interfirm migration of
skilled personnel in the development of technological capabilities. The skills
workers gained through this workplace experience were determined to be
the second most important source of production technology for firms entering export markets (Westphal and others 1981). Interfirm flows of workers
embodying new technology have often been important in creating nuclei of
competence that form the basis for the acquisition of new types of technology. For example, the effectiveness with which the firm that led Korea's
entry into the petrochemical industry acquired foreign technology was
greatly enhanced by the company's ability to draw on engineering capabilities previously accumulated by another firm in the refinery industry (Enos
and Park 1988). Similarly, the engineering and project management capabilities accumulated by the Korean Electric Power utility were subsequently
diffused to enhance the efficiency of firms entering the power engineering
and equipment industries (UNCTAD 1985). More generally, close interactions with customers and domestic users of related foreign products have
been an important stimulus to technological accumulation in the Korean
machine-building industry (Kim and Kim 1985). Behind these flows of
change-generating interactions lies substantial investment in training—not
only in educational and training institutions but within firms themselves.

Business Firms as Creators of Human Capital

The common perspective on human capital in economic growth gives primary emphasis to formal education and training in educational institutions;
firms themselves are seen as the users, not the creators, of the human capi-

---

11. For example, see Mytelka (1978) and Vianna (1985) on some of the smaller
Latin American countries; Farrell (1979) on Trinidad; Quazi (1983) on Bangladesh;
Scott-Kemmis and Bell (1988) on India; Ng and Siy (1986) on the non-NIC Southeast
Asian countries; and Mlawa (1983), Mytelka (1992), Ohiohenuan and Poloamina
(1992), and Wangwe (1992) on a range of African countries.

tal they require. This assumption understates the central importance of businesses in the process of technological learning. In fact, businesses have played an especially significant role in countries such as Japan and Germany, which have effectively exploited the dynamic gains of technological accumulation.[12]

However, educational institutions and firms are not substitutable alternatives: particular kinds of skills and knowledge can be acquired only in firms, through investment in learning by doing or training. But because firms are unable to capture the full returns to their investments (since trained workers can move to other firms), they are likely to underinvest in human capital, from both a social and possibly a private perspective. There are, however, significant differences in labor mobility among countries (notably, the United States and Germany or Japan) and hence in the incentive to provide on-the-job-training.

Although the formal education and training infrastructure has been extremely important in the East Asian NIEs, it has nevertheless accounted for only part of the total education and training effort that has contributed to technological accumulation in industry. Firms themselves have played an important role in this process. There is little information about the importance of their role during the rapid-growth phase of labor-intensive industries, but at that stage hands-on experience may be more important than more organized education and training within firms. In any case, the latter appear to have become increasingly important in Korea and Taiwan, China, as these economies diversified into knowledge-intensive industries.[13] Particularly significant has been the emphasis on training and the accumulation of experience in product and process engineering and project mana-gement (Enos and Park 1988; Amsden 1989). As in the industrialized countries, the East Asian firms are becoming increasingly important not just as employers but as creators of skilled human capital.

---

12. See, for example, Prais (1981) for detailed and careful comparisons of the effects of investments in education and training on levels of and rates of increase in productivity in British and German firms.

13. Fragmentary evidence suggests that even in the 1970s in-plant vocational training was quantitatively more significant than similar training in public organizations. One study, for instance, notes that between 1967–71 and 1977–81 the total annual number of vocational trainees in Korea increased fivefold. The number of technicians trained in public organizations tripled, while the number trained in plants increased sevenfold (Kim 1994).

More recently, the role of firms in training has become more visible: the largest electronics company in Taiwan, China, has set up its own university, the Tatung Institute of Technology. In Korea, the Samsung Advanced Institute of Science and Technology has been established. The Government of Singapore has been particularly skillful not only in mobilizing the financial resources of multinational corporations to establish education and training institutes but also in harnessing these corporations' own human resources to help implement a range of education and training programs in technology and management.

There is surprisingly little information from other developing countries about the role firms play in training. The available data suggest, however, that this kind of complementarity between the public infrastructure and intrafirm training efforts has been moderately significant. Only limited private initiatives have been undertaken in Latin America and India. Among firms in some southeast Asian countries, the prevalance of training programs seems to vary: in Indonesia, for instance, training has been significant in just one or two public sector enterprises; and despite some significant efforts in Thailand, intrafirm human resource development has been absent even in companies involved in information technologies (Hobday and Baba 1990). In Africa, private intrafirm training has been almost completely absent (Mlawa 1983; Mytelka 1992; Ohiorhenuan and Poloamina 1992; Wangwe 1992).

R&D Institutes

R&D needs to be intimately associated with production. Specialized institutes can and do make important contributions to technical change, but links between these institutes and the production activities of firms depend heavily on the strength of technological capabilities within firms themselves.

Most developing countries have established separate government-supported institutes to undertake R&D for industry. In Korea and Taiwan, China, the scale of government-funded R&D in the 1970s was somewhat greater than in most other developing economies, but it was otherwise similar in that it accounted for the major proportion of total industrial R&D—around 80 percent (firms undertook the remaining 20 percent). Its innovative activities made only a limited contribution to technical change in industry.

However, in two other key dimensions, the activities of the Korean and Taiwanese institutes reflect activities common to the development experiences of industrial economies. In these respects, Korea and Taiwan, China, differ from other developing economies.

First, especially since the 1970s, many of the R&D institutes in the East Asian NIEs have emphasized both innovation and the learning or technology absorption aspects of R&D (Cohen and Levinthal 1989). In emphasizing the role of learning rather than concentrating solely on the generation of technological innovations, these institutes undertook activities that differ from those typically undertaken in developing countries. This difference has been especially evident in those institutes set up to support the electronics industry. In Taiwan, China, the Electronic Research and Service Organization of the Industrial Technology Research Institute has acted less as a generator of state-of-the-art technology for industry than as a focal point for acquiring existing foreign technology, assimilating it, training people to use it, and then diffusing both the technology and the trained operators to firms. Naturally, it has also undertaken its own activities, which imitate R&D activities in industrial economies, in order to keep up with the latest technology. A similar emphasis on acquisition, absorption, training, and diffusion (as opposed to generating innovation) has characterized the activities of electronics-oriented R&D institutes established in Korea in the early and mid-1980s and more recently in Singapore.

Second, the apparent dominance of R&D in infrastructural institutions (compared with firms) in the East Asian NIEs in the 1970s is misleading in two ways. Surveys take little or no account of the engineering and related resources that play a major role in generating and managing technical change in industry. If these resources are included alongside R&D activities, the balance between infrastructural and intrafirm technological capabilities tips substantially towards the latter—the typical pattern shown by R&D data for the advanced industrial economies. In any case, even for R&D alone, the balance changed considerably during the 1980s. This change has been most striking in Korea, where, within a rapidly growing total, the 20/80 percent distribution of R&D activity between intrafirm and infrastructural institutions in the 1970s was reversed to 80/20 percent in the early 1990s.

Most other developing countries have continued to maintain a large proportion (80 percent or more) of their R&D capabilities in infrastructural institutions—even countries such as Brazil and Argentina, where substantial industrial expansion began in the early decades of this century. However, more important for many countries is the limited intrafirm accumulation of a much wider range of (non-R&D) engineering and other change-generating capabilities. Even if these are taken into account, however, the distribution of overall technological capabilities between infrastructural institutions and firms frequently remains heavily weighted toward the former, in comparison with the historical experience of the industrial countries or the contemporary experience of the East Asian NIEs.

Summing Up

This chapter has argued that competing in the world market requires not only that firms achieve international benchmarks of productive efficiency but that they make steady technological improvements over time. This process starts, rather then ends, with investment in new industrial plants and productive capacity. Thus, a nation's capability to foster and manage technological change is crucial to its firms' ability to survive and grow in the international marketplace.

While firms in developing countries tend to depend on imported technology in the initial stages or when they are entering new lines of production, there is considerable variation in the gains they derive from adopting and using this technology. In particular, the intensity with which firms accumulate their own capabilities to generate and manage technical change influences a range of important performance variables, including:

- the efficiency of investment in new production capacity—including the economic efficiency of input combinations chosen in the light of local prices, the level of process technical efficiency initially attained, and the initial competitiveness of product quality and specifications;
- the subsequent rate of productivity growth in existing lines of production; and
- the sustained competitiveness of product specifications and designs.

Over longer periods, the intensity with which the change-related resources are accumulated and applied in the process of technical change will influence other variables:

- the strength of both backward and forward linkages to suppliers and customers;
- the ease of structural change toward more technology-intensive lines of production; and
- the ability to enter new product markets successfully.

Technological capabilities are not acquired as an automatic byproduct of investment and production activities. They are accumulated through conscious and continuous investment by firms in specialized, change-generating activities, comprising product design, production engineering, quality control, training, and linkages to foreign sources of technology and change-generating expertise.

The volume and effectiveness of these largely firm-specific investments depend in turn on the technological competence of senior management, the skills of the labor force, the incentives for firms to invest in technological accumulation, and the effectiveness of specialized support institutions (especially R&D laboratories) in providing technological knowledge and training. These conclusions have clear implications for industrial policy that are taken up in the next chapter.

5

The Creation of Comparative Advantage: The Role of Industrial Policy

Sanjaya Lall

Previous chapters of this book have argued that productivity growth is an essential ingredient of sustained economic growth. Productivity growth at the aggregate level is composed of two things: a shift in the production structure toward activities with higher levels of productivity, and the growth of productivity in all existing activities. The evolution of competitiveness in industry reflects both these shifts. As economies mature industrially, manufactured exports tend to move from simpler to more complex activities, use more advanced products and processes within activities, and increase local content in physical inputs, services, and technologies.[1]

This chapter discusses shifts in developing countries' competitive advantage in manufacturing over time and the role that industrial policy can play in encouraging and accelerating such shifts. Industrial policy can be defined as *all forms of conscious and coordinated government interventions to promote industrial development*. In common parlance, industrial policy is associated with import protection and with subsidies that are given to selected "winners." These are not the only forms of such policy: any intervention in capital, labor, skill, and technology markets or institutional

---

1. This is demonstrated statistically for a broad range of countries by Chenery, Robinson, and Syrquin (1986).

change that is directed at promoting industrial development may be counted as industrial policy, whether or not it picks winners.

Two important distinctions must be borne in mind here. First, every use of such interventions does not necessarily count as a coherent industrial strategy. Many governments intervene in industry without having a real strategy that addresses the economic needs of industrial development. It is important to distinguish between such interventions and those that form a coherent strategy. Second, it is useful to draw a distinction between functional interventions, which are not directed at specific activities, and selective interventions, which are. The latter are normally (but often misleadingly) lumped together under the heading "picking winners," while the former are taken to be addressing the development of efficient markets in a manner that is neutral in terms of resource allocation among particular activities. Much debate revolves around this distinction and the relative efficiency of each type of intervention. Later sections take up some of the issues involved.

Two important points should be noted at the start. First, the phrase "picking winners" may not be an accurate depiction of selective interventions in general. Most policies to promote particular activities, or sets of activities, are not aimed at specific technologies, products, or firms, though there are notable exceptions (the Concorde aircraft supported by the British and French Governments, for instance, or some of the very detailed interventions of the Korean Government, which are mentioned later). Most interventions aim to create conditions that will allow winners to emerge from a range of possible technologies and firms rather than to choose who the exact winners will be in advance. Certainly, governments need to avoid "putting all their eggs in one basket" and should hedge against uncertainties related to technology, markets, and X-inefficiency by promoting a fairly broad range of industries. There are, in other words, many levels of selectivity (depending on the nature and efficiency of the relevant markets), and it is vital to distinguish among them. Much of the argument in this chapter relates to levels of selectivity (which have relatively low information requirements and risk levels) rather than to highly detailed levels of intervention (which involve championing particular technologies and enterprises).

Second, the traditional economic argument for industrial policy rests on the efficiency or failures of markets. If markets work perfectly, according to neoclassical models of atomistic competition, they achieve an optimal allocation of resources that cannot be improved by intervention without making someone else worse off. If, on the other hand, there are missing or badly functioning markets, there may be a case for intervention to create markets or improve their efficiency. This method of analyzing the case for intervention is useful, and this chapter relies heavily on it. However, the methodology has some intrinsic limitations. It is derived from static models of com-petition, in which market failures are measured with respect to departures from Pareto optimality. In such models, many kinds of external-ities, dynamic structural change, and interactions between economic actors with missing and fragmented markets are difficult to encompass.[2] The models cannot, as a consequence, deal properly with many strategic issues that governments in developing countries face.

This limitation of the normal economic definition of market failure is important. As described below in reference to the newly industrializing economies (NIEs), different governments had different strategic visions of how their industrial competitiveness could be developed. These strategic visions cannot, as explained later, be captured fully in terms of market fail-ures as defined by reference to static equilibria, and there is no unique set of policies that could lead them to a general optimal solution in the way the theoretical analysis of market failures suggests. For these reasons, it is diffi-cult to model industrial policy in conventional economic terms, even though theory can provide a satisfactory case for interventions when markets fail.

This is not to suggest that every set of interventions undertaken to pro-mote industrialization is justified—quite the contrary. Recent history is replete with cases of inefficient and distorting interventions. The main aim of this chapter is to differentiate between these kinds of interventions and well-designed policies that lead countries to develop their competitiveness to a greater extent than free markets would have allowed. It is useful for immediate analytical purposes to retain the traditional argument for indus-trial policy as a framework for analysis. The larger strategic considerations are brought in where necessary.

The literature on market failures suggests that not every failure neces-sarily calls for policy remedies (Stiglitz 1989). Since each intervention car-ries its own implicit costs and risks, the expected benefits must be weighed against the potential disadvantages. The decision to intervene will depend

---

2. Chenery, Robinson, and Syrquin (1986) provide a succinct analysis of many such deficiencies.

on the extent and cost of the market failures in question, the ability of markets to develop their own solutions to the failures, and the ability of governments to design and implement the necessary measures. Certain interventions may call for a great deal of information and monitoring, and implementing them efficiently may require considerable skill and impartiality on the part of officials. Many of these conditions are not met in developing countries; the result can be *government failures* that need to be considered in the same light as potential market failures. These points are addressed later in the chapter.

Theoretical Antecedents

In received models of comparative advantage theory, there is little or no role for the government in the evolution and realization of comparative advantage. As explained in chapter 2, traditional trade theory (the Heckscher-Ohlin theorem) assumes that all markets are fully efficient. In this simplified model, competition is perfect, with no scale economies; technologies and levels of efficiency in the use of technologies are identical across firms and countries; information is perfect (with no risk and uncertainty); and there are basically two factors of production (capital and undifferentiated labor), homogeneous products, and small firms confined to local markets. Prices reflect relative factor requirements and endowments, and relative endowments change only with the accumulation of capital and the growth of the labor force.

In this neoclassical world, comparative advantage can reflect only differences in national endowments of the two primary factors, *capital* and *labor*. There is no role in competitiveness for such factors as differences in technology or efficiency (since by assumption all firms have access to identical technologies, and these technologies are absorbed instantaneously and without significant costs); skill gaps (since labor is undifferentiated and presumably equally productive); scale economies; or marketing and product differentiation (tastes are identical and products homogeneous). Since all firms are assumed to be small and to have access to the same knowledge, skills, and other inputs, firms cannot create competitive advantages through individual efforts; such advantages can evolve only at a national level. There is, then, no role for the government in influencing comparative advantage (apart from ensuring that the macroeconomic conditions for savings and investment are in place), and free trade—by assumption—ensures the optimal allocation of resources, and—by implication—long-term growth.[3]

One of the earliest amendments to the Hecksher-Ohlin theorem was to admit human capital as a separate factor of production. This addition meant that, other assumptions of perfect competition remaining constant, comparative advantage would reflect the national accumulation of skills (by education and training) as well as of physical capital and raw labor. Given the assumption of efficiently functioning markets, however, there would still be no role for the government. Individuals would decide on the optimal extent and form of education; maintaining appropriate macroeconomic conditions and free product and factor markets would be the only requirements of policy. The neoclassical conclusion on market efficiency again ruled out any role for industrial policy.[4]

There have been several other amendments to traditional trade theory. Within the neoclassical tradition, "new" trade theorists argue that scale and learning economies can play a crucial role in determining competitive advantage (Krugman 1986). Because of market failures, there may be a role for strategic interventions by governments anxious to secure for their firms the advantages of being "first movers." This would enable them to preempt potential competitors by securing scale economies or traveling first down the learning curve. This model is largely of relevance to the industrial rather than the developing countries, since it is generally applied to industries

---

3. However, the theoretical case for free trade does not establish the links between optimal resource allocation in a static sense and higher rates of growth over time. As new growth theories point out, under traditional neoclassical assumptions, with the usual assumptions of diminishing returns to investment, optimizing static resource allocation does not by itself lead to higher rates of growth over a sustained period. A shifting upward of the growth rate can come only from factors (such as education or technology) that offer increasing returns to scale. Thus, Lucas (1988) criticizes the earlier explanations of the success of Asian NIEs as the result solely of liberal trade policies.

4. Some recent analyses of development do admit that certain factor markets, especially those affecting human capital and technology, may not work efficiently because of externalities, public goods, uncertainty, and lumpiness. These analyses provide a case for remedial interventions, but it is argued that such interventions should be functional rather than selective and not influence the allocation of investment resources as driven by free markets (see, in particular, World Bank 1991, 1993a). The distinction between functional and selective interventions is, however, sometimes misleading, as argued below.

with a few large, dominant firms operating in global markets. Moreover, it tends to be assumed that the learning curve is largely predictable and confined to "frontier technologies" (that is, new technologies that are in the process of being mastered). If this theory is applied with the same assumptions to developing countries, which are not creating frontier technologies, it would follow that these economies should still optimize their trading position by engaging in free trade and allowing the free inflow of technologies. There would still be no market failures in any of the important markets that determine comparative advantage.

However, the basic insight of new trade theories—that the existence of scale and learning economies creates a case for intervention to improve a country's competitive position—clearly applies to developing countries. If mature technologies do have unpredictable learning costs that vary across activities, traditional neoclassical theory suggests that selective intervention will improve competitiveness. New trade theorists tend to shy away from drawing this conclusion, not because the economic reasoning is faulty but because of the fear of government failure. This fear is certainly valid, but whether it completely negates the case for industrial policy is not clear.

"Neotechnology" theories of comparative advantage have consciously rejected neoclassical assumptions of efficient markets with identical production functions, equal access to knowledge, identical tastes, small firms and homogeneous products. These theories assign a central role to differences based on technology and taste. Competitive advantage is taken to be created by individual firms operating in imperfect markets rather than by national factor endowments (though national conditions do determine where technologies are created and exploited). The technological differences that drive competitive advantages in these models are based on innovations—that is, major breakthroughs in products and processes—and give rise to international investment as well as to trade. Much of the resulting trade is within rather than among industries with broadly similar factor requirements.

These theories have remained largely analytical rather than prescriptive. Surprisingly, they have not followed up the implications of admitting that widespread market imperfections exist by exploring the possible role of governments in overcoming such market failures to promote competitive advantage. Some recent versions of this approach, in particular those favored by the "business school" analysts of national competitiveness, argue for interventions to strengthen the national base of skills and technology in otherwise freely competitive markets. However, these variants tend to lack a full analysis of market failures and so do not consider the full implications of their analysis for industrial policy as a whole.[5] The concern of neotechnology trade theories with major innovations means that developing countries are treated as largely passive recipients of mature technologies from industrial countries. The best policy for nonindustrial economies remains to be open to free trade and to attract technology through direct investment. Industrial policy can be used only to create an enabling environment for the entry of multinational companies.

Industrial policy receives little or no explicit support from much of trade theory, for several reasons. First, the simplifying assumptions of neoclassical economics rule out the need for interventions (though the theory can readily incorporate them once market failures are admitted). Second, the focus of neotechnology theories on innovations, and the continued assumption that developing countries can both afford and passively absorb new technologies, mean that some critical areas of potential market failure are ignored. Finally, trade theories do not concern themselves with the functioning of factor markets within countries. These markets are taken as given parameters within which trade patterns are determined, and possible market failures here do not appear as legitimate areas for policy concern. Rather, industrial policy is concerned with these markets as they affect industrial development.

Drawing upon the analyses of chapters 2 and 4, the next section provides an account of the complex process by which developing countries acquire industrial competitiveness in the real world. The section describes the market failures this process may be prone to and explains why there may be a need for concerted government action.

How Industries in Developing Countries Become Competitive

The common assumption, which is that technology is selected and absorbed with relative ease and at little cost by developing country firms operating in efficient factor and product markets, is in many instances a

---

5. The business school analysts are represented by theorists such as Porter (1990), who argue that national comparative advantage is highly firm specific and draws on skills, technology, and input markets. Thus, there is a role for governments in strengthening the base of skills, technologies, and institutions that firms and their suppliers can use to develop their own strengths. However, the analysis is not couched in terms of market failures in these markets, and possible failures in product markets are ignored. This omission allows Porter to argue, for instance, that countries like Japan and the Republic of Korea developed national competitiveness by exposing their economies to free-market competition.

misleading simplification. In general, most industrial technologies operate at low levels of technical proficiency in developing countries and thus
tend to be a much larger cause of low productivity than allocative inefficiency (that is, the inefficiency arising from choosing the wrong techniques or investments because of distorted prices). As noted in the
previous chapter, the process of selecting, absorbing, and mastering technology is neither passive nor without risk. *Differences in the efficiency with*
which mastery over new technologies is achieved are thus themselves a major
source of differences in competitiveness between countries. This fact is
neglected in received theory and accounts in part for the general dismissal
of industrial policy as a viable tool. This section shows how the nature of
technological mastery itself can create a case for interventions to support
competitiveness in industry.

The process of mastering a new technology requires the acquisition and
development of new knowledge, skills, organizational forms, and linkages
among enterprises—that is, the building up of *technological capabilities.* As
stressed in the previous chapter, this process is necessarily firm specific, and
there is no predictable learning curve down which all firms must travel.
The process of developing technological competence is not instantaneous,
automatic, or without its costs, even if the technology is well diffused elsewhere. It is risky and unpredictable, and often itself has to be learned: in
developing countries new firms may not even know what their deficiencies
are or how to go about remedying them (Stiglitz 1987).

Developing technological competency is a process that varies according
to the complexity of the technology itself. In simple industries with labor-
intensive technologies, say garment manufacture, setting up production
facilities and learning basic operations may be all that is needed to establish
competitiveness (as long as wages are relatively low). In more complex
industries, such as machinery manufacture, reaching even static "best practice" levels as established in advanced countries involves a longer and more
demanding process, sometimes requiring years of research and hands-on
experience with engineering techniques and production management.[6] The
demands of maintaining dynamic competitiveness within the industry in
the face of constantly changing technologies and market conditions are correspondingly greater. In the end, because of greater or lesser investment in

---

6. For an analysis of the long learning process in the Korean engineering industry, see Jacobsson (1993).

the creation of technological capabilities, rates of technological development vary among firms using the same technology, resulting in very different levels of efficiency.

The important point here is that developing comparative advantage is not just about gaining mastery (in a static sense) of foreign technologies. As economies progress and mature, a more complex process of continual upgrading and diversification is involved. Such deepening of industrial activities can take one or more of the following four forms:

- *Technological upgrading of products and processes within industries,* so that the country engages in greater value-added activities than it starts with. New entrants to industry generally undertake the simplest assembly or processing activities, which have relatively low value added and use the simplest of technologies. As economies develop, it becomes necessary to undertake more complex activities within those industries— activities that yield higher wages and profits and are less exposed to competition from low-wage newcomers.

- *Entry into progressively more complex new activities.* These activities broaden the industrial base, create new areas of comparative advantage in high- value-added activities, and allow skills and capital to be exploited in more sophisticated capital-intensive industries.[7]

- *Increasing local inputs and linkages,* so that the process of assembling imported components or adding minimum value to local resources, with which industrialization normally starts, is broadened and made to contribute to the setting up of domestic suppliers, subcontractors, and specialized service firms. Increasing local involvement allows for the diffusion of industrial technology and skills, helps to keep a larger proportion of the value added by industry within the country, creates new sources of competitiveness, and captures many of the externalities that industrial development entails. In particular, setting up a supporting capital goods industry contributes greatly to the creation and diffusion of new technical knowledge, acting as a "hub" of technical progress (Rosenberg 1986).

---

7. This is the usual pattern of structural transformation that occurs with economic development, as documented by Chenery, Robinson, and Syrquin (1986).

- *Mastering complex technological capabilities within the technologies in use locally.* The capabilities acquired initially relate to simple assembly or processing, and there is a high level of reliance on foreign sources for basic technology as well as for expertise in most complex engineering and adaptation tasks. As industrialization progresses, local capabilities should deepen to include more difficult manufacturing tasks, the adaptation and improvement of technologies, and finally the undertaking of process and product design and development. Such deepening can lead to the importing and absorbing of more complex technologies, reductions in the cost of utilizing technologies, better diffusion of technologies locally, a more diversified base of competitive advantages, and the capturing of some of the externalities that result from technical progress.

Each process involves its own learning costs, which tend to differ by activity acccording to the sophistication of the technology, the extent of local supply linkages, and the level of technological mastery desired. Progressive deepening is to some extent a natural part of industrial development, but it is not inevitable. Its pattern and incidence differ greatly, depending on the nature of factor and product markets facing national firms, the initial levels of skills and capabilities, and the level of the institutional support firms receive. However, the deepening process depends to a large extent on the ability of the government concerned to identify and overcome any market failures that might hinder the development of technological capabilities.

Because there is no set path of successful industrial development, countries can further their industrialization process and deepen their technological capabilities in different ways, depending on the weight given to each of the four components noted above in their development strategies. In other words, countries with different industrial structures, local linkages, levels of technological sophistication, and degrees of reliance on foreign technological inputs can aim for different levels of industrialization.

Market Failures and Policy Needs

This section seeks to synthesize the arguments presented by the capability approach to industrialization and the development of export competitiveness. It draws on the evidence of export success in the developing world to provide insights into the kinds of market failures that enterprises may confront and the policy needs that may arise when the process of export development is accelerated.

The Case for Intervention

As noted at the start of the chapter, the case for intervention in theory rests on the existence of certain kinds of market failures, although in practice the effect intervention may have on entrepreneurship must also be considered. In developing countries, industrial promotion has been commonly viewed as synonymous with the promotion of domestic enterprise, but the outcomes have varied enormously. In some cases (notably East Asia), local enterprises have expanded and matured, while in others interventions have simply encouraged rent-seeking behavior (Latin America, Africa, and elsewhere). This issue is taken up later in the discussion of government failure. Market failures are considered under two broad headings: product markets (dealing with competition for final products) and factor markets (dealing with inputs of various kinds).

PRODUCT MARKETS. There is general agreement that free competition in product markets may not lead to the optimal allocation of resources if there are differing and unpredictable learning costs among activities, economies of scale or scope, and externalities. While scale economies and externalities are well recognized in the literature as sources of resource misallocation, learning processes have not featured prominently in the discussion of industrial strategy. Yet the literature on technological capabilities suggests that learning processes are likely to be more important and pervasive sources of market failure in the context of industrial development than scale economies or externalities. This fact is particularly important for developing countries, which are latecomers to industrialization and thus face established competitors that have already undergone the learning process. In essence, in the presence of high and unpredictable learning costs, latecomers to industrialization also face more costs and greater risks than industrial economies. This fact does not diminish the benefits latecomers can derive from the experience of countries that have led the way in industrial development.

The fact that the learning process requires special attention has long been recognized. John Stuart Mill (1848), after hundreds of pages of arguments on the benefits of free trade, makes the following comment on the case of industrial latecomers:

The only case in which, on mere principles of political economy, protecting duties can be defensible, is when they are imposed temporarily (especially in a young and rising nation) in the hopes of naturalising a foreign industry, in itself perfectly suitable to the circumstances of the country. The superiority of one country over another in a branch of production often arises only from having begun it sooner. There may be no inherent advantage on one part, or disadvantage in another, but only a present superiority of acquired skill and experience . . . . But it cannot be expected that individuals should, at their own risk, or rather to their certain loss, introduce a new manufacture, and bear the burden of carrying on until the producers have been educated to the level of those with whom the processes are traditional. A protective duty, continued for a reasonable time, might sometimes be the least inconvenient mode in which the nation can tax itself for the support of such an experiment. But it is essential that the protection should be confined to cases in which there is good ground for assurance that the industry which it fosters will after a time be able to dispense with it; nor should the domestic producers ever be allowed to expect that it will be continued to them beyond the time necessary for a fair trial of what they are capable of accomplishing.

This perceptive comment on the determinants of competitive advantage presents lucidly and concisely the case argued here. As with much of classical economics, it was ignored by the later literature; its insight was lost amid the simplifying assumptions of the neoclassical analysis. In the context of market failure, however, it can be comfortably incorporated into modern theory. Its conclusion is simple: *a failure to assist firms in overcoming the costs of learning more complex technologies can hinder the development of competitiveness in new technologies.* This failure can keep a country's enterprises from climbing the technological ladder to higher-value-added activities and from increasing the degree of local integration.

Three important points need to be noted here.

- First, since the learning process is very technology and scale specific, it differs greatly by activity and the precise nature of the technology being used. Interventions aimed at helping firms to bear learning costs therefore cannot be uniform. The argument that low uniform levels of overall protection can help to meet infant learning needs has little theoretical validity. Protection must be selective if learning needs are to be addressed—precisely it was in economies like Japan, the Republic of Korea, and Taiwan, China.
- Second, the case for supporting developing country enterprises in acquiring complex technologies differs from that for sponsoring new technologies in industrial countries. Industrial economies may also

suffer from market failures, but these failures are not caused by excessively high learning costs. The element of risk involved in intervening in industrial countries is thus likely to be greater, because major new innovations are involved. It is inherently more difficult to pick advanced technologies successfully than it is to target new activities in developing countries for which technological parameters already exist (information and experience), precisely because others have taken the same path. Carefully designed interventions are therefore more likely to succeed in developing than in industrial countries. The case against picking winners (based on some notorious examples of failure in industrial countries) is not particularly relevant or compelling. It also needs to be recognized that poor investment choices are possible even if no market interventions are involved; there are many examples of poor investment decisions by private investors. As the evidence on East Asia shows, it is as much a question of creating as of picking winners.

- Third, the argument for infant industry promotion applies mainly (but not exclusively) to local enterprises in developing countries. Multinational enterprises face fewer market failures in acquiring complex technologies in developing countries. They have information on and experience in managing the learning process in new locations, a large internal reservoir of skills and capital, and the ability to bear risk. Developing countries cannot, however, depend wholly on multinational corporations to drive industrial development. Local enterprises have an important role to play in low-end technological activities and as suppliers and subcontractors. Even in more advanced activities, there may be arguments for building up the capabilities of locally owned enterprises in order to develop an indigenous base of design and innovation as the industrial structure grows more complex.

Another form of market failure may arise from investment coordination problems in the context of what is termed "technological externalities": in vertically interlinked activities, it is difficult for individual firms to plan their investments rationally so as to anticipate each other's learning processes. In such cases, intervention may be justified in order to coordinate investment decisions to achieve a more desirable allocation of resources. The case for investment coordination in situations where individual firms do not have the necessary information is well recognized in the literature (Pack and Westphal 1986; World Bank 1993a). Only an external agent like the government can anticipate the externalities involved and so ensure that investments are allocated in a way that reflects social interests.

It is important to note that externalities can vary significantly across industries. Some sets of activities may have more beneficial externalities than others, either because they are more "linkage intensive" (that is, they draw on a larger number and variety of local suppliers of goods and services) and so lead to greater diffusion of demand or technologies, or because they create the kinds of technological capabilities that are more conducive to dynamic growth. To some extent, then, there may be a valid case for promoting certain sets of activities over others.[8] Governments in both industrial and developing countries use this rationale to support strategic industries, generally in high-technology areas, that are thought to build greater national competitiveness. Such considerations certainly guided policymakers in East Asia (and continue to do so today). These countries selected entire sets of dynamic activities for promotion, in the belief not just that these activities would provide the most promising areas for future export growth, but also that they would create considerable beneficial spillovers to other activities. Information technology, advanced materials, automation, and specialty chemicals were among these areas.

FACTOR MARKETS. There may be failures in many of the factor markets in which developing country firms operate, including those for labor, credit, and physical infrastructure. Since most of these failures are well known, they do not merit separate consideration here. Instead, the focus here is on two specific and less widely discussed types of failures: those in *skills* and *technology*.

Skills relevant to industrial activity can be imparted both by the formal education and training system and by in-firm training and experience. The need for skills varies by activity and technology. Less advanced or more specialized firms need a smaller range of skills than large-scale and technologically complex industries. But even operating the simplest technology at world levels of efficiency requires a range of worker, supervisory, maintenance, quality control, and adaptive skills. At the lowest end of the technological spectrum, simple literacy and some vocational training, complemented by a few high-level technical skills, may be sufficient to ensure ade-

---

8. This case is argued by some "new" growth theorists, who trace differences in sustained growth rates partly to the ability of some countries to specialize in technology-intensive sets of activities that promote industrial development and growth (Young 1991).

quate technological capabilities, but even garment assembly for export requires good supervisory, layout, and maintenance skills. With sophisticated technologies, the requirements are more diverse and the range of necessary special skills wider. It is important to note that at higher levels of technology, the qualifications and experience required are very specific and therefore difficult to substitute for one another. Thus, the pattern of skill creation has to match, at least in broad terms, the evolving pattern of industrial activity.

Primary and secondary schools provide the necessary foundation for basic capabilities in all activities, regardless of technological complexity. All countries accept the need for the state to support the provision of basic and secondary schooling and to regulate curriculum and quality. These needs are relatively general, and such interventions are essentially functional. However, more advanced and specialized training, especially in technical areas, becomes increasingly important as the industrial structure develops, and most governments also accept a large role in the provision and regulation of such education. Market failures in providing such training can arise from a number of factors, including imperfect information and foresight, risk aversion, lumpiness of facilities, and the need to assure relevance and quality. When the government seeks to promote new industries, however, there is also the risk that the composition of skills created by the training system may not correctly anticipate the needs of the new technologies. The government may then have to guide the system in line with planned needs. Since skill creation must be closely geared to the needs of industrial policy, high-level interventions have to be selective: certain kinds of engineering, scientific, and technical skills must be fostered to support the specific needs of the industries being set up.

Apart from the formal education system, an important part of skill creation takes place during employment, through training within (or financed by) enterprises. While such training is a growing trend in industrial countries, many enterprises in developing countries invest relatively little in upgrading the skills of their employees, for three reasons.

First, managers may not be fully aware of the skills required to use new technologies. Managers may also be rooted in traditional ways of manufacturing and training (such as the apprenticeship system in Africa) that are unsuited to modern technologies or to the upgrading of existing technologies (Lall and others 1994). The level of education of these managers may, in certain cases, make them averse to training their employees further. Such problems are a form of information failure.

Second, firms may not be able to remedy skill deficiencies because of the lack of training institutions or resources such as appropriate in-house trainers. Overseas training may be out of the question, and local institutions, official or private, may not be able to offer the appropriate level and quality of training.

Finally, failures may be caused by the externalities inherent in training: employers may be unsure of recouping the full benefits of their investments, a classic market failure in the economics literature.

INFORMATION AND TECHNOLOGY. Failures in information and technology markets may be further subdivided according to whether they stem from *technology inflows from abroad* or from *domestic technological activity.*

It is evident that developing countries must use large and sustained *inflows of technology* to sustain industrial development. International technology markets are widely known to suffer from various imperfections. They are often oligopolistic, with buyers facing large information gaps on sources of supply, prices, and product quality. There is often considerable scope for bargaining over the terms and conditions of technology transfers (as demonstrated by the early Japanese experience of successfully bargaining for low royalties), but developing country enterprises tend to be at a competitive disadvantage in the early stages of industrialization in these imperfect markets.

There is, moreover, a further complication in trade in technological "products": different modes of importing the same technology may have different impacts on the long-term development of competitive advantages. Trade in these products differs from trade in physical products in that, in technological exchanges, the form of the transaction itself assumes policy significance. In particular, a distinction must be drawn between two broad modes of technology transfer. First are *internalized* modes, such as the traditional forms of direct foreign investment in which the supplier of the technology retains control (and a controlling equity stake); provides the technical hardware and software; manages the start-up, operations, and marketing; and continues to supply technology and skills from the parent company. With *externalized* modes, the second type, technology is purchased at arm's length in the form of equipment, licenses, or other contracts, and the local firm retains control.[9] While both are effective forms of

---

9. There are a variety of intermediate forms of technology transfer that fall between these two extremes, including joint ventures, licensing cum management contracts, and subcontracting.

technology transfer, each has its strengths and weaknesses as far as local technological development is concerned.

Direct foreign investment offers many advantages to developing countries. It is a rapid and effective way of gaining access to new operational technologies. It provides access to advanced technologies local firms cannot purchase outright and keeps subsidiaries abreast of the shifting technological frontier. In addition, it can be a powerful means of expanding certain forms of manufactured exports in situations where brand names, scale economies, international integration of production, and fast-moving technologies are important. More significantly for the creation of the necessary technological capabilities, however, a multinational investor can provide several inputs into the learning process that a typical local firm cannot. Multinationals have large internal capital markets that allow them to finance prolonged learning processes and scale-intensive facilities, as well as reserves of skills and technical know-how local firms lack. There are therefore strong reasons—which probably grow stronger with time, as the pace and costs of technical change increase—for utilizing direct investment as the avenue for importing technology.

However, while foreign investment may be an effective way to introduce new technologies, it may not offer the same long-term benefits for learning as the externalized mode of acquiring technologies, which leaves local firms in control. In the literature, a distinction is drawn between technological know-how (the knowledge and skills needed to efficiently operate a technology) and what is called "know-why" (an understanding of the technical principles underlying the technology, leading to full absorption of the technology and the ability to modify and improve upon it). While the former is essential at all stages of industrial development, the latter becomes increasingly important as the industrial structure grows more complex.

A growing base of know-why is needed, not necessarily to develop major new technologies but to reduce the costs of technology imports, to absorb and to adapt complex new technologies, and to develop new products and processes on the basis of these technologies.[10] Also important are the spillover effects of having a growing local design and innovation base and personnel mobility, both of which can benefit related firms, services, and industries as well as the science and technology infrastructure. For industrial countries, the importance of a strong research base that helps maitain competitive advantage in international markets is generally

---

10. On the significance of R&D to imitation and information collection as well as to innovation, see Cohen and Levinthal (1989).

accepted. It is perhaps less common in the literature to find the argument that a growing research base can also be a vital input into the development of the comparative advantages of newly industrializing countries. Yet there are strong reasons to believe that this is the case, and practically all developing countries with significant industrial sectors take the deepening of their technological capabilities as an objective of policy.

Internalized modes of technology transfer are at a disadvantage as far as the development of know-why is concerned. Though direct investment may be a very efficient means of transferring operational know-how, multi-nationals are naturally reluctant to invest in the process of developing more sophisticated technological capabilities in developing countries (except to the extent needed for adaptation to local materials and tastes). Local firms, especially in export-oriented economies with appropriate policies, are generally found to invest significantly more in research and development (R&D) than comparable foreign affiliates. Multinationals tend, generally for sound commercial reasons, to concentrate their innovative activities in a few centers in industrial countries, which offer advanced science infrastructures, a large and diverse base of specialized skills, a network of established and familiar suppliers, and the advantage of being near major markets and the main centers of corporate decisionmaking. It is more economical for multinationals to centralize their R&D activities in these countries than to invest in the development of similar research capabilities in developing countries. While many corporations are increasing their investments in overseas research and development, most of these activities are still located in the industrial world. The R&D that takes place in developing countries is limited, generally geared to specific adaptive tasks, and concentrated in the few countries with relatively advanced industrial sectors.

The lack of such investment may act as an incentive to domestic technological effort, but appropriate incentives must be in place. Arrow (1962) noted long ago that a free market may fail to ensure optimal innovative activity in industrial countries because of the imperfect nature of returns to R&D. This observation applies also to investment in technological capabilities in developing countries. As noted in the previous chapter, the process of mastering and adapting new technologies is not entirely different from that of investing in costly and uncertain innovation for the individual firm (though the degree of risk may well differ). In developing countries, however, market failures may arise from several specific factors. Many firms in the early stages of industrialization may not understand the deliberate technological effort that is required to achieve efficient operation. They may lack information and technical support services. As these firms undertake more complex activities, they generally have to involve themselves in formal R&D but may be too small to pay for it (or even to raise the necessary funds from the banking system) or to bear the risk of such an investment. Firm size is not always the determining factor, but in some cases promoting larger firms may be one way to counteract the market failure (though this solution may have repercussions for domestic competition policy). R&D also requires effective supporting facilities from a science and technology infrastructure that may not exist in developing countries. Finally, the returns to investments in technology may be greatly reduced by externalities such as the danger of losing the knowledge to other firms.

What Kind of Interventions Are Needed?[11]

The *product market* failures noted here relate to infant industry considerations and the need to coordinate investments across vertically linked activities. In essence, there are two complementary methods of overcoming such market failures in resource allocation: intervening in capital markets, or providing strong signals to investors to enter difficult or strategic activities (and related areas) by providing subsidies or protection against competing imports. Historically, the most important measure, which has been used by practically every industrial country in the early stages of industrialization, has been import protection (Vernon 1989). Direct interventions in allocating investment via the financial system have also been common. In particular, subsidized and directed credit has been extensively employed in East Asia to channel investments into selected industries.

It is evident that as long as there are significant differences in technological learning, scale, linkages, and externalities among activities, interventions to improve resource allocation have to be selective. In simple activities, for instance, the need for protection may be minimal, because the learning period is relatively brief and predictable and information is easy to acquire. In fact, in simple labor-intensive activities such as garment assembly, the wage cost advantage of developing countries may offset the low learning costs completely, making protection unnecessary.[12] In complex

---

11. This subject is explored at greater length in Lall (1993).

12. This offset accounts for the success of export-oriented garment manufacture in many developing countries in recent years, though it must be remembered that in most such activities the special technological capabilities required for international competitiveness have been provided by foreign investors or buyers. Otherwise, the learning costs would be too high for local producers.

activities, usually with difficult technologies, large minimum scales of production, advanced information and skill needs, wide linkages, and intricate organizational structures, the learning process is generally far more costly and prolonged. It can spread over years, even decades.[13] Unless a strong natural resource advantage exists, these activities are difficult for individual investors to undertake in the face of full import competition.

Protection and subsidization are, however, dangerous policy tools. They can create rather than reduce distortions and may eliminate incentives to invest in the development of technological capabilities. If, for instance, protection is granted indiscriminately, without regard to the costs of the learning process and the time involved, and is not accompanied by measures to induce firms to invest in technological capability development, the result can be inefficiency, technological stagnation, and waste. Trade interventions must specifically address the source of market failures and should not be an attempt to compensate for high costs or inefficiency arising from deficiencies in other markets—say, for local production factors (Bhagwati 1988). Otherwise, protection may not improve the allocation of resources to more demanding activities that may reach world levels of competitiveness at the end of the learning period. This is the lesson that can generally be drawn from experiences with import substitution in developing countries that did not use protection selectively to overcome specific market failures but spread it over all activities.[14] This is not the kind of infant industry protection that theory demands. The experience of typical import-substituting regimes should not, therefore, be taken as a test of the general case for protection. The real test lies in the experience of countries that have been selective in their use of the protectionist tool and have managed to combine protection with competitive incentives to invest in the development of technological capabilities.

In export-oriented regimes that have used protection judiciously, the results have been strikingly different from the effects of protection under import substitution. As described below, the incentive to compete in export markets in turn creates a strong incentive to invest in the acquisition and constant upgrading of technological capabilities. In addition, the pressure to promote exports itself disciplines governments and forces them to con-

---

13. See Jacobsson (1993) on the heavy engineering industry in Korea.

14. In addition, as noted later, most export-oriented regimes (in contrast to most import-substituting regimens) also intervened in factor markets to ensure that the needs of their protected industries for certain skills and information were properly met.

fine protection to a relatively few selected activities.[15] The experience of the most successful industrializing economies of East Asia (Japan, Korea, and Taiwan, China) suggests that protection was a necessary condition for diversifying into heavy and technologically advanced industries and developing a strong indigenous technological base. Yet the interweaving of protection and strong export orientation sets these regimes apart from typical inward-oriented regimes.

In terms of *factor markets*, it is worth reiterating an obvious but often neglected point: factor market interventions have to be closely integrated with product market interventions, since one without the other is often likely to be less effective than it would be otherwise (or even completely ineffective). Thus, offering protection or subsidies without attempting to provide the skills and know-how that firms need in order to compete is likely to be counterproductive. Both sets of interventions have to be guided by a broader strategy or vision, since narrow considerations of specific market failure are unlikely to yield a full set of policy guidelines when the failures are difficult to define and the remedies span a range of options.

As far as *the development of skills* is concerned, most development analysts now accept the risk of market failures in skill creation and recommend interventions to promote the formation of human capital. These interventions can take a variety of forms: increasing investments in education in general (not only by the government but also by private individuals and families); improving both access to education for all segments of society and the dissemination of information on the need for education; raising the quality of education and improving retention rates; increasing the relevance of education and training to economic, and particularly industrial, needs; encouraging the establishment of high-quality private training institutions to assess and meet the needs of industry for certain skills; coordinating the skills needs of industry with the design of educational curricula; increasing the emphasis on technical subjects at higher levels of education; increasing industry involvement (including by multinational enterprises) in training at the vocational level; and encouraging in-firm training through tax incentives or training grants.

There is now a large body of literature on the best way for governments to intervene in education and training in both industrial and developing

---

15. See Amsden (1989), Lall (1992b), Wade (1990), and Westphal (1990). The discipline over the government exercised by export orientation is analyzed for Brazil and Korea by Moreira (1995), for Korea by Chang (1994), and for the East Asian NIEs by the World Bank (1993a).

countries. This literature for the most part describes policies to promote human resource development as purely functional and therefore market conforming—a statement that is often unjustified. Many forms of educational investments are nonselective, particularly for primary and secondary schooling and nontechnical higher education, and provide a general base of skills for all activities. However, more specialized forms of tertiary education and vocational training tend to be highly industry specific, and policies to address these needs have to be selective. The need for selectivity increases as policies to promote specific industries are adopted, since it becomes more difficult for the educational system to anticipate the skill needs of future industries.

The need for both functional and selective interventions in education and training is borne out by the experience of the East Asian NIEs. Training in skills essential to new industrial activities was an integral part of industrial policy in East Asia. Industry was closely involved in the design of curricula and the actual training of industrial workers, engineers, and managers. Tax and other incentives were provided to encourage in-firm training. Data on the growth of enrollments in various educational and training programs bear out the efficacy of these policies, though certainly growth itself encouraged private individuals to invest in education because of the increased returns.

In terms of *technology and information,* the first policy need is to strengthen the capabilities of local enterprises to select, bargain for, and buy technologies in international technology markets. Meeting this need requires setting up data bases and information centers that industrial enterprises can easily access. Detailed intervention in the negotiation of technology contracts is not generally required. In fact, experience suggests that highly interventionist strategies on technology imports can choke off the inflow of valuable new technologies, while information support and advice of the sort given in Japan and Korea can be very useful to technology importers (OED 1993).

The second policy need involves influencing the mode of the import. It has been suggested that a policy of passive reliance on foreign investment to meet technological needs can lead to underinvestment both in R&D and in the deepening of technological capabilities. (The contrast in technological effort between Korea and Mexico, which will be discussed in the next chapter, is a striking illustration of this argument.) Policy must be used to increase local R&D capabilities without shutting off the flow of new technologies. One way of achieving this goal is to increase local ownership of industry. However, the mere fact of local ownership is not enough to ensure that technological capabilities will be deepened; local enterprises may choose to remain dependent on foreign sources of technology rather than risk developing their own R&D capabilities. In this case, there is even less technological development than there is with foreign investment, because local firms may not have access to the latest technologies at arm's length and may not be able to export as much as foreign affiliates. What is needed is a combination of policies that both regulate technology imports and encourage and facilitate local R&D. Experience shows that such a combination is both possible and beneficial (OED 1993).

Japan, Korea, and Taiwan, China, the economies that have developed the most innovative capabilities in recent years, have all intervened in both foreign investment and indigenous technological activity to achieve just this policy combination (World Bank 1993a). An economy with technological ambitions may find it necessary at certain stages of industrial development to restrict technology imports selectively in internalized forms and to promote investment in indigenous design and development. This is not an argument for indiscriminate restrictions on foreign investment. While supporting domestic enterprises seems to be a vital component of capability building, a great deal can also be done with foreign investment to increase local technological activity. The Singapore experience shows how an astute policy of selective interventions in foreign investment can induce multinational corporations to increase local design and development activities.

Again, this is not an argument for promoting inefficient local enterprises in an import-substituting framework. There are many countries (India is a prime example) that have sought to promote indigenous enterprises and technological development in a highly interventionist, inward-oriented setting. But these interventions have not been geared to remedying weaknesses in the learning process and thus have resulted in widespread inefficiencies and low levels of technological competence and dynamism. All interventions must be made in the context of incentives that are conducive to investments in local technological development, something that is best done by forcing firms to compete in export markets. Export orientation also offers an important benefit in terms of disciplining the government in its use of interventions—as long as the officials concerned are forced to meet performance targets of their own.

How then can local technological efforts be increased? Of the various forms that technology policy may take, perhaps the most important is the *provision of technical information and support.* Providing such support does not always call for intervention. Many forms of technical information are more or less readily available to firms from journals; contacts with capital goods suppliers and buyers of export products; visits to fairs, plants and conferences; and interactions with subcontractors and other suppliers. More complex or closely held information is available commercially from consultants, more advanced firms (on license), or as part of a package of direct investment.

However, there are many other forms of information and support that markets do not provide in a developing country. There are several technological functions with "public goods" features whose rewards are difficult to appropriate privately. These include encouraging technological activity in general (that is, helping firms to overcome risk aversion and the "learning to learn" barrier); developing special research skills; setting industrial standards and promoting quality awareness; providing metrology (industrial measurement and calibration) services; undertaking contract research, testing, and information searches for firms that lack the facilities or skills; providing other extension services for small enterprises; and undertaking and coordinating basic (precommercial) research activities.[16] Some of these services must be provided as part of the public infrastructure.[17] Others must be stimulated within the private sector through fiscal and other incentives, information support, and public sector participation.

The *financing* of technological activity is another potential area for policy support. Capital market failures are widespread in developing countries (Stiglitz 1989, 1993; World Bank 1993a). Some such failures are policy induced, but others are endemic to the economies of these countries. Financial intermediaries may suffer from inadequate information, especially on small borrowers, and may be exceptionally risk averse, not only because of this problem but because of the difficulty of enforcing contracts. Financial agents may be particularly reluctant to finance technological development because of their lack of knowledge of what is involved (they know even less about it than the firms involved) and because of the risk inherent in all technological activity.

---

16. Some of these services can command a market price as the economy develops and firms come to realize and accept the need for technological activity. In the early stages of industrialization, however, most countries find that they have to subsidize both firms and science and technology institutes in order to overcome the initial lack of knowledge and risk.

17. For a good historical review of institutional support for technological activity in the industrial countries, see Mowery and Rosenberg (1989). The technology support systems of a number of industrial and developing countries are reviewed in Nelson (1993).

Technological capabilities, especially at the basic levels, are often acquired not through formal research activity but through problem solving in the course of production. Financing this form of activity does not generally require special instruments. The capital market failures that may occur here reflect the broader financial failures that affect developing country enterprises in general and have to be addressed in that context. Of more specific concern is the portion of capability development that is based on formal technological effort and thus requires long-term search and experimentation that tends to face considerable market risk. The financing of such technological activity calls for different mechanisms (such as venture capital financing and technology "incubators") to overcome market failures. Market forces may be able to provide some of these institutional solutions, but the government may need to supply the initial impetus and seed money for others.

Promoting technological investments may also call for *subsidized R&D* to induce firms to undertake particularly large and risky projects. Over the longer term, the development of autonomous research capabilities by industrial firms tends to require a certain size (though in industrial countries small technology-based firms are often in the forefront of innovation), and developing countries may have to promote the emergence of large firms to enable entry into highly demanding areas of technology.

Korea undertook most of these measures to stimulate local technology and now has by far the highest ratio of R&D to GDP in the developing world. The Korean Government provided subsidies for R&D and promoted large local firms in order to encourage domestic competitiveness in heavy and high-technology industries. Subsidized credit, direct participation in national research projects, and incentives for collaborating with technology institutions were widely used (OED 1993). The Korean Government also supported technological efforts in several ways. Private sector R&D was directly promoted by incentives such as tax-exempt funds, tax credits for both expenditures and the upgrading of human capital related to research, the establishment of industry research institutes, accelerated depreciation for investments in R&D facilities, a tax exemption for 10 percent of the cost of relevant equipment, reduced import duties for imported research equipment, and a reduced excise tax for technology-intensive products. The commercialization of research results was encouraged by a tax credit and special accelerated depreciation of the relevant investments. Technology transfers were promoted by tax incentives: the transfer costs of patent rights and technology import fees were made tax deductible; income generated by technology consulting was not taxed; and foreign engineers were exempted from income tax.

The Korean Government also gave direct financial grants and long-term, low-interest loans to enterprises that participated in national projects. Tax privileges and official funds were available to private as well as government research institutes to carry out these projects. Small and medium-sized enterprises were offered "shop-floor" advice and guidance in upgrading technical capabilities and productivity by the Korea Production Technology Corporation, which helps the Small and Medium Industry Promotion Corporation to provide technical, training, and other services. Small and medium-sized enterprises are further assisted by the Korea Academy of Industrial Technology, as well as by "technology guidance systems" operated by government research institutes.

Many of these policies to support technological efforts, like those to encourage skill development, can be considered functional, but many others are necessarily selective. Thus, a research facility to support electronics must be geared to the skills and technology needed by electronics manufacturers, not to industry in general. In addition, the resources available to promote technological development tend to be scarce, and it may be more economical to conserve them for a few activities rather than to spread them over all industrial activities. A country may have to concentrate its promotional efforts on a few sectors—those with the most technological promise or the greatest potential spillover effects—in order to derive the maximum benefit. It should, in other words, groom the few winners that offer the maximum externalities and the broadest scope for developing dynamic comparative advantage.

The Risk of Government Failure

The risk of government failure exists whenever interventionist solutions are recommended for market deficiencies. Widespread intervention by well-meaning governments has been the cause of enormous waste and inefficiency in the developing world. This problem has become so common that the current reaction is to treat all governments as incapable of successful intervention. However, governments do not succeed and fail absolutely; as with markets, there are degrees of failure and success. And, as with markets, governments can improve with time and effort. For some tasks, there may be no alternative to government interventions, but in other cases a reasoned judgment has to be made as to whether the costs and benefits of intervention outweigh the possibility of market failure (Shapiro and Taylor 1990).

Government failure may arise at various levels. At the top, it may be caused by a lack of commitment, by corruption on the part of the administration, or by an inability to devise an intervention strategy that is appropriate to the industrial structure and needs of the country. Failure can also occur at the level of implementation, often from a shortage of administrative capabilities to carry out strategies, even those that are well designed. Finally, if the government is unable to maintain its neutrality, failure may arise from the pressures brought by vested interests (within or outside the government) that oppose the strategy. Some of these problems do not admit of easy solutions, especially those that arise from a lack of commitment, from corruption, and from a susceptibility to political pressures. Others may be tackled over time by improving policy design, administrative skills, and the incentive structure for officials.

The difficulties of improving policy design and implementation should not be underestimated, even if the government does not lack political will and honesty. It is well known that in a second-best situation, with many types of market failures and distortions, attempts to resolve one set of problems can make others worse. The promotion of the small-scale sector, for instance, may constrict the growth of larger and more efficient firms, as happened in India. The creation of an autonomous science and technology infrastructure can divert scarce human capital to the pursuit of science rather than technology. Investments in high-level training can create unemployed or "misemployed" scientists and engineers if the existing skill structure does not match the needs of the production structure. Attempts to promote local technological efforts can lead to the hijacking of resources into unrealistic and costly ventures. Such problems are rife in all spheres of development policy, and resolving them calls for great discretion in making policy recommendations.

The existence of such problems does not, however, amount to a case for complete inaction. As long as market failures exist, it is necessary to tackle those that most threaten industrial development and that can be remedied with a reasonable hope of success. The evidence reviewed earlier suggests that policy interventions can be successfully undertaken in this as in other spheres of development.

It is widely accepted that governments should provide basic education and infrastructure services related to technology development in most developing countries. These interventions have been called "market-friendly interventions." However incompetent governments are, there is no realistic alternative to official participation in these areas. The best that can be done is to strengthen governments' capabilities and improve their performance, making them as responsive to market forces as possible. The more serious problems start with the selective forms of intervention that require enormous skills, information, and discipline on the part of governments and are likely to be subject to rent-seeking behavior and pressure from special interest groups. Such policies can be very costly if they are poorly designed and implemented.

Experience in the developing world suggests that selective interventions have determined the nature and success of industrial development in the most dynamic economies and also that such interventions have been well implemented. The real issue is whether the conditions under which these governments operated are replicable in other countries.[18] In other words, do the governments of typical developing countries have the clear economic objectives, information, design skills, implementation and monitoring capabilities, and political will to carry out selective policies in the same way as the NIEs of East Asia?

The answer must be that most do not. The level of selectivity exercised by, say, the Korean government has been so detailed and pervasive that few other countries can hope to emulate it with a comparable degree of success. Korea also had many advantages that may be unique: a homogeneous population, relatively favorable income distribution, and strong nationalist sentiment in response to an external threat. Korea started with a strong base of human capital, which the government was able to enhance dramatically, partly because of local traditions. Industrialization has been driven by the single-minded pursuit of particular economic objectives and is supported by direct economic involvement at the highest political level, close government collaboration with private business, a dedicated and well-trained civil service, and monitoring capabilities that allow for the penalizing of poor performers. Policy design has been closely influenced by the experience of neighboring Japan, with which Korea shares cultural similarities and technological links. There can be few countries that have this unique combination of characteristics.

The complexity and range of Korean interventions may not be replicable. Even so, it is not true that no selective interventions are possible. There are valuable lessons to be learned from Korea—if they are adapted to the economic conditions and political realities of each country. For example, the need to promote learning in infant industries is universal in developing countries. Faced with the capabilities of advanced countries, developing

---

18. The necessary conditions are analyzed in World Bank (1993a); Chang (1994) contains a good review of the political economy of industrial policy.

economies cannot absorb the costs and risks of mastering difficult new technologies unless they are assisted in factor markets and offered some security of markets or profits. However, the interventions need not be as detailed and specific as those in Korea, where the government has intervened at the level of industry, product, technology, and firm. More general levels of protection at the broad subsectoral level may be suited to countries that have limited administrative capabilities. Market forces can then be left to sort out the best enterprises and technologies.

The most useful lesson of the Korean experience is perhaps that many of the potential costs of protection can be overcome by instituting safeguards (such as early entry into export markets) and integrating incentives with interventions on the supply side. Most developing countries have established protection without ensuring that their enterprises have access to the new skills and information they need to become competitive. Unlike the Koreans, these countries have not been truly selective in planning their industrial strategies.

The correct balance of interventions and market forces cannot be decided on a priori grounds. Both governments and markets fail, but both can be improved with effort. Some governments today are capable of mounting effective selective interventions at a fairly complex level, while others are best confined to functional policies or the most general levels of selectivity. The judgment ultimately must be a pragmatic one. General statements on the virtues of markets as opposed to governments are suspect and may be economically harmful.

Conclusions and Implications

Creating competitive advantage remains an important issue of development policy. This chapter has argued that understanding technological capabilities at the microeconomic level is essential to an understanding of competitiveness and the need for industrial policy. The traditional simplistic assumptions, which argue that there are no costs involved in learning new industrial technologies and that efficient production can be launched merely in response to the "right" prices do not do justice to a complex reality. In fact, they often result in misleading policy recommendations. The promotion of capability development has to be a vital part of industrial development strategy; in the presence of market failures, active government involvement is required.

The main considerations of rational industrial policy to promote comparative advantage can be reiterated. In product markets, the best incentive framework for efficient industrial development is one that provides enterprises with constant competition at the international as well as the domestic level. Full exposure to world competition will, however, be tempered by the market failures that arise from the existence of risky, uncertain, and prolonged learning processes. Depending on the extent of the learning costs involved, as well as the efficiency of the relevant factor markets and supporting institutions, there may be a valid case for selective and variable infant industry protection and for the gradual exposure of existing activities to import competition.

Since protection itself reduces the incentive to invest in capability building, however, it has to be carefully designed, sparingly granted, strictly monitored, and offset by measures to force firms to aim for world standards of efficiency. Protection has to be granted to a few activities at a time, because only a few have the capacity to achieve international levels of competitiveness and intervention resources on the supply side are limited (though the risk of failure also mounts with the increase in selectivity). The most effective offset to the disincentives to capability development that arise from protection seems to be strong pressures to enter export markets, as a commitment to exporting disciplines not only firms but also those who design and administer policy. *The success of export orientation lies in this discipline rather than in conforming to static comparative advantage.*

Interventions may also be needed in factor markets. Markets for human capital, technical support, technology, information, and finance in developing countries generally suffer from a number of deficiencies, all of which a sound industrial promotion strategy must address. Moreover, these interventions must be integrated with incentives, so that the activities being promoted are not penalized by the lack of production factors and information. Resources for intervention are scarce, and using them effectively calls for selectivity and coherence. This fact seems so obvious as to sound banal, yet few governments have aimed for such coherence and selectivity. Current adjustment programs not only ignore the supply side of capability building in their overwhelming urge to get prices right and reduce interventions but also underplay the need to be selective in factor markets.

There are many possible strategies for industrial development and export support. The greater the degree of selectivity exercised, the greater the potential benefits—and the risk of government failure, with its heavy economic costs. A few governments have managed to intervene selectively with great success, producing industrial growth rates perhaps unmatched in recent economic history. Most, however, have not. This evidence suggests that government intervention capabilities have to be assessed in drawing up development strategies and that administrative capabilities and incentives themselves have to be developed to the fullest extent possible (Lall 1992b). There is considerable debate about the capability of governments to undertake selective interventions at all, an argument that moves the realm of economics into that of political economy (Streeten 1993; Shapiro and Taylor 1990). The safest strategy seems to be to create the conditions necessary for winners to emerge rather than to try to select these industries. What is undeniable is that many governments have managed such interventions effectively, and that, given imperfect markets, the costs of nonintervention may be high.

Today, the most pressing policy problem in most developing countries is not the setting up of new industries but the restructuring of existing inefficient and technologically stagnant industries. Policy must therefore aim to remove the irrational and inefficient interventions that many governments have undertaken in the past four decades. The analytical approach proposed here is equally relevant: *industrial reform policy must have the same basic elements as industrial development policy.* Industrial reform and restructuring, in other words, must address various determinants of capability development: the incentive framework, the supply of human capital, the supporting technology infrastructure, finance for technological activity, and access to foreign technologies.

However, reform policies will need to differ from conventional industrial policies in that account should be taken of the "relearning" costs and the time required for existing industries to become efficient and to shed the legacy of inherited attitudes, outdated skills, and inappropriate technologies. Similarly, account has to be taken of the costs and time needed for the relevant factor markets to be upgraded to meet the needs of international competition. The design of policy reforms should take these factors into account. The reasoning here suggests that an appropriate reform package should be implemented gradually and aimed at overcoming identified market failures. It would be phased in according to the needs of relearning and factor market upgrading. It would ultimately retain some instruments of intervention in trade and technology, which are necessary to set up new infant industries, so that these industries are not the first casualties of economic reforms.

6

The Creation of Comparative Advantage: Country Experiences

Sanjaya Lall

This chapter reviews the different approaches to industrial development and the creation of competitive strength that have been adopted by the dynamic newly industrializing economies (NIEs) and, with varying degrees of success, by other countries. The experience of the NIEs shows that there have been wide variations in the ways industry is nurtured and also in the countries' success in achieving industrialization. An understanding of these differences, then, is essential to defining the appropriate role of industrial policy.

The Success Stories

The discussion of industrial policy and export performance in the development literature has centered largely around the experience of the four East Asian NIEs—Hong Kong, the Republic of Korea, Singapore, and Taiwan, China—the most successful industrializing economies in the developing world. During the 1980s, it was widely argued that the success of these export-oriented economies validated the standard neoclassical prescriptions of prudent macroeconomic management and liberalized international trade. It was generally taken that export orientation was synonymous with both liberal trade and industrial policies and market-driven resource allocation. Empirical evidence has now more or less demolished this line of argument.[1]

The most recent publication establishing both that there is no unique East Asian model and that there were numerous government interventions, selective and functional, in most of the NIEs, is the World Bank (1993a) study of the East Asian miracle. This study makes an important contribution to the debate on what actually happened in East Asia. However, it does not fully address the specific market failures industrial policies were designed to correct in the larger NIEs and Japan. Its interpretation of the role of industrial policy is thus rather pessimistic, suggesting that policy may have helped marginally in the allocation of credit but did not significantly change the industrial structure or affect comparative advantage.[2]

While this chapter cannot provide a comprehensive analysis of industrial policy in East Asia, it can offer a review from the perspective of capability development and export competitiveness. This perspective provides new insights into the need for policy support of competitive advantage and shows that creating winners can be a practical strategy, with many variations possible on the basic theme.

These variations are best illustrated by Hong Kong and Korea, the two Asian NIEs that provide the most vivid contrast, although both had strong export orientation and high growth rates. **Hong Kong's** virtually laissez-faire trade regime comes closest to the neoclassical paradigm of an ideal industrial strategy. It provides a stable administrative and macroeconomic environment. The government has not intervened in product markets, either to support particular industries or to protect manufacturing in general, nor has it tried to guide investments via the allocation of domestic credit or the entry of foreign investments.

The Hong Kong Government has intervened functionally to provide education and training to workers, subsidized land to manufacturers, and information and support services to its exporters. Its so-called Productivity Center has undertaken various technological services to help producers improve their technologies. The government has even supported the clothing sector by sponsoring a large, well-funded textile and garments design

---

1. See, among others, Amsden (1989), Lall (1990, 1992a), OED (1992), Pack and Westphal (1986), Wade (1990), Westphal (1982, 1990). For a critical review of the early neoclassical arguments on trade strategy in view of the experiences of Korea and Brazil, see Moreira (1995).

2. The arguments of the Bank's study are analyzed by, among others, Amsden (1994), Kwon (1994), Lall (1994), and Fishlow and others (1994).

and training center. However, its interventions have been predominantly nonselective, with few attempts to pick or create winners. Moreover, even its interventions to promote education, while impressive by most developing country standards, have not been as intense as those of the larger NIEs, even if overseas enrollments are taken into account. In particular, Hong Kong has lagged behind other NIEs in the training of scientists and engineers and in vocational training. Its investments in local research and development (R&D) also have trailed those of other industrializers. Though precise data on R&D in Hong Kong are not available, studies of the country's manufacturing sector suggest that there is relatively little formal technology development and that R&D expenditures are probably below 0.5 percent of GDP.

Thus, the level of intervention has been fairly low, and trade has always been free. Hong Kong's growth performance over the past three decades has been impressive, albeit lower in terms of income and export growth than the performance of the large NIEs. Its share in developing country exports of manufactures actually declined over the 1970–89 period. Does this experience have lessons for other industrializing economies? It does, but not necessarily that the laissez-faire approach is the best way to promote competitive manufacturing everywhere. Two important features of the Hong Kong experience have to be noted in this context.

- First, Hong Kong started with several unique advantages that other developing countries, including other free trade centers and tax havens, lacked. Its century and a half of entrepôt experience gave it a range of capabilities and a highly developed infrastructure for trading and finance. The presence of several British business and finance houses (the "Hongs") provided a constant supply of foreign skills as well as externalities in the form of training for local employees. Most important for manufacturing, its textile, garment, and toy industries took off after the communist takeover of China in 1949. Much of the learning for these industries had already taken place, and the technologies were simple enough that subsequent training could be given to a workforce with a good primary education. The free trade environment, combined with existing capabilities in trade and finance and a supply of cheap manpower, enabled these advantages to be fully exploited, mainly by Chinese entrepreneurs from Shanghai, who entered the country along with other Chinese professionals (including engineers and technicians) after the takeover. There was considerable foreign investment, but in manufacturing the lead stayed firmly in local hands—in sharp contrast to what occurred in Singapore.

- Second, the ensuing pattern of industrialization in Hong Kong reflected the government's nonselective industrial policies. The colony started and stayed with labor-intensive light manufacturing, although there was considerable upgrading within this category. The government did not selectively promote more complex industries. Hong Kong's success was based on impressive operational and marketing capabilities, but there was little industrial deepening and diversification. Despite some natural progression up the ladder of industrial complexity, Hong Kong's achievements in this sphere were relatively limited in relation to other NIEs. As wages and land costs rose, the colony had to relocate its manufacturing to other countries, mainly mainland China, and suffered a significant loss of industrial activity at home; in 1986–92 it lost about 35 percent of its manufacturing employment, and this process is continuing (*Financial Times* 1993). The growth of its manufactured exports has slowed considerably and may even have gone into decline in 1993–94.

Hong Kong has been able to continue to grow in services and trade because of its unique location, its connections with the adjoining mainland, and the enormous business opportunities that are opening up with China's liberalization. However, its pattern of industrial success is not open to other developing countries, where recourse to free trade alone is unlikely to lead to such dynamic growth. No other free trade center and tax haven—and there are several in the developing world—has achieved much industrial success; none has been able to undertake even the relatively easy learning required of light industry.

More important, larger economies that attract foreign investments in labor-intensive light manufacturing cannot progress up the ladder of industrial complexity without undertaking interventions to promote the move into advanced activities. Foreign direct investment can make the learning process easier, but the development of local technological capabilities is bound to need supporting selective interventions.

The development of Hong Kong's competitive advantage in industry thus has special characteristics. Hong Kong was able to succeed in existing light industry and then to diversify out of manufacturing altogether instead of taking on the more complex technologies that would have maintained its manufacturing base (but with rising wage costs).[3] By contrast, Switzerland, with roughly the same population, retains a growing and deep industrial sector (with highly sophisticated activities in chemicals, pharmaceuticals, electrical and textile machinery, food processing, and so on) and has much higher wage levels than Hong Kong. The difference lies precisely in the fact that Switzerland has, with judicious periods of protection and promotion, built up a deep technological base over the past century. The industrial success of Hong Kong lies, in essence, in its having deindustrialized without losing out on growth, a feature that has depended crucially on its location and ability to act as a conduit for the mainland.

Korea is at the other extreme. Its record of export development, growth, and industrial diversification and deepening is one of the most impressive in modern economic history (even more so than Japan's, in view of the rapid pace and poor initial conditions).[4] The government intervened extensively, both functionally and selectively, in practically all product and factor markets.[5] It offered high, variable, and prolonged periods of protection to selected activities and forced those that approached competitiveness to export significant portions of their output. It directed domestic investible resources to infant industries and deliberately fostered the emergence of

---

3. The relative lack of depth in its industrial structure has, nevertheless, led to considerable disquiet among Hong Kong's policymakers. As the *Financial Times* (1993), notes in its survey of Hong Kong: "The laissez faire prop against which the Hong Kong government has leaned since 1841 has prevented it from adopting the ambitious strategies that have spawned the computer components and telecommunications products of Singapore, South Korea and Taiwan. But as Hong Kong continues to evolve into a financial and services centre, the pressures of some of the highest land and labor costs in Asia appear to have given the government second thoughts about its stance . . . . The government is taking serious measures to encourage the inflow of overseas technologies, so that Hong Kong can retain some kind of industrial base . . . . The government has toned down its laissez faire inclinations to permit a new applied research and development scheme. This is a $HK 200m. fund, which will match the investment of any start-up company which fulfills certain criteria, in exchange for an equity stake. This represents the first step towards direct government funding for research and development, and by implication, the creation of a Government industrial policy."

4. Korea's manufactured exports grew at 27.2 percent per annum during 1965–80 and at 12.9 percent during 1980–90, compared with Hong Kong's 9.1 percent and 6.2 percent, Singapore's 4.7 percent and 8.6 percent, and Taiwan, China's 18.9 percent and 10.3 percent (World Bank 1993b; and official Taiwanese statistics).

5. The details are now well known and are given in publications such as Amsden (1989), Chang (1994), Moreira (1995), Pack and Westphal (1986), Westphal (1990), and OED (1992, 1993).

giant private conglomerates (the *chaebols*) that could internalize various imperfect markets. It invested heavily in education and selectively promoted technical education; industrialists actively participated in setting the curriculum for technical training. It induced firms to launch employee training schemes. It invested directly in R&D and technology infrastructure institutions, partly by sponsoring national technology projects.[6] At the same time, it undertook various measures to induce local firms to develop their own research capabilities and so reduce the country's dependence on foreign sources of technology, an objective that few countries subscribe to today.[7] These factor market interventions were often selective and were integrated into the overall direction of trade and industrial policies. The policies themselves were guided by a clear and strong strategic vision of industrial deepening and competitiveness.

Perhaps the most interesting aspect of Korea's industrial success is that it was based largely on indigenous enterprises rather than on technology transfer via direct investment. Until recently, the Korean government was highly selective about foreign direct investment and, in some instances, induced Japanese firms to sell out to the *chaebols* after some years in the country. In technological terms, this strategy called for far more domestic skills training and technology creation than one with the same range of industries but a heavy reliance on direct foreign investment. Korea's investments in education and R&D and the fostering of the giant *chaebols* were a necessary part of a nationalist strategy driven by the objective of achieving world-level competitiveness.

Korea's research and manufacturing base is able to copy, adapt, and build upon state-of-the-art industrial technologies to an extent unmatched by other developing countries. This pattern of competitive development is of a completely different order from that of Hong Kong. It is conducive to sustained industrial expansion rather than to deindustrialization. It suggests that the development of indigenous know-why has many dynamic

---

6. Government involvement in Korean R&D is growing rather than diminishing as the country pushes into increasingly complex industries. The latest data released by the government show that it plans to spend $1 billion over the next fourteen years on biotechnology alone and, along with the private sector, a total of $50 billion on eleven "national projects" covering biotechnology, new materials, fine chemicals, satellite rockets, aircraft, maritime technologies, and basic research (*Asian Wall Street Journal* 1994). The promotion of national projects has been an important tool of industrial targeting in Korea in recent years.

7. On Korean technology polices see Kim (1993); for a relevant case study of the electronics industry, see Mody (1990).

benefits: apart from significantly lowering the cost of technology transfers, know-why allows diversification into more advanced areas of industrial exports than does foreign investment (which tends to leave control in the investors' hands).[8] By forcing firms to import technologies at arm's length and to compete in world markets, Korea's policy leads industries to develop skills and technical knowledge that are more advanced than those needed to operate a technology imported in a fully "packaged" form.

The development of local R&D capabilities in Korea has also had several externalities and linkages. It has fed into local capital goods and component production. It has enabled accumulated technical knowledge to be applied by other industries and firms. And it has led to growing linkages between industry and the technology infrastructure (universities, research institutions, quality assurance centers, and so on).

In **Singapore,** the smallest of the NIEs, the government has been highly interventionist, but its interventions have taken different forms from Korea's (Krause 1988; Hobday 1994a). The economy started with a base of capabilities in entrepôt trading, ship servicing, and petroleum refining. After a brief period of import substitution, Singapore moved into export-oriented industrialization based primarily on investment by multinational companies. Unlike Hong Kong, Singapore had a weak tradition of local entrepreneurship and had not enjoyed an influx of technical and entrepreneurial know-how from China. There was a decade or so of light industrial activity (garment and semiconductor assembly), after which the Singaporean Government acted firmly to upgrade the industrial structure. It intervened in foreign investments to guide multinational corporations to high-value-added activities and in education to create the specific high-level technical skills that would be needed.[9] It set up public enterprises to enter those activities it believed would define the country's future comparative advantage; in fact, the public sector in Singapore accounts for a substantial proportion of GDP.

The Singaporean Government selected specific areas of both manufacturing and services (including banking, freighting, and aircraft servicing) for promotion but did not include trade protection among its policy instruments. Instead, it offered a range of incentives and pressures that guided

---

8. The capabilities may be mainly for absorption rather than for innovation, but, as noted, even the absorption, adaptation, and improvement of advanced technologies needs substantial local R&D effort.

9. When the local skill base proved insufficient, the government allowed a controlled import of skilled manpower.

the allocation of resources and lowered the cost of entry into difficult activities by providing the requisite skills and infrastructure. Manufacturing moved into highly specialized processes and products, but there was no deliberate attempt to increase local content. Such specialization, along with a heavy reliance on foreign investments for technology and skill transfers, greatly reduced the need for indigenous technological investments—as compared, say, with Korea. Thus, while selective interventions led Singapore's industry into sophisticated producer and consumer electronics, precision instruments, optics, and so on, the technological depth of its enterprises remained comparatively low. Some design and development activity—a field targeted for the island's future industrial activity—did develop over time, but only with considerable urging and support from the government (Hobday 1994a).

To the extent that an economy with 3 million people is relevant to the developing world, Singapore's experience offers two lessons. First, foreign direct investment can take a small economy a long way if it is carefully selected and guided, supplied with superlative infrastructure and a disciplined and trained workforce, and given a competitive and stable investment environment. Second, it is not necessary to offer import protection to technologically complex activities if the main sources of operational and other technologies are foreign and domestic production is integrated with production in foreign countries (rather than with local suppliers), so that local industries concentrate only on certain tasks. But this strategy requires both functional and selective interventions by the government: the contrasting experiences of Singapore and Hong Kong with respect to the deepening of industrial activity illustrate this fact clearly.

For larger countries that wish to emulate Singapore in developing their competitive advantages, however, this level of selectivity may not be enough. Local enterprises will be able to shoulder the significantly higher learning costs involved only with increased government support through protection or subsidies and the creation of large domestic firms that can partly internalize defective risk, capital, and information markets.

Taiwan, China, which has approximately one-half the population of Korea, has become almost as dynamic as its larger neighbor. Some thirty years ago, Taiwan, China, was considerably more developed than Korea and better endowed with human resources. Like Hong Kong, it had experienced a large influx of capital, skills, and entrepreneurship from mainland China after the communist revolution. Its development strategy contained elements of Korean-style attempts to select and promote local industries through protection, credit allocation, and selectivity in foreign direct investments. However, Taiwan, China's selectivity was far less detailed than Korea's, and the government did not attempt to create giant private conglomerates or to push as heavily into advanced technologies and capital-intensive activities. Its weaker relationship with private industry meant, moreover, that many of Taiwan, China's more ambitious forays into heavy industry had to be undertaken by the public sector. As a result, Taiwan, China, has built up the largest public sector among the NIEs: some 25 percent of manufacturing is in the hands of public enterprises. The public sector has led the economy's entry into the kinds of cutting-edge technologies that are regarded as essential to future export success, such as the manufacture of memory chips and, in 1994, the aerospace industry.

Taiwan, China's strength lies in its myriad small and medium-sized enterprises, which have tapped its large base of human capital and taken advantage of the government's policy of promoting infant industries by helping them to diversify into skill-intensive activities. The resulting industrial structure is "lighter" than Korea's, with greater emphasis on filling market niches and less on mass production. On average, Taiwanese manufacturers conduct far less in-house R&D than their Korean counterparts and invest less in creating international brand names. While small industries are at an inherent disadvantage in terms of spending on technical upgrading, this problem has been offset somewhat by the wide range of technology support services (including R&D) the government provides for Taiwanese manufacturers (Hou and Gee 1993). The flexibility and export orientation of these firms have allowed Taiwan, China, to maintain export growth rates that are nearly as high as Korea's.

The evolution of competitiveness in Taiwan, China, has thus differed from the development of competitiveness in Korea. A large proportion of small enterprises specialize in labor-intensive manufacturing (and face the same problems as Hong Kong's industries). These industries can survive only by relocating overseas, becoming more competitive in their domestic operations, or moving out of simple technologies. If these alternatives prove too costly, Taiwan, China's industries may simply die out. Unlike Hong Kong, however, Taiwan, China, has many firms able to enter high-value-added activities and to upgrade their technologies by tapping the large technology infrastructure. There are also a growing number of larger firms that have developed the capabilities to invest in their own R&D and to create their own brand names, giving Taiwanese industry some of the capabilities arising from industrial depth, as in Korea. It is debatable which of these two economies has the greater competitive strength in the long term—the one dominated by the giant *chaebols*, or the one with the smaller, more nimble, but technologically lighter enterprises.

This brief survey of the experience of the East Asian NIEs has important implications for the analysis of market failures and the role of government. These four dynamic economies have all been successful in creating and extending their areas of competitive advantage in industry and in using their advantages to drive economic development. The evidence suggests that their strategies not only differed greatly but produced very different results in terms of industrial structure and export competitiveness. Unless these differences are taken into account, the role and effects of government intervention cannot be correctly evaluated.

Each NIE started out with a different set of endowments and adopted a unique approach to improving them and to pushing enterprises into more productive activities. The models that emerged were formed by the strategies chosen to tackle market failures. These strategies were fairly effective in addressing functional failures, especially in terms of physical infrastructure and human capital, but their approaches to capital markets and their technology support activities differed. The most important differences, however, lay in trade and industrial policies, which ranged from laissez faire to intense and detailed intervention in the most important aspects of resource allocation, technology transfer, and competition.

The nature of industrial competitiveness in these countries reflects their different strategies. While each country has been successful in coping with world competition, each has developed a different range and level of industrial technologies. Hong Kong has the least technological depth, and its response has been to move to the manufacture of light consumer goods and to shift production elsewhere. Korea has developed a very diverse industrial sector with considerable technological depth and R&D capabilities. It has tackled complex and risky technologies that offer potentially large payoffs, spawning its own large multinational enterprises, creating an international image, and confronting industrial leaders directly. Singapore's and Taiwan, China's strategies lie somewhere between these two approaches.

Industrial policy has been central to this process. Note that this is not an argument for those wholesale and nonselective interventions practiced by classic import-substituting economies. The dangers of such strategies are well known, and it is evident that export orientation, not import substitution, provides the appropriate policy setting for effective interventions. The need to promote internationally competitive activities and tap export markets disciplines both policymakers and enterprises; without this discipline, selective interventions run the risk of going wrong.[10] However, this approach may also run into difficulties as the industrial country markets become more protective and raise barriers against exports from developing countries. This issue is addressed in chapter 7.

Much has been made in the recent literature of the risks of intervening in countries where the political economy and administrative capabilities are not of the order of East Asia's. While it is undoubtedly necessary to exercise less selectivity in interventions when the risk of government failure is present, it is important to recognize that official capabilities can be improved and that a firm commitment to export orientation itself places a check on policymakers. The positive effects of stringent recruitment standards, improved education and training, competitive salary structures, and a degree of insulation for the bureaucracy from the political process are all fairly straightforward lessons that can be learned from East Asia in terms of improving the quality of interventions.[11]

It is also important to be aware of the dangers of not intervening. Given the market failures inherent in the capability-building process, free market policies may lead to stagnation or may slow the evolution of competitiveness in manufactures. It is not easy, however, to assess empirically the impact of nonintervention on the development of competitive advantages. The problems of generalizing from the Hong Kong economic experience have been discussed, and the absence of other successful industrializers with similar laissez-faire policies has been noted. Nearly all other developing countries have intervened to promote industrial development. The fact that most have intervened poorly, using little selectivity, lacking a coherent strategy, and showing a sweeping disregard for market failures means that it is difficult to analyze the impact of the "ideal" industrial policy. However, some of these recent experiences do offer lessons for industrial policy. The evidence is only indirect and suggestive, but it helps to get away from the concentration on East Asia.

---

10. The World Bank (1993a) analyzes how Korean and Japanese policymakers gave selective favors in return for export performance, creating non-market-based "contests" that reduced the dangers of rent seeking.

11. The World Bank (1993a) makes this point. On the political economy of formulating and managing industrial policy, see Chang (1994).

Other Country Experiences

The impact of industrial policy (or its absence) on industrial competitiveness in other developing countries is illustrated by the effects of liberalization. The justification for liberalization is derived directly from the neoclassical theory of comparative advantage. According to this theory, import-substituting strategies are largely wasteful, encouraging uncompetitive industries; free trade gives the best signals for resource allocation in developing competitive advantage; and efficient markets ensure that the supply response to liberalization is strong and uniform across countries (since by assumption there are no differences in capabilities). Liberalization and the withdrawal of government regulation are recommended in all aspects of economic activity. The empirical underpinning for this theory is usually provided by the Asian NIEs, and many developing countries believe that liberalization by itself will lead to the export success enjoyed by Korea or Taiwan, China. One way to examine the case for industrial policy (as opposed to nonintervention in a free market) is to assess how valid these assumptions really are and how countries that have liberalized have actually fared in terms of competitiveness.

In practice, structural adjustment is not a homogeneous process. Developing countries undertake different methods of reform, depending on national economic beliefs and conditions. These countries can be classified into two broad groups, according to their approach. The first comprises countries that liberalize slowly and retain a promotional role for the government during and after reform. This group includes many countries in East and Southeast Asia, including Korea and Taiwan, China. The second group comprises countries that liberalize rapidly across the board, giving free markets the primary role in resource allocation; this group includes several countries in Latin America and some in Sub-Saharan Africa. The impact of nonintervention on the evolution of competitiveness is illustrated by the experience of the second group of countries.

In contrast to the assumptions of standard theory, the "capabilities approach" suggests that the reaction to sweeping and sudden liberalization cannot be uniform across countries. The extent and nature of market failures will differ, as will the economies' ability to respond to the new set of signals, since these responses are dependent on existing stocks of technological and other capabilities that vary considerably. Thus, the countries in the second group may be further subdivided by level of capability development:

- *Countries that are industrially underdeveloped, with low stocks of technological and other skills.* These countries face the risk of massive deindustrialization and a reversion to exports based largely on natural resource endowments.

- *Countries with a larger skill base that have developed a few industrial technologies to world levels of competiveness.* These countries may suffer significant deindustrialization but also may evolve new competitive advantages from their base of capabilities. In the absence of interventions, however, progress may be slow and limited and may not lead to the diversification of exports into activities with costly and prolonged learning processes.

- *Countries with substantial import-substituting sectors and significant technological capabilities that have mastered a wide range of heavy technologies behind protective barriers.* These countries may be able to expand industrial exports into complex activities, but developing new areas of industrial competitiveness depends on government policies to promote specific capabilities or on the economy's ability to attract well-heeled foreign investors able to overcome the market failures that confront domestic enterprises.

The first group of countries includes the so-called least-developed countries, most of which are in Sub-Saharan Africa. **Ghana** has the longest history of rapid and sweeping liberalization in this region. It first undertook structural adjustment in 1986 and, by 1991, had implemented three programs that resulted in a fairly liberal economy. A study of industrial performance for this period shows that manufacturing value added rose rapidly after 1983, when imported inputs were made available to existing industries with substantial excess capacity (Lall and others 1994). The rate of growth was 12.9 percent in 1984, 24.3 percent in 1985, 11.0 percent in 1986, and 10.0 percent in 1987. However, as liberalization spread and excess capacity was used up, exposure to world competition led to a steady deceleration of industrial growth. Thus, the rate of growth of manufacturing value added fell to 5.1 percent in 1988, 3.1 percent in 1989, and 2.5 percent in 1990. There have been few signs of a revival since.

The expectation was that exports of manufactures would grow and diversify rapidly under the new regime. In fact, data show that while manufactured exports have grown since 1986, the absolute values are extremely small—a total of $14.7 million in 1991. The growth has come mainly from wood and aluminum products (both long-established export sectors) and from firms established in export markets, rather than from new products or producers.[12] There were relatively few signs of a broad-based response on the part of Ghanaian manufacturing enterprises, particularly in the country's main area of comparative advantage, cheap labor. Labor-intensive exports such as garments, footwear, toys, and other light consumer goods and metal products (which led the initial export thrust of the NIEs) have been conspicuous by their absence. Yet it is these exports that must lead the new industrial strategy under structural adjustment if the economy is to diversify and grow on a sustained basis.[13]

At the same time, large portions of the manufacturing sector have been devastated by import competition. The adverse impact of liberalization has been strongest in the large-scale, modern areas of the industrial sector, which have the most complex technologies and so have suffered most from the lack of technological capabilities. Industrial survivors and new entrants are clustered in activities with natural protection; they operate on a very small scale, making low-cost or indigenous products, goods with high transport costs, or items that require some processing of local raw materials. Apart from the enclave operation of aluminum processing or protected activities such as government-owned petroleum refining, these activities include some food processing, furniture, cement, simple metal products, and uniforms for the army or schools. The important low-technology, entry-level manufacturing activities such as garments and footwear, in which Ghana should be developing a competitive edge, have been unable to survive the import threat. The generally low level of capabilities and skills needed to upgrade manufacturing to world levels means that liberalization has led to significant deindustrialization, and the growth of new activities has been too limited to provide the momentum to exports or production that would transform Ghana into a "new NIE" in Africa.

It is particularly relevant to reiterate that, despite very low wages, cheap labor has not so far emerged as a source of comparative advantage for Ghanaian industry. Conventional wisdom suggests that cheap labor should be

---

12. The values of the main nontraditional manufactured exports in 1991 were aluminum, $5.5 million; wood products, $6.2 million (of which furniture accounted for $3.6 million and other wood products for $2.6 million); canned foods, $0.3 million; tobacco, $0.4 million; soaps, $0.6 million; machetes and iron rods, $0.8 million; and others, $1.3 million.

13. In wood products, for instance, some 95 percent of furniture exports come from one foreign affiliate, while scores of local manufactures operate with such low efficiency and poor quality that they cannot enter world markets. Most of their exports continue to be of builder's products, the lowest category of wood manufacturing.

the main source of comparative advantage in manufacturing for newly industrializing countries. This has not happened because the ability to compete internationally even in low-technology, labor-intensive industries requires a level of labor productivity and managerial and technical skills that is at present lacking in Ghana. The few relatively well-managed firms that exist are largely foreign owned; among local enterprises, the better ones have entrepreneurs that are well educated. The typical local firm, on the other hand, has entrepreneurs with little education, a poorly skilled workforce, and no way to improve technological capabilities. Most lack the ability even to perceive and define their technological problems.

Exposure to market forces per se is thus retarding the development of Ghana's comparative advantage. The rapid pace of exposure to world competition is killing off not just inherently uneconomic activities but also some that could be the basis for new manufactured exports. The lack of policies to upgrade skills, as well as of technical information and technological support, is exacerbating market failures in inputs essential to developing competitive capabilities. Ghana's comparative advantage is likely, in this policy framework, to evolve very slowly unless there is a rapid inflow of foreign manufacturing investments. However, the lack of industrial capabilities means that foreign investors prefer to invest in other developing countries. The expectation in Ghana that it could "do a Korea" by liberalizing and minimizing the role of the government was unrealistic. A more appropriate set of policies might have included gradual liberalization and closely integrated measures to improve skills and technologies.

The countries in the second group have a relatively strong skill base but have not been able to develop a broad range of efficient industries behind import-substitution barriers. **Chile** is a particularly interesting case because, while it has never adopted a formal structural adjustment program (its reforms predate such programs), it has had the longest experience of sweeping liberalization in the developing world (some twenty years). Of all the developing countries, it is the one that most closely approximates the neoclassical ideal of development strategy (and the early depiction of the East Asian model): rapid opening up to international competition, very low and uniform rates of protection, no picking of industrial winners, opendoor policies for foreign investment and technology, and reasonable macroeconomic stability. Though Chile's liberalization led to massive deindustrialization, with about half of manufacturing employment disappearing within a short period, this result may have been desirable in terms of the efficiency of resource allocation in the long run. The real test of the need for industrial policy lay in subsequent manufacturing growth and export performance. The cost in job losses would have been worthwhile if Chile had been able to fulfill neoclassical expectations and "do an NIE" in the East Asian mold.

Liberalization began in Chile in 1973. Chile's manufacturing production had been rising at a rate of 0.6 percent a year during 1965–80. In 1980–90, the rate climbed to 3.6 percent. During the same two periods, commodity exports rose at 7.9 percent and 5.2 percent a year, respectively. This level of growth may reflect a better performance than other Latin American countries turned in during the 1980s, but it is rather modest by the standards of most Asian economies, even those with massive interventions.[14] The total value of Chile's manufactured exports came to $1.3 billion in 1992, compared with $70.0 billion for Taiwan, China, in the same year. Chile's population is around two-thirds that of Taiwan, China, so in terms of size the two economies are not so different. But Chile exported $96 per capita, Taiwan, China, $3,500.[15] During 1980–87, by which time liberal policies were well established in Chile, the rate of growth of manufactured exports was 3.3 percent per annum, compared with 13 percent for Taiwan, China. Unlike Taiwan (China) 1and other East Asian NIEs, whose export dynamism was driven by diversification into non-resource-based activities and encompassed increasingly skill- and technology-intensive activities, Chile's export growth in manufactures was based largely on the further processing of natural resources. As a result, the skill and technology content of its exports diminished over time.[16] Thus, the share of high-wage products in total manufactured exports (an indicator of skill intensity) fell over the period 1966–86, as did the share of products that rely heavily on technical and engineering manpower (an index of technological intensity). In Taiwan, China, by contrast, these shares rose sharply.

This is not to say that there has been no dynamism in Chilean exports. In agriculturally based activities, Chile has introduced new products and developed new markets. Chile has always had a resource advantage in its traditionally strong agricultural sector (aided by the fact that its seasons dovetail nicely with those of countries in the northern hemisphere), a good base of agricultural skills, and government support for biotechnology

---

14. For instance, India's rates of growth in these periods were 4.5 percent and 6.7 percent for manufacturing and 3.7 percent and 7.4 percent for exports.

15. Data from World Bank, *World Development Reports,* various years.

16. For a full analysis of Chile's export performance and its industrial policy in the broad sense, see Pietrobelli (1994a and 1994b). For a more general analysis of Chile's reforms, see French-Davis and Muñoz (1991).

research. (Interestingly, this support was the only intervention in export-related fields that the Chilean government had undertaken until recently.) This base has provided Chilean enterprises with the needed incentives to invest in technological activities related to agricultural exports. Thus, much of Chile's export growth has been in manufactures based on its natural resources, and its learning process has been stimulated by export prospects and a degree of natural protection.

The capability approach not only provides a good explanation of the pattern of export growth that has resulted from Chile's liberal policies but offers additional useful insights. The primary one is that despite two decades of stringent policy reforms intended to free its economy from government intervention, Chile has failed to transform its manufacturing sector into an engine of export growth. It has not been able to "do a Taiwan, China." It is not that Chile lacks the human resources it needs to develop its industrial exports. It has one of the best educational systems in Latin America, as well as a base of entrepreneurship and substantial experience with industrialization as far back as the nineteenth century. However, because of the failure of its earlier ·governments to devise and implement effective industrial policies that addressed market failures, it has never managed to build up competitive capabilities that could succeed in world markets. After liberali-zation, the presence of human capital was not sufficient on its own to dynamize Chile's industrial competitiveness. This is an important point to note, in view of the emphasis currently being placed on human resources (as opposed to industrial policy) as the main explanation of the Asian miracle (World Bank 1993a). As noted earlier, however, it is the combination of education and appropriate interventions in other factor and product markets that accounts for the success of the Asian NIEs. The presence of human capital has helped Chile in boosting resource-based exports, but the creation of new competitive advantages in industry has been severely constrained, in the absence of policy support, by the learning costs inherent in upgrading and deepening industry.

The third category includes developing countries that have already mastered a range of complex technologies behind protectionist barriers and have been able to take advantage of their existing comparative advantage in the first stages of liberalization. **Mexico** may be taken as an example. A long history of inward-oriented industrialization, combined with a sizable internal market, a respectable base of natural and human resources, and a location next to the world's most powerful industrial nation, have enabled Mexico to build up a large and diverse industrial sector. The expansion of manufacturing output during its import-substitution phase was impressive: the three decades before 1980 showed average annual growth rates of 6.3 percent, 8.8 percent, and 7 percent, respectively (OED 1993). For several decades, Mexican manufacturing value added ranked third in the developing world, after China and Brazil. In recent years, Mexico has been overtaken by Korea, but the two industrial sectors are fairly comparable in size.

The 1980s witnessed a considerable slowdown, accompanied by severe fluctuations, as macroeconomic disturbances and accompanying stabilization policies took their toll on the economy. In the mid-1980s, Mexico launched a sweeping and thorough process of economic liberalization. It changed its trade orientation drastically, privatized many state enterprises, and generally reduced the role of the state in economic activity. More recently, it has negotiated entry into the North American Free Trade Agreement (NAFTA), in which there will be a phased reduction of all import protection among the three members. Mexico's recent experience is thus of interest both in terms of the accomplishments of the past import-substituting regime and of the impact of liberalization on the country's competitive advantage. The policy reforms envisioned that Mexico's most heavily protected import-substituting activities would fade out after liberalization and be replaced by new activities that became attractive as a result of the new set of price signals. But has this change taken place? An examination of recent developments in Mexico reveals some interesting facts.

Mexican manufactured exports performed well over 1981–91. In current dollar terms, they grew more than threefold, and in real terms around twofold. However, much of the growth took place following two massive devaluations (and well before liberalization started to affect domestic competition) in 1983–84 and 1986–87. Exports were also affected by the severe recession caused by stabilization. After 1987, the rate of export growth declined steadily, falling to 16 percent in 1988, 6 percent in 1989, and 3.5 percent in 1990—far below the rates for East Asia in the same periods. The timing of the growth in exports suggests that recession and devaluations played a larger part in this growth than any efficiency-enhancing impact of import liberalization (Ros 1994). In the end, Mexico's structural reforms seem to have had little effect on export expansion.

There are two particularly interesting points about this performance. First, the most dynamic of Mexico's manufactured exports over the 1980s were produced by heavy, import-substituting industries, mostly in the socalled maquiladoras, or export-processing zones, close to the U.S. border. Mexico was evidently exploiting competitive advantages that already existed; the improved incentives for exports allowed these advantages to be deployed fairly quickly for exports to the neighboring U.S. market. This fact is quite clear from the sectoral composition of the expanded exports in the 1980s. The largest exporter in 1989 by far was the engineering subsector (led by automobiles, which continued to be highly protected): it accounted for 45 percent of the total, growing 2.7 times between 1985–89. The next largest was basic metals, accounting for 15 percent of the total and growing three-fold. In all, heavy industry—defined as including engineering, chemicals and petrochemicals, basic metals, nonmetallic minerals, plastics, and rubber—accounted for 82.3 percent of Mexican manufactured exports in 1989 and for 88 percent of the increase in these exports over 1980–89. These industries entail complex processes, intensive in the use of technical and engineering skills. As noted above, their efficient operation calls for lengthy learning periods during which technological information is assimilated and adapted and supplier and technical information networks are developed.

Second, the progressive slowing of manufactured export growth in recent years suggests that once the existing comparative advantage was used up, the industrial sector was unable to sustain rapid export growth. It lacks the base of technological capabilities that would allow it to generate continuous productivity rises or to independently introduce new or adapted products. The unselective nature and prolonged application of protection, together with the lack of a coherent technology strategy, has deprived Mexican industry of the technological dynamism of the larger NIEs of East Asia. R&D in industry has been limited, and the supporting science and technology infrastructure is weakly linked to production needs. A large number of small enterprises operate with low skill levels and few technological capabilities.

In general, there has been a tradition of technological dependence in Mexican industry, compared with industrial sectors in countries like Korea or Taiwan, China. Mexico has relied too heavily on imported capital goods for a country of its industrial size and sophistication. This dependency has been accompanied by a similar and widespread reliance on inflows of foreign know-how, licenses, and expertise. Despite the government's nationalistic stance, foreign multinational enterprises retain a large presence in practically all advanced sectors of Mexican industry.[17] These enterprises have tight links with their centers of innovation and advanced design abroad. Thus, a diverse industrial sector with a reasonable mastery of technologies coexists alongside the small, low-technology enterprises. Mexico

---

17. Mexico has traditionally had the largest stock of foreign direct investment in the developing world after Brazil. After a slackening following the debt crisis, large direct investment inflows have again resumed.

spent about 0.5 percent of GDP on R&D in the early 1980s, but recession and fiscal austerity caused this amount to decline to only about 0.3 percent of GDP by 1990; the figure for Korea was 2.1 percent. Of Mexico's total R&D expenditures, only around 10 percent came from industrial enterprises, in contrast to 80 percent for Korea.

The lack of investment in domestic R&D may not have prevented the transfer and utilization of new technologies, but, by holding back the development of deeper capabilities, it has retarded further diversification, development, and diffusion. It has also restricted the ability of Mexican industry to move autonomously into technologically dynamic or sophisticated industries. Korea used import substitution to foster industrialization and simultaneously pursued a strategy of independent industrial technological development. Because Mexico has never been as export oriented, nationalistic, and technologically ambitious as Korea, it has failed to create similar competitive pressures for technological effort. The comparison serves to highlight the need for coherent interventions in technology markets to promote deeper technological capabilities, at least in larger countries. The upgrading of Mexican competitive advantages in industry will depend largely on foreign investment inflows. Some such upgrading is bound to happen, given the country's location and labor cost advantages. However, whether this process moves much beyond the point of taking on new assembly functions in export activities and gives industries the dynamism and high-technology edge Korea enjoys remains to be seen.

The Mexican experience shows that past interventions have had both positive and negative effects. The interpretation of the experience here is different from the view that regards Mexico's early strategy as wholly wasteful and liberalization as an unparalleled boon to the country's comparative advantage. A different pattern of interventions in the past might in fact have given Mexico a far more dynamic industrial structure structure, but with the present structure and tradition of low-technology activity, even wholesale liberalization may not lead to a widespread upgrading of the country's comparative advantage. It seems extremely unlikely that even a liberal Mexico will be able to "do a Korea."

7

The World Trading Environment

Carl Dahlman, Irfan ul Haque, and Kenji Takeuchi

The previous chapters have been concerned with approaches to building the competitive strength of a country. It was noted that building competitiveness requires a multidimensional strategy involving effective macroeconomic management; a deliberate, focused, and planned approach to accumulating technological capabilities; and an articulated industrial policy to develop new areas of competence. The arena in which a country's competitiveness is tested, of course, is the world market. The textbook view of the world market is highly idealized, consisting of atomistic decisionmakers that produce and trade goods and services in perfectly competitive markets where prices are more or less given. Where the possibility of market imperfections is considered, as in the new trade theory, it is confined to specific product markets and taken more or less as the exception; the world market view remains basically unchanged. But reality is far removed from this idealized picture and is becoming increasingly so, largely on account of technological developments. This chapter attempts to describe the real world of competition and its consequences for developing countries.

The first section discusses the evolution of the globalization that has characterized the past several decades and that has been a major force behind the increasing preoccupation with international competitiveness. Two key factors affecting this phenomenon have been the rise of the multinational corporation (MNC) and increasing capital mobility, both of which have exerted an enormous influence on world trading relations. The second section traces the impact on the process of production of certain trends in global technology that are changing the basis of specialization in production and of success in the world market, with significant implications for international competition. This section is followed by a review of the "rules of the game" of world trade as they have evolved since the end of World War II. The last section examines the implications of the evolution of the world economy and trading relations for the newly industrializing economies (NIEs), including countries in transition, particularly in light of recent rapid technological change.

The Globalization of Industry

The term "globalization" refers to the increasing interaction of domestic economies with the world economy. With the rise of globalization, it has become quite unrealistic to discuss the problems of a single economy without considering their international dimensions. Globalization is reflected in the rising share of international trade in world output and in the extraordinary rise in capital mobility, including foreign direct investment. Accompanying these developments has been the rise in both strategic alliances among firms and international trade within some corporate entities, with the MNCs playing a prominent role. Such developments have been brought about largely by the rapid technological progress of the postwar period.

The Increasing Share of World Trade

As noted in Chapter 1, one of the clearest signs of the globalization of economic activity is the growth of exports as a share of world output, a trend that has persisted for almost two centuries (except during the interwar period) and that has been particularly marked during the postwar period. In 1965–90, the share of exports in world GDP increased from 11 to 20 percent, a trend reflected in all major groupings of economies (Table 7.1).

The increase in the share of trade is the result of several factors, but especially of technological progress. First, rapid advances in technology have reduced the costs of transportation and communication—expenses that had been tantamount to trade barriers. Second, technological advances have increased the range of products and, in turn, specialization and exchange, including intraindustry trade. Third—and this factor is also related to technology—large economies of scale make it more efficient to produce in quantities that often exceed domestic demand, forcing firms to seek foreign markets. In addition, for industries in which research and

Table 7.1. Exports as a Share of GDP, 1965 and 1990
(in percent)

Country Grouping	1965	1990
By income		
Low income [a]	8	18
Middle income	17	—
Lower middle income [b]	17	28
Upper middle income [c]	19	—
High income	12	20
By region		
Sub-Saharan Africa	22	29
East Asia and Pacific	8	31
Southern Asia	6	9
Europe	—	29
Middle East and North Africa	26	—
Latin America and the Caribbean	13	15
OECD	12	19
World	11	20

Source: World Bank 1992.
a. 43 developing economies with per capita incomes ranging from $80 to $600.
b. 41 developing economies with per capita incomes ranging from $600 to $2,490.
c. 17 developing economies with per capita incomes ranging from $2,490 to $7,050.

development (R&D) is particularly important, the often high costs must be amortized over greater production volume, further encouraging exports.

The Increase in Foreign Direct Investment

Foreign direct investment is a second indicator of globalization. After stagnating in the early 1980s, foreign investment grew rapidly. Between 1983 and 1989, direct investment by countries of the Organization for Economic Cooperation and Development (OECD) grew at an average annual rate of 31.4 percent, compared with only 11.9 percent for gross fixed capital formation, 11.0 percent for trade, and 10.4 percent for GDP (OECD 1992c). Several factors were responsible for the increase in foreign investment. One factor accounting for increased investment in the European Union by other European countries, the United States, and Japan was the prospect of an enlarged Single Market.[1] Another reason was the fear of increased protectionism in the industrial countries—a fear that explains the heavy foreign investment in the United States, especially by the Japanese and Europeans, and has fueled increased U.S. and Japanese investment in Europe.

Trends in trade and foreign investment in services underscore the need to take a more integrated view of the move toward globalization. Between 1970 and 1985, the share of services in world trade only increased from 29 to 32 percent, while the share of the service sector in economic activity increased considerably more. However, the share of services in the total stock of foreign direct investment increased from 25 to 50 percent over the same period. The reasons for this sharp divergence are that services tend to be nontraded goods and that an increasing number of services are being undertaken within firms. It has been estimated that 70 percent of transnational data flows are intracorporate, although for some economies, such as Canada, the figure reaches 90 percent (OECD 1992c).

Another feature of the emerging global economy is the increasing concentration of foreign direct investment and trade within what has been called the "Triad" of the United States, the European Union, and Japan. Between 1980 and 1988, intra-Triad foreign investment stock nearly tripled, growing from $142 billion (30 percent of the worldwide total) to $410 billion (39 percent of the worldwide total). Intra-Triad trade also rose from 13 percent of world trade to 17 percent over the same period (OECD 1992c).

These trends have several implications for developing economies. First, developing economies appear to be receiving a smaller share of foreign investment. Second, since direct investment is one of the primary conduits for technology inflows, developing economies' access to foreign technology may be becoming more limited. Third, if there is indeed an increase in protectionism within the two members of the Triad, the United States and the European Union (assuming that Japan does not retaliate), developing countries' access to industrial country markets will be further compromised, with a subsequent negative impact not only on the ability of these economies to generate foreign exchange through exports but also on their access to foreign technology, since exporting provides many technological externalities.

---

1. The rapid growth of foreign investment inside the OECD has included accelerated cross-border mergers and acquisitions. See OECD (1992c, pp. 215–16) for relevant data, especially for Europe.

The Changing Structure of World Trade

Along with the overall increase in the share of trade in world output, there has been a rise in manufactured products and a fall in the share of primary commodities in trade (Table 7.2). The rapid growth of manufactured exports is basically the result of higher income elasticity of demand for manufactured products as compared with primary products. Technological change, with the resultant declining costs and greater range and diversity of manufactured products, has also been a key factor.

Table 7.2. The Structure of Merchandise Exports, 1965 and 1990
(in percent)

	World		Industrial countries		Developing countries	
Export	*1965*	*1990*	*1965*	*1990*	*1965*	*1990*
Total primaries	43.7	21.9	30.8	19.1	85.0	34.1
Nonfuel	34.2	15.9	27.4	14.9	56.2	20.3
Food	18.8	9.6	15.0	8.9	31.2	2.7
Nonfood agricultural	8.2	2.9	6.5	2.8	13.5	3.4
Minerals	7.2	3.4	5.9	3.2	11.5	4.2
Fuel	9.5	6.0	3.4	4.2	28.8	13.8
Total manufactures	56.3	78.1	69.2	80.9	15.0	65.9
Machine/transportation equipment	24.2	38.1	30.9	41.6	3.0	23.5
Other manufactures	32.1	40.0	38.3	39.3	12.0	42.3
	Asian NIEs		United States		Japan	
	1965	*1990*	*1965*	*1990*	*1965*	*1990*
Total primaries	41.6	11.5	34.6	21.9	8.9	2.6
Nonfuel	33.7	6.6	31.1	18.6	8.5	2.1
Food	19.2	3.9	21.1	11.2	4.4	0.6
Nonfood agricultural	12.0	1.5	5.5	4.4	2.5	0.6
Minerals	2.4	1.2	4.5	3.1	1.6	0.9
Fuel	7.9	4.9	3.5	3.2	0.4	0.5
Total manufactures	58.4	88.5	65.4	78.1	91.1	97.4
Machine/transportation equipment	7.6	38.0	37.1	46.8	31.3	65.7
Other manufactures	50.8	50.5	28.3	31.3	59.9	31.7

Source: United Nations BESD database, and authors' calculations.

For the world as whole, the drop of over 20 percentage points in the share of primary products in total merchandise exports between 1965 and 1990 has been offset by a corresponding increase in the share of manufactured products. For industrial economies, the change has not been as great, as these countries started with a much lower share of primary commodities in their exports. On the other hand, for the developing economies, the change has been dramatic—a shift of almost 50 percentage points. Because of this shift, the structure of trade of the Asian NIEs—Hong Kong, the Republic of Korea, Singapore, and Taiwan, China—has now come to resemble that of the industrial economies. An indication of the speed and depth of their transformation is that the share of primary commodities in their exports has fallen further, and from an initially higher level, than the share of these commodities in the exports of industrial economies. By 1990, the East Asian NIEs had a greater share of manufactured exports than (on average) the industrial economies. However, there are strong variations even among the latter, as can be seen from the contrast in the shares of primary and manufactured products in total imports between the United States and Japan. The Asian NIEs are somewhat closer to Japan in their export pattern than they are to the United States, in part because, like Japan, they are relatively poor in natural resources.

The changing composition of exports can be probed further by looking at the primary sources of competitive advantage for each industry, using the five-way classification system developed by the OECD (1988a). The data show that the share of resource-intensive industries (such as food, leather, wood, petroleum, and nonferrous metals) in world trade of manufactures has fallen from almost one-third to less than one-fifth (Table 7.3). While the shares of labor-intensive industries (such as textiles, garments, and furniture) have stayed about the same, the shares of those industries classified as scale intensive (paper, chemicals, iron and steel, cars and trucks, for example), differentiated (including electrical and nonelectrical machinery and photographic products), and science based (other chemicals, computers, professional and scientific equipment, and aircraft) rose. Thus, there has been a clear shift toward industries that tend to require a greater use of technology.

As noted earlier, the fall in the share of resource-intensive products has been smaller in industrial than in developing countries, primarily because industrial economies started with a lower share of these products in manufactured exports. On the other hand, there has been a small fall in the share of labor-intensive products. The changes in the shares of the other categories are not significantly different from the changes for world trade as a

Table 7.3. The Structure of Manufactured Exports, 1965 and 1990
(in percent)

	World		Industrial countries		Developing countries	
	1965	*1990*	*1965*	*1990*	*1965*	*1990*
Resource intensive	31.2	18.9	24.6	17.5	76.5	25.7
Labor intensive	15.5	15.1	15.6	12.3	14.2	28.2
Scale intensive	27.1	30.0	30.3	32.4	5.8	18.9
Differentiated	19.0	23.3	21.5	24.2	2.1	19.4
Science based	7.2	12.7	8.0	13.7	1.4	7.9
	Asian NIEs		*Japan*		*United States*	
	1965	*1990*	*1965*	*1990*	*1965*	*1990*
Resource intensive	30.9	11.9	9.1	2.9	20.3	14.9
Labor intensive	46.5	29.8	26.1	6.3	10.3	7.6
Scale intensive	13.6	18.0	43.6	40.2	25.2	25.4
Differentiated	6.8	28.1	19.1	39.6	29.4	26.3
Science based	2.2	12.2	2.1	11.1	14.8	25.9

Source: United Nations trade data; OECD (1988) classification of industry types; and authors' computations.

whole, although industrial countries have slightly higher shares of scale-intensive, differentiated, and science-based goods.

For developing economies, the changes in the shares are considerably greater. The share of resource-intensive products fell more than 50 percentage points. Almost one-third of this decline was actually a shift to labor-intensive products; the remaining two-thirds has been divided among the other three categories, though at lower shares than for the world as a whole. For the Asian NIEs, the shares of labor-intensive and scale-intensive products are similar to the shares of these products for developing countries as a whole. However, because of their poor natural resource endowments, the Asian NIEs have a much lower share of resource-intensive exports.[2] Somewhat surprisingly, the Asian NIEs display a higher share of differentiated products and a very similar share of science-based products in comparison with industrial countries. This situation is largely the result of the Asian

---

2. In fact, it is the inclusion of Singapore, with its significant petroleum product exports from its local processing of imported crude, that raises the Asian NIEs' share of resource-intensive products.

economies' export-oriented strategies, which have focused on manufactured goods, particularly electronics-based products.

The Growth of Intrafirm Trade

The rise of MNCs has meant that a large proportion of world trade is accounted for by the exchange of goods and services within a single firm based in different countries. Intrafirm trade implies virtual replacement of market transactions by arrangements worked out within firms that may or may not conform to the competitive rules of the market. This development has obvious implications for government policy and institutional regulations governing international trade. These implications are discussed later in the chapter.

While there are anecdotal accounts of the growth of intrafirm trade, there are few hard data on its magnitude, as world movements of goods and services are recorded by product category and origin and not by firm. Even if data were compiled on the transactions of MNCs, these data would not paint a complete picture because of difficulties in definition and the complex arrangements governing global firm–subsidiary relations. A recent OECD (1993) study made a systematic attempt to measure intrafirm trade, but owing to the paucity of data, the study had to be confined to the United States and Japan. The study found that over one-third of U.S. merchandise trade was conducted within firms but that (contrary to what is generally believed) this proportion had shown few signs of increasing over the period reviewed (1977–89). Intrafirm trade in the United States was concentrated in industries such as transportation equipment and machinery, which have invested heavily in R&D and human capital. The Japanese data did not allow for an estimate of the overall importance of intrafirm trade but did show that it was relatively more important in the machinery industries, including transportation equipment. Reflecting the importance of Japanese corporate networks, a significant share of intrafirm trade was accounted for by retail and wholesale trade. All in all, a sizable proportion of world trade is conducted on the basis of corporate goals and strategies rather than in markets characterized by arm's-length competition.

The Evolution of the Production Process

Technological change has been a major force behind the globalization of production and the changes in the structure of trade that have led to increasing competitive pressures. This section first describes the broad elements of the technological changes that have occurred in recent years and then explains how technology has affected production relations and processes. The main source of technological advancement is still the leading industrial countries, but some of the industrially more advanced developing countries are increasingly contributing to this process and are even beginning to influence the nature of world competition (OECD 1988).

Elements of Technological Change

The last decade has witnessed an unexpected and dramatic acceleration in the pace of innovation that has been called the "third industrial revolution" (Perez 1985; Freeman, Clark, and Soete 1987). Contrary to the expectations that prevailed only twenty years ago, which held that the rate of innovation would slow, technological change has continued unabated, bringing with it an explosive growth in information and technical knowledge unprecedented in human history, as the following quotation explains:

> It took from the time of Christ to the mid-eighteenth century for knowledge to double. It doubled again 150 years later, and then again in only 50 years. Today it doubles every 4 or 5 years. More new information has been produced in the last 30 years than in the previous 5,000 (Linowes 1990).

Much of the recent technical progress consists of developments in microelectronics, biotechnology, and new materials and is the outcome of both demand and supply factors. On the demand side, economic multipolarization and intense competition for world markets has given rise to technological rivalry among nations and industrial firms. On the supply side, technological progress has been pushed by a series of breakthroughs in material sciences, solid state and plasma physics, and genetic engineering, and by substantial improvements in scientific instrumentation. Key to the "technological revolution" are the falling costs of information storage and retrieval: the real costs of storing, processing, and transmitting a unit of information have fallen at a rate of 20 percent a year over the last forty years, while the decline in energy costs that fueled the industrial revolution was only 50 percent over thirty years (Hanna 1991). R&D has also hastened the pace of innovation, in turn feeding the demand for the formal education and further R&D required to keep up with technical innovations and to adapt them for commercial use. Over the last decade, R&D expenditures as a proportion of GNP have risen not only in the industrial economies but also in the most rapidly industrializing developing economies in East Asia.

Another feature of recent technological progress has been that the new technologies often have a broad application. Some of the most influential developments have been in electronics and telecommunications processes and pro-ducts and have affected a wide range of other sectors. These developments include process control in such industries as steel and petrochemicals; automation in assembly-type industries, such as automobiles and other consumer durables; and automated data processing and communications in service industries, such as banking and insurance, that require recording and tracking large numbers of transactions. For example, although sales by information technology industries accounted only for between 0.9 percent and 2.3 percent of GNP in 1984 in the United Kingdom, France, Germany, and Japan, estimates for the same year indicate that about two-thirds of manufacturing firms in those countries adopted some form of microelectronics technology (OECD 1988).

At the same time, the increase in automation made possible by new electronics-based technologies has resulted in a decline in the direct labor share of production costs. For example, the share of labor costs in textile production has fallen from 30 percent to as low as 4 percent in automated assembly lines and to less than 3 percent in the production of, for instance, printed circuit boards. Increased automation means that cheap labor may no longer be a sufficient basis for competitiveness in some industries. On the one hand, this trend tends to work against the developing countries, whose most abundant resource is cheap unskilled labor; on the other, the development of automated technologies—such as numerically controlled machine tools, computer-aided design, automated accounting and management systems, and expert intelligence systems—can substitute for skilled labor and, in some cases, even for white-collar professionals in business and technical fields such as architecture and medicine. This substitutability may relieve some of the technical skill constraints that handicap many developing countries, although adopting these technologies will require a new set of operational and maintenance skills, as well as a flexible labor force equipped with multiple skills.

Another development has been a general reduction in the use of traditional industrial inputs. Increased process control has led to increased energy efficiency in energy-intensive process industries such as steel and cement. Better integration between design and production and new optimization techniques have brought about material savings. Synthetics are replacing many traditional materials such as natural rubber fibers (notably cotton and jute) while composites such as plastics and ceramics are being substituted for steel and aluminum and optical fiber is replacing copper. This displacement has a direct impact on many developing countries that are important producers and exporters of some of the natural materials.

Finally, the increased importance of environmental issues is beginning to redefine the agenda for future technological developments. The need to protect the environment has stimulated the search for and development of environmentally friendly technologies intended to reduce harmful by-products and emissions through recycling, further processing, or the adoption of production processes that do not create these by-products. In light of the tightening environmental regulatory regime in the OECD countries, there is likely to be strong demand for these technologies, and a large market is expected to develop.

Implications for the Production Process

Technological progress has always had a profound impact on production processes and relationships. For one thing, the rapid pace of technological change, the rising number of innovators, and the accelerated diffusion of technology have led to shorter technological life cycles for both production processes and products. In consumer electronics, for example, a product's lifespan has fallen from one or two years to just a few months as products or models with new features are introduced and displace older models. This shorter product life cycle applies even to some consumer nondurables. For instance, retailers and fashion designers, who used to introduce two to three fashion lines every year, now introduce as many every season. Thus, there is increasing pressure to capture technological rents as quickly as possible before an innovation becomes obsolete. In this race to outpace obsolescence, major firms develop new competitive strategies and form strategic alliances with overseas firms. For example, of the recorded international cooperation agreements among firms between 1982 and 1985, 28 percent were for distribution and marketing, 26 percent for integration of R&D activities, 17 percent for technology transfer, 16 percent for integration of production, 6 percent for supply, and 7 percent for other activities (OECD 1988; Mody 1988). In the case of semiconductors, international R&D cooperation agreements among firms increased from 43 in 1983 to 90 in 1985 and to over 100 in 1989 (OECD 1992a).

Another major change is taking place in the organization of production. Some observers have characterized this change as a shift in the organizational paradigm. Pioneered by the Japanese, the new mode involves the concepts of "just in time" inventory, zero defects, and total quality control, which have reduced costs, improved quality and flexibility, and helped to make the Japanese formidable competitors across a wide range of products and markets. An increasing number of producers are attracted to these organizational techniques, which also require that labor become more fungible—that is, that it acquire multiple skills that can be applied to a variety of different tasks.

Moreover, the Japanese management and organizational model dictates a different relationship between final assemblers and suppliers that generally requires geographic proximity (as opposed to distant facilities that tie up a larger amount of capital in inventories). It is common for suppliers in Japan to make several deliveries of parts and components to their principals each day. To the extent that the Japanese model prevails over the U.S. model, which is based on the concept of worldwide sourcing from distant, low-cost locations, the markets for some developing country suppliers in a few subsectors (such as auto parts) may decline in the future.[3] Increased intrafirm trade and closer links between assemblers and component producers also suggest that it is the systems or networks rather than individual firms that are in competition. The success of developing countries therefore depends increasingly on becoming part of these global systems.

In short, quality and speed of delivery to the market have now become key elements of competitiveness. A move to computer-integrated manufacturing is under way that involves technologies such as computer-aided design and manufacturing, numerically controlled machine tools, industrial robots, automatic guided vehicles, automated warehouses, and automated order and distribution systems. These innovations have dramatically reduced the period between the design and production of new products and have enabled firms to respond rapidly and with more flexibility to customer specifications, increasing the diversity of products and promoting competition in design, distribution, and service.[4] At the same time, production costs have become a declining proportion of the total costs of developing and delivering a product to the market in a number of industries. For example, the cost of producing a differentiated product with a large design compo-

---

3. For an elaboration of this development in the engineering and electronics industries, see Hoffman (1989), Castells and Tyson (1988), and Kaplinsky and Hoffman (1988).

4. There are many examples of reductions in product development time by different firms. Stalk and Hout (1990) note that Honeywell reduced the product development time in the core of thermostats from 4 years to 1. Navistar reduced it for trucks from 5 to 2.5 years, while Hewlett Packard reduced it for printers from 4.5 to 2 years.

nent, such as a fashion garment, is now only about 10 percent of the total delivered cost (Stalk and Hout 1990).

These developments, which are still confined to a subsector of industry, have some important consequences for the production process. First, the notion of "given factor endowments" has become less relevant with the increasing importance of what might be called "created" endowments—that is, human and physical capital and management skills. The proportion of trade based on natural resources, as seen above, has greatly diminished, while the relative abundance of cheap labor has become less significant in determining the pattern of specialization today.

Second, it is no longer a safe strategy for producers to take market conditions as givens to which firms can respond by providing goods at the lowest possible cost. With the dramatic decline in the response times of suppliers, even small countries need to anticipate market trends and adapt their production decisions accordingly in order to secure a place in the world market. An important element in the success of the four East Asian "Tigers"—Hong Kong, Korea, Singapore, and Taiwan, China—has been their ability to mold the world market in significant ways by promoting new fashions, designs, and even products. Creating market opportunities itself is an innovative, entrepreneurial process.

Finally, whether they involve developing new products or processes or simply accessing the market, "strategic alliances" among producers or between buyers and sellers have become increasingly important in international trade. Few producers in developing countries have the capability or resources to mount large marketing drives. Further, the trend toward increasing specialization at lower levels of production and the rising importance of standards and specifications in international trade (whether in automobile parts or garments) have created a need for effective production and trading links.

The Rules of the Game

For the last forty-five years, the GATT (now evolved into the World Trade Organization) provided the institutional basis for the conduct of world trade. It was an extraordinary achievement, designed to save world trade from the self-defeating "beggar-thy-neighbor" policies of the interwar period. In pursuit of freer world trade, the GATT has operated on four broad principles: (i) multilateralism and nondiscrimination, or the application of the most-favored-nation (MFN) principle to all contracting parties; (ii) the expansion of trade through the reduction of trade barriers; (iii) the reciprocity of the rights and obligations of members; and (iv) the establishment of a set of universal rules for the conduct of trade policy (Bhagwati 1991). While this framework has on the whole served the world community well, and while international trade has flourished, international trading relations have nevertheless been strained.

The Evolution of the GATT-Based Global Trading Regime

"Contracting parties," as they are called in the GATT, have since the agreement's inception attempted to stretch the established trading rules. The developing countries have always stressed their weak bargaining position in a system based on reciprocity and have invoked the "infant industry" argument to defend the "differential and preferential treatment" the GATT rules have allowed. Of late, however, the industrial countries, in view of their varying performances in international trade and the emergence of large trade imbalances, have started to complain about unfair trading practices not just in other industrial countries but in developing countries as well. Such complaints have resulted in rather contradictory attempts at more rigorous enforcement and efforts to broaden the scope of the agreement and to bypass the established GATT rules altogether.

Several rounds of multilateral trade negotiations were conducted to liberalize the world trading environment. In the first two decades of the GATT, successive rounds of multilateral negotiations—notably, the Dillon Round (1960–62) and the Kennedy Round (1962–67)—resulted in remarkable reductions in tariff barriers and the subsequent growth of world trade. The Tokyo Round (1973–79) also succeeded in producing substantial reductions in tariff barriers. While tariff barriers have continued to be reduced since the early 1970s, nontariff barriers (NTBs) have increased, seriously compromising the success achieved in tariff reductions (Laird and Yeats 1990; UNCTAD 1993). Bhagwati (1988) distinguishes two classes of NTBs: those that bypass GATT rules (high track) and those that capture and pervert them (low track). High-track NTBs are relatively visible, politically negotiated restraints on exports by trading partners and consist of what are called voluntary export restraints and orderly marketing arrangements. Low-track restraints on imports consist of countervailing duties and antidumping provisions that are technically within the scope of GATT rules but can easily be abused. The use of both high-track and low-track NTBs has been on the rise for the last two decades, although there is some evidence of a levelling off in the 1990s (Low 1993). The Tokyo Round endeavored to control low-track restraints on imports without any tangible success. More recently, regional trading arrangements have been proliferating. These arrangements generally represent attempts to reduce or eliminate trade barriers among a group of countries and involve discriminatory treatment for outsiders, thus going against the spirit of nondiscrimination of the GATT.

Implications of the Uruguay Round

The latest round of multilateral trade negotiations was the Uruguay Round, which was negotiated over a period of seven years and concluded only toward the end of 1993. The negotiations encompassed a far wider range of issues than any previous round and resulted in a number of substantive changes in international trading rules as well as the creation of the World Trade Organization (WTO) to replace the GATT.

The negotiations focused on the following areas:

- reductions in tariff and nontariff barriers;
- the expansion of GATT disciplines to agriculture and textiles and clothing;
- reform of the GATT rules, most notably those on subsidies, countervailing duties, dumping, and safeguards;
- the extension of multilateral rules to new areas, namely, trade in services, trade-related intellectual property rights, and trade-related investment measures; and
- institutional reforms relating to the settlement of trade disputes and the functioning of the GATT system.

The reforms are to be implemented gradually over ten years, and only after the formation of the WTO. However, the successful completion of the Uruguay Round has produced one immediate benefit by avoiding the costs that would have been associated with failure of the negotiations—that is, a serious deterioration in the world trade environment (World Bank 1994).

Under the terms of the Uruguay Round, tariffs in industrial countries will be reduced by a trade-weighted average of 39 percent, although the average reduction is only 34 percent when weighted by imports from developing countries (World Bank 1994). For textiles and clothing and leather products (the main export items of developing countries), the average reduction is only about 20 percent. However, the relatively meager achievements in tariff reductions in these products will be supplemented by the elimination of NTBs such as the Multifiber Arrangement and voluntary export restraints, especially on footwear, electronics, and travel goods.

Most of the liberalization of NTBs will take place in agriculture, textiles and clothing, and sectors subject to voluntary restraints. In agriculture, initially all NTBs will (in principle) be converted to their equivalent in tariffs and then reduced by an average of 36 percent over a six-year period. It remains to be seen whether all voluntary export restraints and similar measures will be notified and eliminated; at present, about eighty are in force on a range of industrial goods and textiles and clothing.

The elimination of voluntary restraints could provoke the intensified use of safeguards, countervailing duties, and antidumping measures. In order to reach the agreement on eliminating these restraints, the Uruguay Round negotiators consented to compromises on nondiscrimination and compensation under the safeguard provisions. The round was also able to achieve some clarification of the rules on subsidies.[5] However, despite concerted efforts negotiators were unable to tighten antidumping rules, which have increasingly become the cutting edge of discriminatory restrictive trade policy (Finger 1993). Antidumping remains subject to discretionary interpretations by national laws.

The Uruguay Round broke new ground in extending the multilateral framework to several new areas. It concluded a framework agreement for trade in services, but the results of this agreement in terms of market access will not be known for another two or three years, as negotiations in many key subsectors are still under way. Most preliminary offers include commitments on computer-related services, although construction, professional services, and tourism are also covered. Most offers so far seem to maintain rather than lower existing levels of protection.

Of particular significance from the viewpoint of the use of technology are the agreements on trade-related intellectual property rights that aim to develop rules to protect intellectual property by establishing disciplines on trade in counterfeit goods. Another new area for the multilateral framework are the agreements on trade-related investment measures limiting the use of local content requirements and trade balancing, among other things. These measures are to be eliminated within set time limits.

The active and widespread participation of developing countries in the Uruguay Round reflected the increased interest and confidence of these countries in the international trading regime and contrasts with the rise of protectionist lobbies in industrial countries. So far, developing countries

---

5. Subsidies are now classified as prohibited, allowable but actionable, and allowable and nonactionable. Thus, certain subsidies now prohibited will be eliminated within established time limits.

have been exempted from certain GATT regulations under the "special and differential treatment" provisions. However, in this round many developing countries were more interested in defining adjustment periods within which commitments would come into force than in securing open-ended exemptions from GATT rules. The least-developed countries will continue to be fully exempted from any tariff reduction commitments.

Now that the Uruguay Round has been completed with some success, will the rising tide of "new protectionism" in the industrial countries be reversed? Certainly, the outright collapse of the Uruguay round would have augured ill for the future of the world trading system. The negotiations succeeded in bringing some of the so-called gray area trade measures under tighter disciplines or, alternatively, in increasing transparency in these areas. But many problems in these areas are still unresolved, and, most importantly, a high degree of uncertainty remains in the enforcement mechanism for controlling these protectionistic measures. This uncertainty leaves the door open to growing demands for fair trade and a level playing field that, if met, will ultimately lead to the increased unilateral use of low-track protectionist measures against imports from developing countries perceived to have unacceptably low environmental and labor standards.

The New Regionalism

Regionalism in international trade has been on the rise in the recent years. The further integration and enlargement of the European Union and the establishment of the North American Free Trade Agreement (NAFTA) have established regionalism as a new dimension of the world trade regime. Many other regional trading arrangements have also been established or are under negotiation, especially among developing countries. An exhaustive count of all regional trading arrangements runs to more than sixty if those formally proposed but not acted upon are included. The proliferation of regional trading arrangements—which are in the nature of preferential trading arrangements—has given rise to two major concerns: what these arrangements mean for the open global market all GATT member countries subscribe to; and what these arrangements mean for developing countries that are in the catch-up stage of industrialization and have developed export promotion strategies but do not yet belong to any of the blocs.

The new regionalism, however, seems to be different from traditional regionalism in several respects (Braga 1994). New regional integration agreements tend to go beyond trade in goods, often covering trade in services and providing for the free movement of capital and/or labor, the harmonization of various regulations, and the coordination of domestic policies that influence international competitiveness (deep integration). Another new trend is the banding together of northern and southern countries, as in NAFTA and, potentially, the European Union. In agreements among developing countries, emphasis seems to have shifted to developing an outward orientation, in contrast to earlier schemes that emphasized the enlargement of protected markets for import substitution.

The key question is whether the proliferating regional arrangements will become stumbling blocks to or building blocks for further improvements in the open global trading system. In working toward the goal of increasing global trade liberalization, countries may find that the multilateral approach is the first-best because of the discrimination inherent in the regional approach to trade liberalization. However, as the experience of the Uruguay Round shows, multilateral negotiations take much longer to conclude: the Uruguay Round lasted seven years, while NAFTA took only around two years to negotiate. As a second-best approach to trade liberalization, regionalism has the virtue of being both relatively easy to implement and effective. Recent reviews of trends in the new regionalism seem to suggest that existing and currently envisaged regional trade arrangements are, on balance, more likely to contribute to than to detract from global trade liberalization (Braga 1994).

Implications for the NIEs

Recent technological changes, along with the new organizational forms of production and new bases of international competition, have important implications for industrial development in developing and transition economies. A country's ability to enter and remain competitive in export markets depends ultimately on domestic industries' ability to match and then exceed international benchmarks of productive efficiency, which rise with every innovation. Knowledge and the ability to exploit it for economic ends is now recognized as a critical factor of production, giving rise to what has been called the "symbolic economy," in which power rests with those who control information (Toffler 1990).

Rapid technological change, then, can be viewed as a blessing or a threat, depending on whether a country is able to take advantage of the opportunities offered by new technologies and new forms of organization. For instance, synthetic substitutes have posed a threat to producers of natural products for several decades, but countries that invested in technological improvements in the production and quality of natural products (such as Malaysia, which exports natural rubber) have been better able to withstand competition than countries that did not make such investments. Similarly, the introduction of automated technologies and the increasing globalization of production, although threatening to some developing countries, also offer opportunities for technological advancement and better integration with the global economy, as will be explained below.

As developing countries strive to integrate themselves into the global economy and to create internationally competitive productive structures, they face the challenge of having to cope with both rapid technological progress and stresses in the world trading environment. It is primarily the industrially advanced developing countries that compete directly with industrial countries and are therefore more exposed to the technological and other developments outlined above. But these issues have become of increasing importance to virtually all developing countries as they progress industrially. Raising living standards in an increasingly competitive global environment involves developing the ability to exploit new technological opportunities while dealing with the twin threats of protectionism and the rise of "technonationalism" (that is, national protection of technology transfer) in industrial countries.

There is also the question of how far the world market can go in absorbing manufactured exports from developing countries, given the already large share of these exports in industrial country markets. The answer to the export pessimists who usually raise this question is that if the exporters also import, the process of globally integrating production and increasing international trade can continue more or less indefinitely. This process does imply, however, that successful exporters will increasingly be pressed to reciprocate by taking in more imports, as is happening with Japan and other East Asian suppliers.

Sustaining Economic Success

The impressive performance of some developing countries in trade is evidence of competition and dynamism in the world market. The initial success these countries enjoyed lay in making large inroads into industrial country markets with traditional items such as footwear, clothing, cork and wood products, and furniture, largely on the basis of cheap labor. Now, the more advanced among these countries, notably the newly industrializing economies (NIEs) of East Asia, are challenged on two fronts. First, the countries' own success has led to a substantial rise in real wages that is beginning to erode the cost advantage in labor-intensive industries.

Less-developed, lower-wage economies such as China, Indonesia, and Thailand are now successfully competing in world markets with many traditional products. Second, as noted earlier, the diffusion of microelectronics technology has resulted in the increasing use of automation in these previously labor-intensive industries (Castells and Tyson 1988; Hoffman and Rush 1982; Mody and Wheeler 1989). The spread of automation has opened up opportunities for industrial economies to regain their competitive edge in those labor-intensive sectors in which developing economies had begun to dominate. In addition, there has been a general shift to more design-intensive modes of production and greater product differentiation, a development that militates against comparative advantage based solely on low wage costs.

In short, the industrially advanced developing countries are being squeezed by competition from lower-wage producers in developing countries and the increasing technological sophistication of industrial economies. In order to sustain economic progress and stay competitive, these countries need to move into more complex products, traditional products with higher value added, and new high-technology products. There are basically four approaches to dealing with the competitive squeeze, which is likely to be experienced by other countries as they move up the development ladder. These approaches are not mutually exclusive.

The first is to specialize in products that require large production runs to reach minimum efficient scales in order to counteract the labor cost disadvantage some developing countries face from competitors with lower wages. Korea has been able to use this tactic successfully in such scale-intensive industries as steel, cement, bicycles, and other traditional products.

A second approach is to focus on specialty products with higher value added that require a rapid response to new fashions and market trends. To a large extent, this is what Hong Kong and Taiwan, China, have done in clothing and footwear. Taiwan, China, is also applying this concept to a traditional product (bicycles) by focusing on the high-end recreational bicycle market rather than the low-quality mass market that Korea has exploited through large production runs.

A third approach is to step up automation to combat rising labor costs, as Korea, Singapore, and Taiwan, China, are doing on a large scale. A complimentary trend is to relocate production in countries with lower wages. Hong Kong, for example, has invested heavily in China; to a smaller extent, the other three Asian Tigers are also investing in Asian economies with an abundance of cheap labor, such as Indonesia, the Philippines, and Thailand.

Finally, there is the option to go for new technology- and design-intensive products. This approach is riskier and requires more groundwork but can produce higher returns, since competition from new entrants squeezes profit margins out of traditional manufactures. The approach is being used in several different ways. Singapore has chosen to attract foreign firms to undertake activities with higher value added by providing state-of-the-art physical infrastructure and a highly skilled labor force. Korea has begun to do the same thing in automobiles and some high-technology products through a combination of joint ventures, technology licensing agreements, and R&D. Taiwan, China, is also developing its electronics industry through joint ventures and local R&D efforts. An impressive example of this approach is Acer computers, which has developed its own brand name and is aiming to become the fifth-largest computer company in the world, thanks largely to its own R&D efforts.

In each case, the best combination will depend not only on the available technological capabilities but also on the existing industrial base and supporting infrastructure. Singapore, for example, did not have many options because of its small size and initially very limited technological base. Korea has been able to develop its own brand names in automobiles and electronic equipment in large part because of the technical and financial capabilities of the *chaebols*, which have been able to take the risks involved and to join some large multinational competitors. Taiwan, China, has taken fewer risks mainly because its firms are smaller and more fragmented, but it has tended to focus more on exploiting a few specialty niches.

Protectionism in Industrial Countries

The successful NIEs made their biggest export drives in the 1960s and early 1970s, a period of rapidly expanding world trade. In the face of sluggish world economic growth, fiscal imbalances, and currency instability, protectionist pressures in industrial countries have increased, making today's world trading environment much less hospitable. Some influential businessmen and politicians have started to push for more restrictive trade regimes among countries at comparable stages of development—that is, with similar wage levels (Goldsmith 1994).

The more advanced developing economies are especially vulnerable to protectionist threats because of the weight of manufactures in their exports and the prominence of these exports in industrial country markets. The principal targets, however, are the economies with large trade surpluses. Korea and Taiwan, China, are already being subjected to increasing scrutiny and have had to raise their exchange rates with respect to the U.S. dollar, but similar pressures are being applied to other large exporters, including Brazil, China, and India. The biggest source of this pressure is the United States, which has a persistently large trade deficit.

Response to protectionist threats can take different forms. One is to further open up developing country markets to imports from industrial countries. An increasing number of developing countries have been doing precisely that, although perhaps not enough to defuse concerns about their export success in industrial countries.

Another response is to seek greater diversity in export markets. In this respect, again, the four East Asian Tigers have gone further than other developing countries. However, the process of diversifying markets is complicated by the fact that many exports are being produced by subsidiaries for their home parents or other affiliates, or under subcontracting agreements for large merchandisers, particularly those in the United States.

There has also been some movement of production to third countries with underutilized export quotas (where they are applied) and to countries whose export volumes are not high enough to trigger adverse reactions in the industrial world. These countries include Bangladesh, Indonesia, Morocco, the Philippines, Thailand, and various countries in Latin American and the Caribbean, where textile and garment production is carried out primarily for the U.S. market. Hong Kong's investment in Mauritius in the early 1980s was aimed at penetrating the European market. Some East Asian producers have started to invest in assembly or even production in the target countries. So far this investment has been primarily in North America, notably by Hyundai of Korea, which has an automobile plant in Canada, and Acer of Taiwan, China, which assembles computers in the United States.

In general, it seems likely that because of slow economic growth and rising protectionism in industrial countries, access to these countries' markets will be more constrained than before. Growth in world trade can therefore be expected to come increasingly from expanding markets in developing countries and transition economies. While most developing countries seem to be rather indifferent to this prospect, it is significant that producers in industrial countries have already started to position themselves to exploit the demand for material goods by what is being hailed as the large middle class that is emerging in the rapidly growing developing economies.

Technonationalism

Until the 1980s, suppliers of technology were more willing than they are now to transfer technology at relatively low prices. Because markets were less international, the sale of foreign technology tended to be seen more as an additional source of income than as a contribution to a potential competitor. In their initial stages of development, for example, Korea and Taiwan, China, were able to obtain much of their technology either by importing capital goods, subcontracting with foreign buyers, or arranging for licensing and technical assistance contracts (Westphal, Kim, and Dahlman 1985). However, many economies that for many years were not considered competitive threats have now matured into strong competitors, and industrial country firms are now more hesitant to grant licenses. Some studies, such as Mansfield, Romeo, and Wagner (1979), show that, other things being equal, MNCs prefer to supply technology to foreign markets by first exporting the products there, then setting up local subsidiaries, and then participating in local joint ventures. Only after exhausting all these possibilities do MNCs license technology to third parties.

A direct consequence of increasing globalization is that as technology becomes a key element of international competitiveness, more efforts are being made to privatize knowledge by placing greater emphasis on intellectual property protection, secrecy, and the exploitation of "first mover" advantage. No hard data on technology transfers are available, but there is some evidence that transfers to developing countries are slowing down. For example, technology payments from developing countries increased from about $1 billion a year in the early 1970s to $2.5 billion a year in 1981–1983. However, between 1985 and 1987, they remained below $2 billion annually (United Nations 1988). The economic downturn may be one reason for the slowdown in technology acquisition, but greater hesitancy on the part of technology producers to supply technology is certainly another.

In addition, foreign direct investment (which is one of the primary conduits for new technology transfer) to developing economies as a whole fell during the late 1980s, particularly in Latin America. This decline was due in large part to the economic stagnation and political uncertainty in many developing economies. Korea and Taiwan, China, have responded by liberalizing royalty and other restrictions on foreign technology purchases and foreign direct investment. They have also substantially raised their R&D expenditures (Korea had already been spending close to 3 percent of GDP on R&D). This type of response has several advantages. First, it helps to increase bargaining power in negotiating technology transfer agreements, as the success of the transfer of VCR technology to Korea shows. Japanese technology suppliers had been unwilling to license some elements of VCR technology until a Korean R&D institute undertook research in the relevant field. Faced with the prospect of losing royalties if these local efforts were successful, the Japanese producers agreed to a technology transfer.

Second, increased R&D helps in assimilating foreign technology, whether that technology is acquired through formal or informal transfers. There is evidence that local producers in some countries have had to demonstrate a high capacity for absorbing technology in order to be selected as joint venture partners. Further, developing local R&D capability has also become increasingly important as a way not only to break into areas in which it is hard to obtain technology from abroad but to participate in the strategic alliances that are emerging around technology sharing in some high-technology areas (Mody 1989b). So far, these strategic alliances have tended to be among firms in industrial economies that share a certain level of technological expertise. Alliances involving developing economies have been limited to arrangements between firms from industrialized economies able to provide R&D and design expertise and those from developing economies able to carry out sophisticated manufacturing processes at low cost. This kind of alliance has been common between firms from the United States and the NIEs, permitting the former to remain competitive in areas such as automobiles and electronics that were losing market share to Japanese firms. Developing country firms have benefited from the opportunity to acquire experience in manufacturing more sophisticated products.

Another strategy pursued by Korea and Taiwan, China, has been to invest in high-technology firms and research facilities in industrial economies, particularly the United States. Thus far such investments have been concentrated primarily in electronics firms, but there may well be future invest-ments in and acquisitions of biotechnology and "new materials" firms in the United States and Europe.

The Latin American NIEs have not yet faced problems as severe as those that have confronted the Asian NIEs in acquiring new technology. For one thing, the competitive threat from Latin American economies, which are still not large exporters, is not considered as serious as the threat from Korea and Taiwan, China. For another, a much larger share of Latin America's manufactured exports is produced by affiliates of foreign firms that are more or less included in global sourcing arrangements and thus pose little competitive threat to local firms. Latin America's immediate concern is to attract the foreign investments that have the greatest spillover and externality effects in order to foster economic development. But ultimately, these economies too must invest in developing their own technological capabilities and skill base in order to position themselves for competition in technologically more sophisticated industries.

8

Epilogue: The Role of Public Policy

Irfan ul Haque

"It matters little if the cat is white or black so long as it catches rats." Deng Xiaoping

Competing in the world market can be likened to participating in a world sporting event for which the participant must fulfill three basic conditions. First, there must be a desire to compete in the event, even though there may be little chance of winning. Second, the "rules of the game" must be understood and accepted, although in practice considerable ingenuity goes into bending them. And, finally, there must be a certain amount of preparation for the event. In this volume, the first condition has been taken for granted. The importance of international trade is now generally recognized, and virtually all countries today seek closer integration into the global economy. The second condition is discussed in chapter 7, where we note that the rules of the world trading "game" are currently in a state of flux. This uncertainty is not a reason for abandoning the world market but for participating more actively in the process of defining the rules.

The book's main concern, however, has been with the third condition: how countries can prepare themselves for world competition. Closed-door, inward-oriented policies do not work in the long run, and active participation in world commerce offers benefits that go beyond the static gains of exploiting the comparative advantage. Apart from the gains that accrue from specialization and economies of scale, perhaps the most significant benefit of competing in the world market is the stimulus it gives to the flow of ideas by creating new "wants" and exposing consumers and producers to new products and processes.

International competitiveness at its root concerns a nation's capacity to maintain and raise living standards while exploiting the opportunities offered by international trade. Productivity growth is at the heart of international competitiveness, for it represents improvements in efficiency and shows that the potential exists for living standards to rise. The basic premise of the preceding chapters has been that the ability to take advantage of the world market varies widely across countries but can be improved through private initiative and public policy. The central thesis can be summed up as follows:

- From the point of view of long-term income growth, it matters a great deal which sectors a country chooses to specialize in, since the absolute level of productivity and its potential for growth vary considerably across sectors and industries.

- Changes in the sectoral composition of output and improvements in plant- or industry-level productive efficiency require investment in new machinery and equipment as well as improvements in human capital (that is, the education and training of the work force). Existing productive capacity and worker skills can be viewed as representing a certain level of productive efficiency, but competing in the world market—where the benchmarks of efficiency are constantly being raised—requires conscious efforts at continually improving that efficiency. Countries must develop the capabilities needed to generate and manage technological change.

- Part of the process of structural change and technological improvement is autonomous and is facilitated and promoted by the market as investors seek out profitable opportunities. But this process may be too slow in relation to changes taking place elsewhere.

- A certain amount of technological learning and of improvement in skill levels is a natural byproduct of experience. But firms (and countries) vary remarkably in their ability to generate and manage technological change, and those that lag behind find not only that their living standards rise more slowly but that it is increasingly difficult to maintain a market position and sustain their earnings. There is a close association, at least in the long term, between economic dynamism and investment in plants and equipment, human capital, and technological capabilities.

- It would be an oversimplification, if not a mistake, to view the process of productivity growth and competitiveness as unidirectional. In fact, there seems to be a virtuous circle of trade, technology, and international competitiveness that is self-reinforcing and self-sustaining and that leads to economic growth. Breaking into this virtuous circle requires deliberate efforts on the part of both the government and the private sector.

- The principal agents of change are firms, and the general attitude and quality of their managers determine firm-level policies and strategies with regard to investment and worker training. However, the general economic environment and national institutions (notably financial institutions) often play a decisive role in determining the culture, responses, and attitudes of domestic firms. The state, therefore, plays a crucial role in designing incentives, policies, and institutions that facilitate and promote structural and technological change.

Two Questions of Policy

The preceding chapters have identified areas in which market mechanisms may fail, requiring some form of government intervention. However, government promotion of international competitiveness remains a matter of considerable debate, not least because there is ample evidence of misdirected policies and disastrous results. Basically, two distinct issues are involved. The first is the question of whether government promotion of industries (and firms) disturbs the "level playing field" of the world market and risks unleashing a series of retaliatory actions that will leave every country worse off in the end. The second asks whether public policy interventions can improve on free market outcomes in the first place.

Whether government interventions hurt the global economy depends basically on their nature and aim. In general, interventionist policies that help to expand markets and stimulate economic growth may not hurt other nations. These policies do not improve the economic performance of one country at the expense of another, although there may be political and other consequences in countries that are left behind. Thus, it seems implausible that policy interventions in the rapidly growing East Asian economies during the last several decades—to the extent that they have been instrumental in promoting exports and the rapid growth of domestic economies and incomes—have actually harmed the global economy. Indeed, it can be argued that their success has stimulated the world economy and been a source of technological dynamism. To put the matter differently, the world trading environment could be hurt by contractionary macroeconomic policies that depress demand, output, and employment, even though such policies might not directly interfere with the free flow of international trade.

In short, the context and aim of policy are what determine whether one country gains at the expense of another. However, in practice policy objectives are often unclear, and governments try to take advantage of each other. In designing the postwar multilateral trading system, the world's leading industrial nations played it safe and opted for the principle of free trade—a rule that is simple, clear, and relatively easy to enforce—even as significant departures from it were allowed.

Because complex practical and conceptual issues are involved, the second question has a less simple answer. The neoclassical approach to economic analysis, which relies on the rigorous deduction of conclusions from clearly specified assumptions, provides a framework for policy discussion. It highlights the conditions under which free markets, atomistic competition, and maximizing behavior on the part of consumers and producers yield Pareto optimal equilibrium outcomes, or situations in which no one can become better off without making someone else worse off. Guidance on economic policy is provided by what have been called the "basic theorems of welfare economics," which delineate the acceptable domains of state action (Stiglitz 1990). The message is that policy interventions, if required, should take the form that least disrupts the free functioning of the market and that leaves consumer and producer decisions on the margin unaffected as much as possible. Thus, lump-sum taxes are to be preferred over graduated taxes and proportional tariffs over quantitative controls.

These policy conclusions, however, rest basically on underlying stringent assumptions concerning producer and consumer behavior and the institutional basis of perfect competition that may not hold true in the real world. A great deal of attention has therefore been given to the "second-best" world, in which some of the specified conditions are not fulfilled, often resulting in market failure. In this case, the situation is such that either markets do not exist or, if they do, competitive behavior on the part of producers and consumers does not yield a Pareto optimal equilibrium (Ledyard 1987). When this happens, a case can be made for government intervention, although it is increasingly recognized that not all market failures call for government action and that interventions entail costs that must also be considered (Chang 1994). Nevertheless, views have tended to converge on the several sources of market failure—such as externalities, increasing returns to scale, uncertainty, and asymmetric information—and to agree on the need for some form of government intervention.

In general, the market is recognized as an efficient and potent source of information for economic decisionmaking; the costs of ignoring market signals, as the failure of central planning has demonstrated, can be enormous. The market also permits the exercise of individual freedom in a way that the dicates of a bureaucracy clearly do not. But defining the government's role solely in terms of market failure is not an entirely satisfactory approach. For one thing, income distribution across classes and generations is often a fundamental concern, one which the notion of Pareto optimality does not encompass. Market signals reflect the prevailing distribution of income, and these signals will be unsatisfactory if income distribution is unsatisfactory, including intergenerational income distribution—that is, if there is too little investment or if the natural wealth is being depleted in the absence of offsetting investment in real assets. Beyond such concerns, it is often the case, as social psychologists have demonstrated, that collaboration and cooperation among economic agents yield results that are socially and economically superior (Kohn 1986; Lane 1991). Thus, for example, if there is no danger of price fixing, collaboration among firms may reduce the costs of competitive advertising or save scarce resources in precompetitive generic research. More generally, issues of nation building, such as economic development, are better resolved collectively than by the market.

While there are costs associated with government intervention—for collecting information and administration, among other things—government failure is not the same as market failure (Haque 1994). Most sources of market failure are institutional, stemming from the workings of the market itself, and thus no competitive market situation can remedy them. But the causes of government failures tend to vary widely, and some governments are more efficient than others. Government failure can arise out of problems of information, administrative capability, transparency, accountability, or impartiality (Stern 1989). These aspects of governance differ a great deal among countries and over time. Governments in some of the East Asian countries have shown themselves to be more adept at intervening in economic life than, say, governments in Latin America or Africa. Some attribute the success of economic policy in East Asia to the "hardness" of the state, a rather vague concept that relates to a government's ability to govern (Briggs and Levy 1991). According to this argument, countries with a "soft" state must not try to emulate East Asian policies. However, "softness" is not absolute, for countries show widely differing governance capabilities. Sen (1990) observes, "Quite often what appears as softness is the responsiveness of the state to the public asserting itself and demonstrating that the state should take heed of the public's welfare. This need be no bad thing" (p. 425). It is important not to dismiss the government's efforts if they have been effective but to explore how the costs of government failure can be reduced and interventions made more efficient.

Finally, it seems rather restrictive to think only in terms of the government and the market when intermediate solutions exist for both market and government failures. The growth of cooperatives and, more recently, the rise of nongovernmental organizations (NGOs) are manifestations of imaginative ways of dealing with both types of failures. This area is underdeveloped and needs to be explored further from the viewpoint of fostering international competitiveness.

Domains of Public Policy

Three areas of public policy have been identified in this volume as key to achieving international competitiveness: macroeconomic management; technology promotion; and industrial policy. The focus on public policy does not imply that the private sector is passive and that its responses to policy can be taken for granted. Quite the contrary. The success of policy depends on the private sector's trust and confidence in the government and its policies. The question of the interaction between government and business is addressed in the next section.

Macroeconomic Management

Macroeconomic management is fundamentally the government's responsibility. Notwithstanding the debate on discretionary fiscal policy and the influence of monetarism in the 1980s, few would deny that macroeconomic policy is an important lever of state power and, at a minimum, needs to be conducted in a way that keeps inflation under control and protects the value of the currency. Policies must also maintain employment levels and create an environment conducive to private investment and rising living standards. But the appropriate components of macroeconomic policy are a matter of keen debate, especially when it comes to choosing between direct regulation and market-based solutions (for example, between trade policy and exchange rate adjustment). An issue that presents particular difficulty in the design of policy is the trade-off between inflation control and economic growth.

Our conclusion in chapter 3 was that while high inflation hampers economic expansion and productivity growth and should be avoided, at moderate rates (say, 10 percent or lower) its impact on growth is less clear. In recent years, macroeconomic policy in the industrial countries has been guided largely by the fear of inflation, even though unemployment levels in most countries have been at historically high levels and economic growth has been relatively modest. However, in countries (such as the transition economies) where output has actually fallen over the years, economic expansion and inflation control should in principle be compatible goals, since policies that tap existing unemployment and excess capacity may not be inflationary. Economic stability and growth are therefore not necessarily sequential goals of economic policy but can be mutually reinforcing; the one need not always precede the other. Fiscal deficits—often the principal source of economic instability—are easier to reduce and have less inflationary impact in an expanding economy than in a stagnant one.

Macroeconomic policy also affects investment, though the relationship is not straightforward. Private investment is sensitive to expectations about the future of an economy, so that a stable environment, including stable policies, is most conducive to investment. Sudden policy changes, however purposeful, often deter investors. General economic liberalization and deregulation may encourage private investment if the reforms are seen as credible, but often they are not, as the recent experience of a number of Latin American and African countries has shown. In such situations, much can be achieved by simply streamlining existing regulations; eliminating excessive, redundant, and conflicting controls on foreign trade and investment; and investing public funds in infrastructure that attracts and supports private investment.

Technology Policy

Chapter 4 explains why the common notion that technology can be bought and sold as an economic good is inaccurate, since market failures in this area are common. On the one hand, to the extent that knowledge cannot easily be appropriated (that is, if others can easily imitate a technological advance), private firms may be discouraged from investing resources in producing it—for example, through R&D. Patents, a form of state intervention, are intended to protect innovators' monopoly rents but are seldom completely effective. On the other hand, if patents are rigorously enforced or knowledge is somehow kept secret, too much may be spent on creating knowledge as firms compete for the position of "pioneer " in order to capture monopoly rents from an innovation. In other words, the market may cause either too much or too little investment in knowledge generation and thus fail to yield an efficient outcome. This does not mean that firms' efforts at R&D are necessarily wasted, since the process of knowledge accumulation is at the heart of the process of building up technological capabilities, which in turn positions a firm to take advantage of technological advances (Nelson 1981).

Further, the market in technology either may not exist or may be highly imperfect because knowledge is a "nonrival" good, or one that does not diminish with use (in fact, it is normally through sharing and use that knowledge is augmented). Thus, the more widely knowledge is shared, the greater is the social benefit. But new knowledge and thus new technologies will not be readily provided privately unless the returns are significantly more than the marginal cost of delivery, which is zero (or virtually so). Decentralized market-based decisions on how much and what types of R&D should be undertaken will therefore not yield an optimal outcome (Romer 1992).

A further complication is that knowledge is cumulative, and the way in which a new idea is exploited depends very much on the user's prior knowledge. Even though engineering blueprints are easily transferred, for instance, the proficiency with which they are used can vary enormously, despite the availability of necessary engineering skills. And, as chapter 4 stressed, in practice the distinction between innovation and diffusion is not sharp; the notion of "best practice" is ambiguous because of the need to adapt and develop technologies locally, something that requires the capability to innovate. In the face of rapid technological change, however, producers that lag behind technologically will find it virtually impossible to catch up if all they do is imitate the practices of the industrial leaders. For one thing, perfect imitation is virtually impossible. More importantly, by the time current technologies have been imitated, the "technological frontier" will have shifted and other, improved technologies will be in use. Under these conditions, the optimal strategy for a producer may not be to adopt currently known techniques or practices but to anticipate future trends. For example, it may not be economically sound for developing countries to imitate or borrow existing techniques that impose high environmental costs when the trend is toward environmentally friendly technologies. Choosing the appropriate strategy is by its nature a rather uncertain (albeit creative) process that involves adapting existing technological knowledge and developing new approaches. It is in this context of generating and managing change that technological capabilities are seen as essential to a producer's ability to compete.

Governments can influence technological development through three primary channels: general education (codified knowledge), training to upgrade skills, and the building up of technological capabilities. There is relatively little disagreement about the appropriate role for government in promoting education, which is accepted as a public good with externalities. Governments may also determine the orientation of education—that is, its availability at different levels and in certain disciplines, although market trends cannot be entirely disregarded. To some extent, the same is also true of skills training. Firms themselves benefit directly from a better-trained work force but, out of ignorance or the fear that workers will move to other jobs (a case of nonappropriability), tend to underestimate the value of training and thus to underspend on it. While formal education and training are extremely important in the East Asian NIEs, for instance, the firms themselves have always been the primary source of technological accumulation. If these economies are any indication, a case can be made for government intervention when the market fails to provide sufficient worker training. Germany, Japan, and the East Asian NIEs have all used incentives such as tax rebates and subsidies to increase firms' willingness to provide worker training. They have also established public institutions to provide additional training.

But an educated and skilled labor force does not by itself ensure that firms will be responsive and successful in a changeable, competitive world market. The third component of a technology strategy must therefore involve building up the capabilities to generate and manage technical change that are crucial to the catching-up process. Opening up an economy to world competition can spur improvements in productive efficiency, but these improvements are seldom, if ever, enough. Beyond the measures and approaches that firms may adopt, there are several important actions governments can take to encourage the development of technological capabilities. First, to the extent that such capabilities depend on the nature and depth of industrial development, defining the direction of domestic industrial development can help guide firms in developing their own strategies. The catch-up process, which involves considerable innovation, cannot be left entirely to the market to work out, especially in developing countries, where there are serious problems in acquiring and disseminating information and firms generally lack the necessary capabilities. Second, governments can help firms learn about technological changes occurring in the outside world through information exchange. Third, by defining the rules and regulations governing direct foreign investment, governments can facilitate technology transfers. Many countries view technology transfers and technology creation as substitutable processes, with the consequence that countries tend to have been either altogether closed to technology imports or too dependent on them. The fact is that the two are complementary: the benefits a country can derive from an imported technology depend on the ability of local firms to exploit it. For example, Singapore relied heavily on technology imports but also invested significantly in the development of domestic skills and capabilities.

Industrial Policy

Industrial policy is a highly controversial tool, for it runs counter to some of the fundamental precepts of mainstream economics. The issue is not one of policy as such—for there is hardly a country where industrial development is not fostered and regulated—but of treating industrial development as a strategically important goal that warrants the attention of government policies and institutions (Singh 1991). The case for industrial policy rests basically on the perceived importance of industry to the economy and the failure of competitive markets, in certain situations, to stimulate industrial growth. Both of these premises have been questioned, even though it is generally accepted that manufacturing is important to economic prosperity because of its relatively high productivity, growth potential, and linkages with other sectors.

The main criticism of industrial policy is directed at the practice of choosing and promoting specific industries, or "picking winners," which some argue interferes with a country's comparative advantage. According to this line of reasoning, the government is driven by diverse objectives and does not have the competence or relevant knowledge to make rational economic decisions regarding the selection of industries. This mistrust is backed up by ample evidence of the failure of such efforts. However, as explained in chapter 5, the key factor is the level of industrial selection: it is one thing to choose a direction for industrial development and quite another to promote individual plants or product lines, as some industrial policy measures have tried to do. The thrust of industrial policy in East Asia, outside of public sector industrial projects, has generally been to promote the development of what are held to be key industries. These industries are important from the viewpoint of both learning and productivity growth and have offered significant spin-off benefits through interindustry linkages (defined in terms of the "density" of input-output relations) (Wade 1994). While the process of choosing an industrial direction is complex, it is somewhat easier for the late industrializing countries because they can draw on the experience of the more advanced economies. Thus, Japanese policymakers, relying on the experience of more advanced countries, paid special attention to such indicators as the income elasticity of demand, the scope for learning, and the potential for productivity growth in choosing industries for promotion (Scott 1985).

Another consideration is the process by which industrial policy is formulated and industries are identified for promotion. There is little question that bureaucrats—however competent and well-intentioned—are not ideally placed to select target industries. Since industrial development is a national issue that concerns many economic sectors and players, formulating industrial policy needs to be a participatory process involving businesses, consumers, labor unions, academics, and other social and political groups. The government can then take advantage of the knowledge of these diverse groups and address their respective concerns. This approach is less likely to result in the egregious mistakes of other approaches to formulating industrial policy, such as central planning, under which decisions are typically made by individuals who are more or less detached from the business world. In East Asia, approaches to policy design varied across countries, with the Japanese approach being the most participatory, but industrial policy was rarely, if ever, devised by bureaucrats working in isolation.

Finally, as stressed in chapter 5, winners are not chosen but made. This point can be clarified using the earlier analogy of a team preparing for a sporting event. The selection of good players is obviously important, but success depends largely on the effort the team puts into training. It is not unusual for an apparently weak team to end up being the winner by dint of better training and organization. There was not a great deal of difference among developing countries regarding the choice of industries for promotion, but there were vast differences in the success these countries had in competing in the world market. The problem was not the choice of industries, even though protection was often targeted at activities that were unsuitable, given national factor endowments. The success of the NIEs in creating competitive advantage points to a more important reason. Governments in the less successful industrializing countries tended to view protection alone as sufficient to promote their industries, disregarding the need both to create an enabling environment that provided essential industrial inputs and physical infrastructure and to develop appropriate capabilities for learning and adapting new technologies. Thus, the fact that a number of countries tried unsuccessfully to develop textile or garment industries while others succeeded does not necessarily reflect poor industrial choices; rather, it indicates a lack of attention to the supportive factors that determine competitiveness in the world market.[1]

Any attempt at industrial promotion by definition implies a change in incentives in favor of industries that otherwise would not be created or, if they already exist, would not survive in the free market. In this sense, industrial policy interferes with a country's existing comparative advantage, inasmuch as it promotes import substitution and discourages exports. The point is often made that the successful industrializing countries (that is, the East Asian NIEs) have adopted export- or outward-oriented industrial strategies, whereas the countries that have failed or that lag behind in industrial development have been characterized by import substitution or inward orientation (for instance, India and some Latin American economies). However, apart from the conceptual and practical problems of distinguishing between the two strategies when factors of production, broadly defined, are not only being accumulated but undergoing qualitative change, the East Asian experience suggests that import substitution and export promotion can complement each other (Amsden 1989; Wade 1990; World Bank 1993a).

There is, however, no question that the successful industrializing countries have been singularly aggressive in promoting exports, although it is unlikely that this is the sole significant explanation of their success (Rodrik 1994). As well as enjoying the benefits of exporting that have already been noted, export-promoting countries appear to have been better able to cope with balance of payments constraints and have therefore been in a relatively good position to sustain economic growth. Import substitution—even when efficient—by definition has limits, since only a certain proportion of imports can be domestically substituted. The expectation that replacing imports with domestically produced goods can solve the balance of payments problem has seldom, if ever, been realized. Another factor that has restrained economic growth in some countries (notably India, Pakistan, and many African economies) is that import substitution has been made to serve two distinct objectives: to promote industry, and to curtail imports in order to protect the balance of payments. Consequently, in the face of foreign exchange stringency—and it has been more or less perennial in the countries noted—the second objective has tended to take precedence, cur-

---

1. It is rather ironic that the proponents of both free trade and protection are inclined to view trade policy alone as an adequate explanation for the success or failure of industrial development.

tailing imports (often including essential inputs) and frustrating efforts to achieve the first objective.

The need for industrial policy to overcome various market failures has been discussed at length in chapter 5. In particular, we have stressed that a country's ability to compete depends on such factors as accumulated skills and knowledge and that firms in developing and transition economies are therefore at a distinct disadvantage vis-à-vis industrial country firms. The traditional view in the development literature has been that infant industries in developing countries need only time and experience to mature into competitive firms; according to this view, protection ensures that fledgling industries have that support. This has been found to be only partially true: industrial policy is also needed to foster and develop the capabilities to create and manage change.

There are other reasons why industrial policy may be required, especially in developing countries. First, the world market is not characterized by atomistic competition (that is, a competitive environment in which firms are so small and so numerous that no single firm can influence the market). Developing country firms are generally much smaller than those in industrial countries, whose size offers certain advantages (such as easy access to capital) and allows for the spread of lumpy fixed costs (such as advertising and R&D) over a much larger output. Large firms can also reduce various transaction costs by bargaining or internalizing them.[2] Thus, a case can be made for promoting and nurturing developing country firms in order to give them a chance to compete in the world market. Protection is not the only means of achieving this objective; partnerships and other alliances with industrial country firms have often been important.

Second, in order for developing country producers to compete in the world market on more or less equal terms, production conditions must not differ widely from those of competitors. Developing country firms need access to imported inputs at international prices and require adequate physical infrastructure. Such factors are important to all industries but matter particularly to export-oriented firms.

Finally, a case for industrial policy can be made on the grounds that such a policy is necessary to ensure adequate investment in the domestic economy in an environment where capital moves relatively freely but labor does not. As we saw in chapter 7, this concern is particularly prominent in those

---

2. The relationship between firm size and the ability to compete is actually rather complex. In many industries, firms of different sizes coexist and successfully compete with each other.

countries where wages have risen, thanks to the success of past development, and is also an important political issue today in the industrial countries. Investors have little incentive to invest in raising productivity in industries that can move relatively easily to lower-wage countries. There may be a case for some restraints on purely speculative capital flows—as some have argued—but such restraints are difficult to impose. The alternative is for governments either to assume a bigger role in domestic investment or to ensure that investing domestically remains a sufficiently attractive activity. In the second case, there are two choices: either to reduce wages (generally through devaluation) or to raise productivity growth by improving production processes. From the viewpoint of raising living standards, the second alternative is clearly the more attractive.

If the government accepts the principle of selectively promoting industry, it must then decide what criteria should guide its choice. Our view is that choosing an industry is rather like choosing a profession after high school. Inherited abilities (factor endowments) and personal interests (national aspirations) must be considered, and market trends in both cases must be evaluated, for it is safer from the point of view of future earnings to opt for a career (industry) for which demand is increasing. But whether the selected profession or industry pays off depends ultimately on hard work, perseverance in the chosen field, and ingenuity in securing a market niche.

Clearly it is much more difficult for a government to decide the future direction of a country than for a young person to choose a career. We believe that three considerations can serve as useful guides in identifying industries for promotion: income elasticity of demand, industrial linkages, and the potential for productivity growth. The importance of market trends cannot be overemphasized, and income elasticity of demand provides a practical criterion that is relatively easy to measure. The existence of externalities, which cause one industry to spawn or help another, also provides a strong case for government intervention.

The potential for productivity growth is the key factor in the choice, however. For late industrializers, the important thing is not the pace at which "frontier" technologies are improving (a consideration that evidently guided the Japanese in their choice), but a country's ability to catch up and establish a market niche for itself in the selected sectors. Catching up involves considerable innovation in terms of product features and production processes, but it also means that a country must be realistic in its choice of industries. In general, a country should not opt for industries in which it cannot catch up within a reasonable time frame—that is, industries in which the productivity differential between the country and the world leader is enormous and the required inputs are not easily available. (However, it is worth remembering that the East Asian economies have promoted several sophisticated industries, notably electronics, television, and semiconductors; these choices have entailed dramatically redefining comparative advantage in the countries involved.) At the same time, the targeted industries should also demonstrate reasonable productivity potential, so that the technological possibilities are not quickly exhausted and the scope for further improvements constrained by world technological trends.

Policies to promote selected industries must be accompanied by rigorous performance standards that are defined basically in terms of the chosen sectors' ability to compete in the world market. Enforcing such standards requires some system of rewards and penalties, as the experience of the East Asian NIEs has shown. Performance standards are essential not just to ensure that firms make the needed efforts to improve their productive efficiency but also to keep the choice of industries realistic, for industrial policies to support "winners" can be justified only if the selected industries cease to need special treatment within a reasonable time.

The Interaction between Business and Government

Any discussion of public policy is not complete without some consideration of the impact on and responses from the agents (notably business firms) that are the targets of policy interventions. Business firms are key players in the domestic economy, and their success in the world market reflects a country's overall competitive strength. Among the factors determining business performance, we have noted those that are essential: investment in physical and human capital; the development of capabilities to generate and manage technological change; and adept, flexible, and responsive management. To these could be added a culture within firms that encourages a long-term view of profit possibilities. Although these are all basically firm-level factors, business strategies and approaches are also influenced by the general economic and financial environment (defined in terms of government policies and institutions) in which firms operate. Some environments tend to be more conducive to the emergence of dynamic and progressive firms than others, as shown by the differences across countries in overall business performance. The incentives (or the system of rewards and penalties) firms face are obviously important in determining responses, but there are two other issues that need to be considered: the government's perceived role in economic life and its ability to direct the economy and get the desired results.

This last depends to a large extent on how businesses and government interact in formulating and implementing national policies.

The existence of a broad agreement within a country on the appropriate role of government matters more than the degree to which the government intrudes into economic life. For one thing, major economic reforms are virtually impossible in countries where the government's role in regulating economic rules, redistributing national wealth, and investing in productive assets remains in doubt. A striking example of the correlation between economic reforms and uncertainty about the government's role is the contrast between the transition experiences of China, which for the present seems to have more or less resolved the role issue, and most of the countries of the former Soviet Union, which are still struggling with it. Private investors are generally put off more by instability in economic rules and regulations than by the regulations themselves. Private foreign investors are evidently more willing to invest in China or Viet Nam, despite the state's continuing dominance, than (say) in Pakistan or Nigeria, which are comparatively lightly regulated but highly unstable.

Even among industrial countries, however, the role of government and relations between businesses and the state vary widely. In fact, the end of the Cold War, by virtually eliminating the communist alternative, has made such differences far more prominent (Ostry 1990). In particular, the differences between the U.S. and the Japanese systems have excited enormous interest because of Japan's remarkable postwar economic performance and the recent successes of the other East Asian NIEs, some of which have closely emulated the Japanese model. There has also been much discussion of the European "social market economy" model, but mainly from the viewpoint of providing social welfare.

The differences among the market systems tend to lie not so much in the extent as in the nature of government involvement in the economy and in relations between government and business. The share of the Japanese Government in the national economy (as measured by public expenditures) does not differ greatly from government shares in other industrial countries, but there are significant differences in the way Japan uses its levers of power, in particular in its approach to economic policy and its relationship with the private sector. The government's influence on the country's industrial development, which has already been mentioned, has been profound. Despite the considerable use of coercion—which took the form of both incentives and penalties—to make the private sector carry out national plans, the Japanese Government is generally regarded as probusiness. At the same time, businesses are viewed not just as economic agents but as social organisms and are generally expected to make substantial contributions to social welfare, including offering lifetime employment, health care benefits, and worker training. There is considerable corruption, but the responsibility of businesses to society is heavily stressed. Thus, such matters as industrial layoffs or firm takeovers are seen not as purely commercial decisions but as developments with significant social impact.

The situation in the United States (and in some other countries that have adopted similar approaches) is quite different. Individualism is greatly cherished, and there is considerable hesitancy to allow the government to become involved in the promotion of the productive sectors, even though the government has played a highly successful role in the development of agriculture and continues to protect domestic industrial interests in international trade relations. Businesses can hire or fire workers, regardless of the social consequences, and, thanks to the New Deal and the Great Society, the government so far has been the principal guardian of social welfare. In short, the government is responsible for protecting consumer interests and providing economic security to its citizens, but as far as industry is concerned, the best policy is held to be minimal government regulation and interference (Scott 1985). On the whole, government in the United States is cast as an adversary or a nuisance, and "getting the government off the people's backs" has become a popular political demand.[3] Still, the United States is an example of outstanding economic success, especially from the point of view of long-term economic development, and has shown remarkable adaptability and resilience in the face of adversity. The recent industrial turnaround, notably in the automobile industry, is testimony to that.

Each market system has its strengths and weaknesses, and none can claim to be universally applicable or to represent the perfect model for attaining the fundamental goals of economic growth, equity, and freedom to which most nations aspire. Nevertheless, the economic success of the East Asian NIEs offers encouragement to and can provide lessons for other developing countries and the transition economies. As Felix Rohatyn observes in his foreword to Albert (1993): "The arguments about the most effective forms of capitalism are much more than interesting theological

---

3. The literature comparing the Japanese and American systems is large and growing (see Scott 1985; Ostry 1990; Albert 1993). A reevaluation is going on, in light of more recent experiences, as the economic performance of the United States has improved, while the Japanese economy has suffered a series of setbacks. The U.S. Government has in recent years become much more vocal about protecting its business interests in international trade negotiations.

arguments. They are completely relevant to the present efforts of the Eastern European as well as the former Soviet Republics to make the transition from communist systems to market systems and democracy" (p. xv).

In the end, what matters is how well a system is adapted and responds to a country's circumstances and the government's ability to aggregate national aspirations and turn them into a national economic agenda. Among the conditions that enabled the East Asian NIEs to succeed, perhaps the most important were a measure of domestic political stability (albeit often forced rather than spontaneous), equitable income distribution, and the ability to mobilize national resources against an external economic or military threat. Why have other developing countries not fared as well? The key difference probably lies in the so-called developmental state that prevails in many of the successful East Asian NIEs. The governments of the East Asian NIEs not only see economic development as key to national economic survival but work together with the private sector toward that goal.

Making the private sector responsive to national needs and ensuring that it contributes to economic development has become particularly important as capital mobility increases, exerting a growing influence on national economic management, even in the industrial countries. The matter is also important to developing countries that are liberalizing their capital accounts, as recent events in Mexico have demonstrated. Once again, the East Asian experience provides a sharp contrast to Latin America. Capital flight (both in and out) has been a perennial feature in the latter, but—whether because of good policies, better regulation, or just coercion—no significant examples of capital flight can be found among the East Asian NIEs, despite occasional lapses in macroeconomic management.

Governments obviously need to pay attention to business interests in devising policies and institutions and to establish consultative mechanisms to mobilize the private sector's support. A great deal of attention in recent years has been given to improving the business environment and eliminating labor market rigidities so that businesses can reduce wages and lay off workers as conditions dictate. But something more is needed. The domestic private sector also needs to make a commitment to national development. Regulation and incentives that encourage domestic investment can help, but ultimately there must be a general sense of social or national responsibility. This sense of responsibility gives rise to a "virtuous circle" within which harmony among businesses, labor, and other social groups and the ability to govern feed on each other. This convergence of interests is easier to realize in conditions of economic growth than of economic decline. Clearly, nothing succeeds like success.

References

Albert, Michel. 1993. *Capitalism vs. Capitalism*. New York: Four Walls Eight Windows.

Amsalem, Michael A. 1983. *Technology Choice in Developing Countries: The Textile and Pulp and Paper Industries*. Cambridge, Mass: The MIT Press.

Amsden, Alice. 1989. *Asia's Next Giant: South Korea and Late Industrialization*. New York: Oxford University Press.

_____. 1994. "Why Isn't the Whole World Experimenting with the East Asian Model to Develop? A Review of the East Asian Miracle." *World Development* 22(4): 627–34.

Arrow, Kenneth. 1962. "Economic Welfare and the Allocation of Resources for Innovation." In *The Rate and Direction of Innovative Activity*, ed. Richard R. Nelson. Princeton, N.J.: Princeton University Press.

Asian Wall Street Journal. 1994. Special Advertising Supplement on Korea, April 25, p. 12.

Atkinson, Anthony B., and Joseph E. Stiglitz. 1969. "A New View of Technological Change." *Economic Journal* 79: 573–78.

Barro, Robert J. 1991. "Economic Growth in a Cross Section of Countries." *Quarterly Journal of Economics* 106 (May): 407–43.

Baumol, William J., Sue Anne Blackman, and Edward N. Wolff. 1989. *Productivity and American Leadership: The Long View*. Cambridge, Mass.: MIT Press.

Bell, Martin, and Geoffrey Oldham. 1988. "Oil Companies and the Implementation of Technical Change in Offshore Operations: Experience in Development Drilling and the Design and Operation of Production Facilities in the North Sea." SPRU Mimeo Report. Science Policy Research Unit, University of Sussex.

Bhagwati, Jagdish N. 1988. *Protectionism*. Cambridge, Mass.: MIT Press.

_____. 1989. "Is Free Trade Passé After All?" *Weltwirtschaftliches Archiv* 125: 17–44.

_____. 1991. *The World Trading System at Risk*. Princeton, N.J.: Princeton University Press.

Blecker, Robert A. 1992. *Beyond the Twin Deficits: A Trade Strategy for the 1990s.* New York: M.E. Sharpe, Inc.

Blinder, Alan S. 1990. "There Are Capitalists, Then There Are the Japanese." *Business Week* (October 8), p. 21.

Blomström, Maagnus, Robert E. Lipsey, and Mario Zejan. 1993. "Is Fixed Investment the Key to Economic Growth?" NBER Working Paper 4436. Cambridge, Mass.: National Bureau of Economic Research.

Bloom, M. 1992. *Technological Change in the Korean Electronics Industry.* Paris: OECD Development Center.

Braga, Carlos A. 1994. "The New Regionalism and Its Consequences." International Economics Department. Washington, D.C.: World Bank. Mimeo.

Briggs, Tyler, and Brian Levy. 1991. "Strategic Interventions and the Political Economy of Industrial Policy in Developing Countries." In *Reforming Economic Systems in Developing Countries*, ed. Dwight H. Perkins and Michael Roemer. Harvard Studies in International Development. Cambridge, Mass.: Harvard University Press.

Cainarca, Gian Carlo, Massimo G. Colombo, and Sergio Mariotti. 1992. "Agreements Between Firms and the Technological Life Cycle Model: Evidence from Information Technologies." *Research Policy* 21: 45–62.

Castells, Manuel, and Laura D'Andrea Tyson. 1988. "High-Technology Choices Ahead: Restructuring Interdependence." In *Growth, Exports, and Jobs in a Changing World Economy*, ed. John W. Sewell and Stuart K. Tucker. U.S. Third World Perspectives 9. New Brunswick, N.J., and London: Transaction Books for the Overseas Development Council.

Chang, Ha-Joon. 1994. *The Political Economy of Industrial Policy.* London: Macmillan.

Chesnais, Francois. 1988. "Technical Co-operation Agreements Between Firms." *STI Review 4.*

Chenery, H. B., S. Robinson, and M. Syrquin. 1986. *Industrialization and Growth: A Comparative Study.* New York: Oxford University Press.

Chhibber, Ajay, Mansoor Dailami, and Nemat Shafik, eds. 1992. *Reviving Private Investment in Developing Countries.* Amsterdam: North Holland.

Choi, Y. 1993. "Evolutionary Concurrent Techno-Capability of Mass System." Ph.D. Diss. Roskilde University Center, Denmark.

Cohen, W. M., and D. A. Levinthal. 1989. "Innovation and Learning: The Two Faces of R&D." *Economic Journal* 99(4): 569–96.

Commission on Industrial Competitiveness. 1985. *Report of the President's Committee on Industrial Competitiveness.* Washington, D.C.: Government Printing Office.

Corden, Max W. 1990. "Macroeconomic Policy and Growth: Some Lessons of Experience." In *Proceedings of the World Bank Annual Conference on Development Economics*, ed. Stanley Fischer, Dennis de Tray, and Shekhar Shah. Washington, D.C.: World Bank.

Dahlman, Carl J., and Fernando Fonseca. 1987. "From Technological Dependence to Technological Development: The Case of the USIMINAS Steel Plant in Brazil." In *Technology Generation in Latin American Manufacturing Industries*, ed. Jorge Katz. London: Macmillan Press.

Dahlman, Carl J., Bruce Ross-Larson, and Larry E. Westphal. 1987. "Managing Technological Development: Lessons from Newly Industrializing Countries." *World Development* 15(6): 759–75.

David, Paul. 1975. *Technical Choice, Innovation and Economic Growth*. Cambridge,U.K.: Cambridge University Press.

Deiaco, Enrico. 1992. "New Views on Innovative Activity and Technological Performance: The Swedish Innovation Survey." *STI Review* 11 (December).

De Long, Bradford, and Lawrence Summers. 1993. "How Robust is the Growth-Machinery Nexus?" Paper submitted at the conference "How Do National Policies Affect Long-Run Growth?" World Bank, Washington, D.C.

De Melto, Dennis, Kathryn McMullen, and Russel Wills. 1980. "Innovation and Technological Change in Five Canadian Industries." Discussion Paper 176. Ottawa: Economic Council of Canada.

Dertouzos, Michael L., Richard K. Lester, and Robert M. Solow. 1989. *Made in America: Regaining the Productivity Edge*. Cambridge, Mass.: MIT Press.

Dollar, David, and Kenneth Sokoloff. 1990. "Patterns of Productivity Growth in South Korean Manufacturing Industries, 1963–79." *Journal of Development Economics* 33(2): 309–27.

Dornbusch, Rüdiger. 1990. "Policies to Move from Stabilization to Growth." In *Proceedings of the World Bank Annual Conference on Development Economics*, ed. Stanley Fischer, Dennis de Tray, and Shekhar Shah. Washington, D.C.: World Bank.

_____. 1992. "The Case for Trade Liberalization in Developing Countries." *Journal of Economic Perspectives* 6(1): 69–85.

Dornbusch, Rüdiger, and Stanley Fischer. 1993. "Moderate Inflation." *World Bank Economic Review* 7(1): 1–46.

Dosi, Giovanni, Silvia Fabiani, and Christopher Freeman. 1993. "On the Process of Economic Development." Department of Economics, University of Rome. Mimeo.

Dosi, Giovanni, Keith Pavitt, and Luc Soete. 1990. *The Economics of Technical Change and International Trade*. London: Harvester Wheatsheaf.

Easterly, William, and K. Schmidt-Hebbel. 1993. "Fiscal Deficits and Macroeconomic Performance in Developing Countries." *World Bank Research Observer* 8(2): 211–37.

Easterly, William, Michael Kremer, Lant Pritchett, and Lawrence Summers. 1993. "Good Policy or Good Luck? Country Growth Performance and Temporary Shocks." NBER Working Paper 4474. Cambridge, Mass.: National Bureau of Economic Research.

Enos, John, and Woo-Hee Park. 1988. *The Adoption and Diffusion of Imported Technology: The Case of Korea*. London: Croom Helm.

Ernst, Dieter, and David O'Connor. 1992. *Competing in the Electronics Industry: The Experience of Newly Industrializing Economies*. Paris: OECD.

Fagerberg, Jan. 1988. "Why Growth Rates Differ." In *Technical Change and Economic Theory*, ed. Giovanni Dosi, Christopher Freeman, Richard R. Nelson, Gerry Silverberg, and Luc Soete for the Maastricht Economic Research Institute on Innovation and Technology. London and New York: Frances Pinter, Ltd.; distributed by Columbia University Press.

Farrell, Trevor. 1979. "A Tale of Two issues: Nationalization, the Transfer of Technology and the Petroleum Multinationals in Trinidad and Tobago." *Social and Economic Studies* 28(1): 234–81.

Financial Times. 1993. "Survey of Hong Kong." May 4, p. 6.

Finger, J. Michael, ed. 1993. *Antidumping, How it Works and Who Gets Hurt*. Ann Arbor, Michigan: The University of Michigan Press.

Fischer, Stanley. 1993. "The Role of Macroeconomic Factors in Growth." *Journal of Monetary Economics* 32(3): 485–512.

Fishlow, Albert, Catherine Gwin, Stephen Haggard, Dani Rodrik, and Robert Wade. 1994. *Miracle or Design: Lessons from the East Asia Experience*. Washington, D.C.: Overseas Development Council.

Freeman, Christopher. 1991. "Catching Up in World Growth and World Trade." In *Economic Crisis in Developing Countries: Policies for Recovery and Development*, ed. Machiko Nissanke. London: Frances Pinter, Ltd.

Freeman, Christopher, John Clark, and Luc Soete. 1987. *Unemployment and Technical Innovation: A Study of Long Waves and Economic Development*. London: Frances Pinter, Ltd.

Ffrench-Davis, Richard, and Oscar Muñoz. 1991. "Economic Development, Instability and Political Disequilibria in Chile: 1950–89." In *Towards a New Development Strategy for Latin America: Pathways from Hirschman's Thought*, ed. Simon Teitel. Baltimore: Johns Hopkins Press.

Fukasaku, Yukiko. 1986. "Technology Imports and R&D at Mitsubishi Nagasaki Shipyard in the Pre-War Period." *Bonner Zeitschrift für Japanologie* 8: 77–90.

Gerstenfeld, Arthur, and Lawrence Wortzel. 1977. "Strategies for Innovation in Developing Countries." *Sloan Managerial Review* 19(1): 57–68.

Girvan, Norman, and Gillian Marcelle. 1990. "Overcoming Technological Dependency: The Case of Electric Arc (Jamaica) Ltd., a Small Firm in a Small Developing Country." *World Development* 18(1): 91–107.

Goldsmith, John. 1994. *The Trap*. New York: Carrol and Graf.

Grossman, Gene M., and Elhanan Helpman. 1991. *Innovation and Growth*. Cambridge, Mass.: MIT Press.

Hagedorn, John, and Jos Schakenraad. 1992. "Leading Companies and Networks of Strategic Alliances in Information Technologies." *Research Policy* 21: 163–90.

Hanna, Nagy. 1991. "Informatics and the Developing Countries." *Finance and Development* 28(4): 45–47.

Haque, Irfan ul. 1994. "International Competitiveness: the State and the Market." In *The State, Market and Development: Beyond the Neoclassical Dichotany*, ed. Amitava K. Dutt, Kwan S. Kim, and Ajit Singh. Aldershot, U.K.: Edward Edgar.

Hatsopoulos, George N., Paul R. Krugman, and Lawrence Summers. 1988. "U.S. Competitiveness: Beyond the Trade Deficit." *Science* 24(15): 299–307.

Havrylyshyn, Oli. 1990. "Trade Policy and Productivity Gains in Developing Countries: A Survey of the Literature." *World Bank Research Observer* 5(1): 1–24.

Hobday, Michael G. 1994a. "Technological Learning in Singapore: A Test Case of Leapfrogging." *Journal of Development Studies* 30(4): 831–58.

_____. 1994b. "Export-led Technology Development in the Four Dragons: the Case of Electronics." *Development and Change* 25(2): 333–61.

Hobday, Michael G., and Yasunori Baba. 1990. "ISDN in Thailand: Developing Country Strategies in Digital Telecommunications." *Information Technology for Development* 5(1): 1–21.

Hoffman, Kurt. 1989. "Technological Advance and Organizational Innovation in the Engineering Industries." Industry and Energy Department Working Papers, Industry Series Paper 4. Washington, D.C.: World Bank.

Hoffman, Kurt, and Howard Rush. 1982. "Microelectronics and the Garment Industry: Not Yet a Perfect Fit." In *IDS Sussex Bulletin Special Issue* 13(2): *Comparative Advantage in an Automating World*, ed. Raphael Kaplinsky.

Hollander, Samuel. 1965. *The Sources of Increased Efficiency: A Study of DuPont Rayon Plants*. Cambridge, Mass.: MIT Press.

Hou, Chi-Ming, and S. Gee. 1993. "National Systems Supporting Technical Advance in Industry: Taiwan." In *National Innovation Systems: A Comparative Analysis*, ed. Richard R. Nelson. Oxford: Oxford University Press.

Hsing, Mo-huan. 1992. "On the Measurement of Aggregate Production Functions." *Cambridge Journal of Economics* 16(4): 463–74.

Imai, Masaaki. 1986. *Kaizan: The Key to Japan's Competitive Success*. New York: McGraw-Hill.

Jacobsson, Staffan. 1993. "The Length of the Infant Industry Period: Evidence from the Engineering Industry in South Korea." *World Development* 21(3): 407–20.

Kaldor, Nicholas. 1967. *Causes of the Slow Rate of Economic Growth of the United Kingdom*. Cambridge, U.K.: Cambridge University Press.

Kaplinsky, Raphael, and Kurt Hoffman. 1988. *Driving Force: The Global Restructuring of Technology, Labor, and Investment in the Automobile and Components Industry*. Boulder, Colo.: Westrien Press.

Katz, Jorge M., and Nestor Bercovich. 1993. "National Systems of Innovation Supporting Technical Advance in Industry: The Case of Argentina." In Nelson, *National Innovation Systems*.

Kim, I., and C. Kim. 1991. "Comparison of Korean to Western R&D: Project Selection Factors for New Product Development." Department of Industrial Project Management, Science and Technology Policy Institute, KAIST, Seoul, Korea.

Kim, L., and Y. Kim. 1985. "Innovation in a Newly Industrializing Country: A Multiple Discriminant Analysis." *Management Science* 13:312–22.

Kim, Linsu. 1980. "Stages of Development of Industrial Technology in a Developing Country: A Model." *Research Policy* 9: 254–77.

_____. 1993. "National Systems of Industrial Innovation: Dynamics of Capability Building in Korea." In Nelson, *National Innovation Systems*.

Kim, Young Woo. 1994. "Industrialization and Human Resource Development: Korea's Experiences." Paper prepared for the ASCA Seminar on Science and Technology and Regional Innovation, Science and Technology Policy Institute, Seoul, Korea.

Kleinknecht, Alfred, and Jeroen O.N. Reijnen. 1992. "Why Do Firms Cooperate on R&D? An Empirical Study." *Research Policy* 21: 347–60.

Kohn, Alfie. 1986. *No Contest: The Case Against Competition*. New York: Houghton Mifflin.

Krause, L. B. 1988. "Hong Kong and Singapore: Twins or Kissing Cousins?" *Economic Development and Cultural Change* 36(3): 45–66.

Krugman, Paul R., ed. 1986. *Strategic Trade Policy and the New International Economics*. Cambridge, Mass.: MIT Press.

_____. 1987. "Is Free Trade Passé?" *Journal of Economic Perspectives* 1(2): 131–46.

_____. 1994. "Competitiveness: A Dangerous Obsession." *Foreign Affairs* 73(2): 28–44.

Kwon, Jene. 1994. "The East Asia Challenge to Neoclassical Orthodoxy." *World Development* 22(4): 635–44.

Laird, Sam, and Alexander Yeats. 1990. "Trends in Nontariff Barriers of Developed Countries, 1966–86." *Weltwirtschaftliches Archiv* 126(2): 299–325.

Lall, Sanjaya. 1990. *Building Industrial Competitiveness in Developing Countries*. Development Center Studies. Paris: OECD Development Center.

_____. 1992a. "Technological Capabilities and Industrialization." *World Development* 20(2): 165–86.

_____. 1992b. "Technological Capabilities and the Role of Government in Developing Countries." *Greek Economic Review* 14(1): 1–36.

_____. 1993. "Policies for Building Technological Capabilities: Lessons from the Asian Experience." *Asian Development Review* 11(3): 72–103.

_____. 1994. "The East Asia Miracle Study: Does the Bell Toll for Industrial Strategy?" *World Development* 22(4): 645–54.

Lall, Sanjaya, Giorgio Barba Navaretti, Simon Teitel, and Ganeshan Wignaraja. 1994. *Technology and Enterprise Development: Ghana Under Structural Adjustment*. London: Macmillan Press.

Lane, Robert E. 1991. *The Market Experience*. Cambridge, U.K.: Cambridge University Press.

Lawrence, Peter. 1980. *Managers and Management in West Germany*. London: Croom Helm.

Leamer, Edward E. 1987. "Leontief Paradox." In *The New Palgrave*, ed. John Eatwell, Murray Millgate, and Peter Newman. New York: Macmillan.

Ledyard, John O. 1987. "Market Failure." In *The New Palgrave*, ed. John Eatwell, Murray Millgate, and Peter Newman. New York: Macmillan.

Lee, Jinjoo, Zong-tae Bae, and Dong-Kyo Choi. 1988. "Technology Development Processes: A Model for a Developing Country with a Global Perspective." *R&D Management* 18(3): 235–50.

Lee, K-R. 1993. "The Role of the User in Technological Innovation: The Case of Machine Tools in Korea and Japan." D. Phil. Thesis, Science Policy Research Unit, Sussex University.

Levin, Richard, Alvin Klevorick, Richard R. Nelson, and Sidney Winter. 1987. "Appropriating the Returns from Industrial Research and Development." *Brookings Papers on Economic Activity* 3(0): 783–820.

Linowes, David F. 1990. Speech to the White House Conference on Libraries and Information Services (October). Washington, D.C.

Lucas, Robert E. 1973. "Some International Evidence on Output-Inflation Tradeoffs." *American Economic Review* 63(3): 326–34.

———. 1988. "On the Mechanics of Economic Development." *Journal of Monetary Economics* 22(1): 3–42.

Lundvall, Bengt-Ake. 1988. "Innovation as an Interactive Process: From User-Producer Interaction to the National System of Innovation." In *Technical Change and Economic Theory*, ed. Giovanni Dosi, Christopher Freeman, Richard Nelson, Gerry Silverberg, and Luc Soete. London: Frances Pinter, Ltd.

———. 1992. *National Systems of Innovation: Towards a Theory of Innovation and Interactive Learning*. London: Frances Pinter, Ltd.

Mansfield, Edwin, A. Romeo, and S. Wagner. 1979. "Foreign Trade and U.S. Research and Development." *Review of Economics and Statistics* 61(1): 49–57.

Metcalf, Stan. 1988. "The Diffusion of Innovations: An Interpretative Survey." In *Technical Change and Economic Theory*, ed. Giovanni Dosi, Christopher Freeman, Richard Nelson, Gerry Silverberg, and Luc Soete. London: Frances Pinter, Ltd.

Meyer-Stamer, Jong, Christopher Rauh, Hady Riad, Sabine Schmitt, and Tilman Welte. 1991. *Comprehensive Modernization on the Shop Floor: A Case Study on the Brazilian Machinery Industry*. Berlin: German Development Institute.

Mill, John Stewart. 1848. *Principles of Political Economy*.

Mitchell, G., and W. Hamilton. 1988. "Managing R&D as a Strategic Option." *Research Technology Management* 31: 15–22.

Mlawa, Hasan M. 1983. "The Acquisition of Technology, Technological Capability and Technical Change: A Study of the Textile Industry in Tanzania." D. Phil. Thesis, University of Sussex.

Mody, Ashoka. 1990. "Institutions and Dynamic Comparative Advantage: The Electronics Industry in South Korea and Taiwan." *Cambridge Journal of Economics* 14(3): 291–314.

Mody, Ashoka, and David Wheeler. 1989. "Emerging Patterns of International Competition in Selected Industrial Product Groups." Industry and Energy Department Working Paper, Industry Series Paper 2. Washington, D.C.: World Bank.

Mody, Ashoka, Rajan Suri, and Jerry Sanders. 1992. "Keeping Pace with Change: Organizational and Technological Imperatives." *World Development* 20(12): 1797–816.

Moreira, Mauricio M. 1995. *Industrialization, Trade and Market Failures: The Role of Government Intervention in Brazil and the Republic of Korea.* London: Macmillan Press.

Mosley, Paul, and Weeks, John. 1993. "Has Recovery Begun? Africa's Adjustment in the 1980s Revisited." *World Development* 21(10): 1583–1606.

Mowery, David C., and Rosenberg, Nathan. 1989. *Technology and the Pursuit of Economic Growth.* Cambridge, U.K: Cambridge University Press.

Myers, Stewart. 1984. "Finance Theory and Finance Strategy." *Interfaces* 14: 126–37.

Mytelka, Lynn. 1978. "Licensing and Technological Dependence in the Andean Group." *World Development* 6(4): 447–59.

_____. 1992. "Ivoirian Industry at the Crossroads." In *Alternative Development Strategies in Sub-Saharan Africa*, ed. Frances Stewart, Sanjaya Lall, and Samuel Wangwe. London: Macmillan Press.

Nakaoka, Tetsuro. 1987. "On Technological Leaps of Japan as a Developing Country." *Osaka City University Economic Review* 22:1–25.

Nelson, Richard R. 1981. "Research on Productivity Growth and Productivity Differences: Dead Ends or New Departures?" *Journal of Economic Literature* 19(3): 1029–64.

_____, ed. 1993. *National Innovation Systems: A Comparative Analysis.* New York: Oxford University Press.

Ng, C. Y., R. Hirono, and R. Y. Siy. 1986. *Effective Mechanisms for the Enhancement of Technology and Skills in ASEAN: An Overview.* Singapore: Institute of Southeast Asian Studies.

Nishimizu, Mieko, and John M. Page, Jr. 1982. "Total Factor Productivity Growth, Technological Progress and Technical Efficiency Change: Dimensions of Productivity Change in Yugoslavia, 1967–1978." *Economic Journal* 92(368): 920–36.

_____. 1989. "Productivity Change and Growth in Industry and Agriculture: An International Comparison." In *The Balance between Industry and Agriculture in Economic Development*, ed. Jeffrey G. Williamson and Vadiraj R. Panchamukhi. London: Macmillan Press.

Odagiri, Hiroyuki, and Akira Goto. 1992. "Technology and Industrial Development in Japan." Tskuba University, Japan. Mimeo.

OECD (Organization for Cooperation and Development). 1988. *Structural Adjustment and Economic Performance*. Paris.

_____. 1992a. *Technology and the Economy: The Key Relationships*. Paris.

_____. 1992b. *The Globalization of Industrial Activities*. Paris.

_____. 1992c. *Industrial Policy in OECD Countries: Annual Review 1992*. Paris.

_____. 1993. *Trade Policy Issues: Intra-Firm Trade*. Paris.

OED (Operations Evaluation Department), World Bank. 1992. *World Bank Support for Industrialization in Korea, India and Indonesia*. Washington, D.C.

_____. 1993. *Study Of Bank Lending For Industrial Technology Development: Case Studies Of Korea, India, Indonesia, Mexico, Spain and Hungary*. Washington, D.C.

Ohiorhenuan, John F. E., and I. D. Poloamina. 1992. "Building Indigenous Technological Capacity in African Industry: The Nigerian Case." In *Alternative Development Strategies in Sub-Saharan Africa*, ed. Frances Stewart, Sanjaya Lall, and Samuel Wangwe. London: Macmillan Press.

Ostry, Sylvia. 1990. *Governments and Corporations in a Shrinking World*. New York: Council on Foreign Relations Press.

_____. 1991. "Lessons from the Triad." In *International Competitiveness: Interaction of the Public and Private Sectors*, ed. Irfan ul Haque. Economic Development Institute Seminar Series. Washington, D.C.: World Bank.

OTA (Office of Technology Assessment), U.S. Congress. 1984. *Computerized Manufacturing Automation: Employment, Education*, and the Workplace. Washington, D.C.: Government Printing Office.

Ozawa, Terutomo. 1974. *Japan's Technological Challenge to the West, 1950–1974: Motivation and Accomplishment*. Cambridge, Mass.: MIT Press.

_____. 1980. "Government Control over Technology Acquisition and Firms' Entry into New Sectors: The Experience of Japan's Synthetic-Fibre Industry." *Cambridge Journal of Economics* 4(2): 133–46.

_____. 1985. "Macroeconomic Factors affecting Japan's Technology Inflows and Outflows: the Postwar Experience." In *International Technology Transfer: Concepts, Measures, and Comparisons*, ed. Nathan Rosenberg and Claudio Frischtak. New York: Praeger.

Pack, Howard. 1987. *Productivity, Technology and Industrial Development: A Case Study in Textiles*. Oxford: Oxford University Press.

_____. 1988. "Industrialization and Trade." In *Handbook of Development Economics*, ed. Hollis B. Chenery and T. N. Srinivasan. Amsterdam: North Holland.

_____. 1992a. "Technology Gaps Between Developed and Developing Countries: Are There Dividends for Latecomers?" In *Proceedings of the World Bank Annual Conference on Development Economics*, ed. Lawrence H. Summers and Shekhar Shah. Washington, D.C.

_____. 1992b. "Learning and Productivity Change in Developing Countries." In *Trade Policy, Industrialization and Development*, ed. Gerald K. Helleiner. Oxford: Clarendon Press.

_____. 1993. "Productivity and Industrial Development in Sub-Saharan Africa." *World Development* 21(1): 1–16.

Pack, Howard, and Westphal, Larry E. 1986. "Industrial Strategy and Technological Change: Theory versus Reality." *Journal of Development Economics* 22(1): 87–128.

Patel, Pari. 1994. "Localized Production of Technology for Global Markets." *Cambridge Journal of Economics* 19: 141–53.

Patel, Pari, and Keith Pavitt. 1994. "National Systems of Innovation: Why They Are Important, and How They Might Be Measured and Compared." *Economics of Innovation and New Technology* 3(1): 77–95.

Pavitt, Keith. 1984. "Sectoral Patterns of Technical Change: Towards a Taxonomy and a Theory." *Research Policy* 13: 343–73.

Pavitt, Keith, and Pari Patel. 1988. "The International Distribution and Determinants of Technological Activities." *Oxford Review of Economic Policy* 4(4): 35–55.

Perez, Carlotta. 1985. "Microelectronics, Long Waves and World Structural Change: New Perspectives for Developing Countries." *World Development* 13(3): 441–63.

Pietrobelli, Carlo. 1993. "Manufactured Exports Performance: How Successful Has Chile Been?" In *The Legacy of Dictatorship: Political, Economic and Social Change in Pinochet's Chile*, ed. A. Angell and B. Pollack. University of Liverpool Monograph Series 17. Liverpool: Institute of Latin American Studies.

_____. 1994a. "Technological Capability and Export Diversification in a Developing County: The Case of Chile Since 1974." D. Phil. Thesis, Oxford University.

_____. 1994b. "National Technological Capabilities: An International Comparison." *Development Policy Review* 12(2): 115–48.

Pindyck, Robert S., and Solimano, Andres. 1993. "Economic Instability and Aggregate Investment." Policy Research Working Paper WPS-1148. Washington, D.C.: World Bank.

Porter, Michael. 1990. *The Competitive Advantage of Nations*. New York: Free Press.

Poznanski, Kazimierz. 1984. "Competition between Eastern Europe and Developing Countries in the Western Market for Manufactured Goods." Evidence Prepared for the Joint Economic Committee of the U.S. Congress, Washington, D.C.

Prais, Sig. 1981. "Vocational Qualifications of the Labor Force in Britain and Germany." *National Institute Economic Review* 98: 47–59.

Quazi, H. A. 1983. "Technological Capacity and Production Performance in the Fertilizer and Paper Industries in Bangladesh." D.Phil Thesis, University of Sussex.

Ray, George. 1991. *Innovation and Technical Change in Eastern Europe*. London: National Institute for Economic and Social Research.

Riedel, James. 1988. "Economic Development in East Asia: Doing What Comes Naturally?" In *Achieving Industrialization in East Asia*, ed. Helen Hughes. Cambridge, U.K.: Cambridge University Press.

Rodrik, Dani. 1994. "King Kong Meets Godzilla: The World Bank and The East Asian Miracle." In Fishlow and others, *Miracle or Design*.

Romer, Paul. 1986. "Increasing Returns and Long-Run Growth." *Journal of Political Economy* 94 (October): 1002–37.

_____. 1992. "Two Strategies for Economic Growth: Using Ideas and Producing Ideas." In *Proceedings of the World Bank Annual Conference on Development Economics*, ed. Lawrence Summers and Shekhar Shah.

Ros, Jaime. 1994. "Mexico's Trade and Industrialization Experience Since 1960: A Reconsideration of Past Policies and Assessment of Current Reforms." In *Trade Policy and Industrialization in Turbulent Times*, ed. Gerald K. Helleiner. London: Routledge.

Rosenberg, Nathan. 1972. "Factors Affecting the Diffusion of Technology." *Explorations in Economic History* 10(1): 3–33.

_____. 1986. *Perspectives on Technology*. Cambridge: Cambridge University Press.

Rothwell, Roy. 1977. "The Characteristics of Successful Innovators and Technically Progressive Firms." *R&D Management* 7: 191–206.

Salter, W.E.G. 1966. *Productivity and Technical Change*. Cambridge, U.K.: Cambridge University Press.

Scherer, Frederic M. 1992. *International High-Technology Competition*. Cambridge, Mass.: Harvard University Press.

Scherer, Frederic M., and Keun Huh. 1992. "Top Managers' Education and R&D Investment." *Research Policy* 21: 507-11.

Schumpeter, Joseph. 1934. *The Theory of Economic Development*. Cambridge, Mass.: Harvard University Press.

_____. 1942. *Capitalism, Socialism and Democracy*. New York: Harper and Row.

Scott, Bruce R. 1985. "National Strategies: Key to International Competition." In *U.S. Competitiveness in the World Economy*, ed. Bruce R. Scott and George C. Lodge. Boston: Harvard Business School Press.

Scott-Kemmis, Donald. 1988. "Learning and the Accumulation of Technological Capacity in Brazilian Pulp and Paper Firms." Employment Program Research Working Paper. Geneva: International Labor Organization.

Scott-Kemmis, Donald, and Martin Bell. 1988. "Technological Dynamism and the Technological Content of Collaboration: Are Indian Firms Missing Opportunities?" In *Technology Absorption in Indian Industry*, ed. A. Desai. New Delhi: Wiley Eastem.

Sen, Amartya. 1983. "Development: Which Way Now?" *Economic Journal* 93(372): 742–62.

_____. 1990. "Development Strategies: The Roles of the State and the Private Sector." Panel Discussion. In *Proceedings of the World Bank Annual Conference on Development Economics*, ed. Stanley Fischer, Dennis de Tray, and Shekhar Shah. Washington, D.C.: World Bank.

Sercovich, Francisco. 1980. "State-Owned Enterprises and Dynamic Comparative Advantage in the World Petrochemical Industry: The Case of Commodity Olefins in Brazil." Development Discussion Paper 96. Cambridge, Mass.: Harvard Institute for International Development.

Serven, Luis, and Andrés Solimano. 1992. "Private Investment and Macroeconomic Adjustment: A Survey." In Chhibber, Dailami, and Shafik, *Reviving Private Investment*.

Sheikh, Anwar. 1987. "Humbug Production Function." In *The New Palgrave*, ed. John Eatwell, Murray Millgate, and Peter Newman. New York: Macmillan.

Shapiro, Helen, and Lance Taylor. 1990. "The State and Industrial Strategy." *World Development* 18(6): 861–78.

Singh, Ajit. 1991. "International Competitiveness and Industrial Policy." In *International Competitiveness. Interaction of the Public and Private Sectors*, ed. Irfan ul Haque. Economic Development Institute Seminar Series. Washington, D.C.: World Bank.

Smith, Keith, and Tor Vidvei. 1992. "Innovation Activity and Innovation Outputs in Norwegian Industry." *STI Review* 11 (December).

Solow, Robert M. 1956. "A Contribution to the Theory of Economic Growth." *Quarterly Journal of Economics* 70: 65–94.

_____. 1957. "Technical Change and the Aggregate Production Function." *Review of Economics and Statistics* 39: 312–20.

Stalk, George, Jr., and Thomas M. Hout. 1990. *Competing Against Time: How Time-Based Competition is Reshaping Global Markets*. New York: Macmillan.

Stern, Nicholas. 1989. "The Economics of Development: A Survey." *The Economic Journal* 99(397): 597–685.

Stigler, George. 1956. "Industrial Organization and Economic Progress." In *The State of the Social Sciences*, ed. Lawrence White. Chicago: University of Chicago Press.

Stiglitz, Joseph E. 1987. "Learning to Learn, Localized Learning and Technological Progress." In *Economic Policy and Technological Development*, ed. Partha Dasgupta and Paul Stoneman. Cambridge, U.K.: Cambridge University Press.

_____. 1989. "Markets, Market Failures and Development." *American Economic Review Papers and Proceedings* 79(2): 197–202.

_____. 1990. "Development Strategies: The Roles of the State and the Private Sector." Panel Discussion. In *Proceedings of the World Bank Annual Conference on Development Economics*, ed. Stanley Fischer, Dennis de Tray and Shekhar Shah. Washington, D.C.: World Bank.

_____. 1993. "The Role of the State in Financial Markets." In *Proceedings of the Annual Conference on Development Economics*, ed. Michael Bruno and Boris Pleskovic. Washington, D.C.: World Bank.

Streeten, Paul. 1993. "Markets and States: Against Minimalism." *World Development* 21(8): 1281–98.

Tanaka, Masami. 1978. "Industrialization on the Basis of Imported Technology: A Case Study of the Japanese Heavy Chemical Industry 1870–1930." M.Phil. Thesis, University of Sussex.

_____. 1992. "Technology Transfer in the Petrochemical Industry." The MIT Japan Program, MITJP 92-06. Massachusetts Institute of Technology, Cambridge, Mass.

Teranishi, Juro. 1992. "Inflation Stabilization with Growth: The Japanese Experience During 1945–50." Discussion Paper Series A (243). The Institute of Economic Research, Hitotsubashi University, Tokyo.

Toffler, Alvin. 1990. *Power Shift: Knowledge, Wealth and Violence at the Edge of the 21st Century*. New York: Bantum Books.

Tyson, Laura D'Andrea. 1993. *Who's Bashing Whom: Trade Conflict in High-Technology Industries*. Washington, D.C.: Institute for International Economics.

U.N. (United Nations). 1988. *Recent Trends in International Technology Flows and Their Implications for Development*. Geneva.

UNCTAD (United Nations Conference on Trade and Development). 1985. "Technology Issues in the Energy Sector of Developing Countries: Technological Impact of the Public Procurement Policy: The Experience of the Power Plant Sector in the Republic of Korea." TT/60. Geneva: United Nations.

_____. 1993. *Trade and Development Report*. UNCTAD/TDR/13. New York: United Nations.

UNIDO (United Nations Industrial Development Organization). 1992. *Industry and Development: Global Report 1992/93*. Vienna.

Vernon, Raymond. 1989. "Technological Development: The Historical Experience." Economic Development Institute Seminar Paper 39. Washington, D.C.: World Bank.

Vianna, H. A. 1985. "International Technology Transfer, Technological Learning and the Assimilation of Imported Technology in State-Owned Enterprises: The Case of SIDOR Steel Plant in Venezuela." D. Phil. Thesis, University of Sussex.

von Hippel, Eric. 1988. *The Sources of Innovation*. Oxford: Oxford University Press.

Voss, Christopher A. 1988. "Implementation: A Key Issue in Manufacturing Technology: The Need for a Field of Study." *Research Policy* 17: 55–63.

Wade, Robert. 1990. *Governing the Market: Economic Theory and the Role of Government in East Asian Industrialization*. Princeton: Princeton University Press.

Wade, Robert. 1994. "Selective Industrial Policies in East Asia: Is the East Asia Miracle Right?" In Fishlow and others, *Miracle or Design*.

Wangwe, Samuel. 1992. "Building Indigenous Technological Capacity: A Study of Selected Industries in Tanzania." In *Alternative Development Strategies in Sub-Saharan Africa*, ed. Frances Stewart, Sanjaya Lall, and Samuel Wangwe. London: Macmillan Press.

Westphal, Larry E. 1982. "Fostering Technological Mastery by Means of Selective Infant-Industry Protection." In *Trade, Stability, Technology, and Equity in Latin America*, ed. Moshe Syrquin and Simon Teitel. New York: Academic Press.

_____. 1990. "Industrial Policy in an Export-Propelled Economy: Lessons from South Korea's Experience." *Journal of Economic Perspectives* 4(2): 41–59.

Westphal, Larry E., Linsu Kim, and Carl J. Dahlman. 1985. "Reflections on Korea's Acquisition of Technological Capability." In *International Technology Transfer: Concepts, Measures, and Comparisons*, ed. Nathan Rosenberg and Claudio Frischtak. New York: Praeger.

Westphal, Larry E., Yung W. Rhee, and Gary Purcell. 1981. "Korean Industrial Competence: Where It Came From." World Bank Staff Working Paper No. 469. Washington D.C.: World Bank.

Williamson, John. 1990. "Comments on Macroeconomic Policy and Growth." In *Proceedings of the World Bank Conference of Development Economics*, ed. Stanley Fischer, Dennis de Tray, and Shekhar Shah. Washington, D.C.: The World Bank.

World Bank. 1989. *World Development Report.* Washington, D.C.

_____. 1991. *World Development Report.* Washington, D.C.

_____. 1992. *World Development Report.* Washington, D.C.

_____. 1993a. *The East Asian Miracle: Economic Growth and Public Policy.* Oxford: Oxford University Press for the World Bank.

_____. 1993b. *World Development Report.* Washington, D.C.

_____. 1994. "The Uruguay Round: A Preliminary Assessment." In *Development Issues: Presentation to the 48th Meeting of the Development Committee.* Washington, D.C.

Young, Alwyn. 1991. "Learning by Doing and the Dynamic Effects of International Trade." *Quarterly Journal of Economics,* 106(2): 369–405.

Index

(Page numbers in italics refer to material in tables or figures.)